WHERE BEARS ROAM THE STREETS

WHERE BEARS ROAM THE STREETS

A RUSSIAN JOURNAL

Jeff Parker

HarperCollins*PublishersLtd*

Published by HarperCollins Publishers Ltd

First edition

Portions of this book previously appeared in slightly different form in
The Globe and Mail, the *St. Petersburg Review*, and *The Walrus*.

Some of the names used in this book have been changed.

HarperCollins books may be purchased for educational, business,
or sales promotional use through our Special Markets Department.

HarperCollins Publishers Ltd
2 Bloor Street East, 20th Floor
Toronto, Ontario, Canada
M4W 1A8

www.harpercollins.ca

Library and Archives Canada Cataloguing in Publication
information is available upon request
ISBN 978-1-55468-381-9

Printed and bound in the United States of America
RRD 9 8 7 6 5 4 3 2 1

Игорю

CONTENTS

PROLOGUE

You can't call a summer night in St. Petersburg, Russia, night. You can, but you'll be lying. They call them white nights, but that's a lie too. They're not night, and they're not white. Usually, at the darkest point, they're a purplish hue. I'd seen that colour before my first trip there. I'd seen it in oil floating on the surface of water, and on the back of a skink.

One of these so-called white nights in the summer of 1999, I was crossing the bridge along Nevsky Prospekt at around three in the morning when I heard a splashing in the Griboyedov canal below. I was with a Canadian woman, also a tourist there for the same writers' conference. Jennifer seemed inclined to have an affair with pretty much anyone except me. So, naturally, I was drawn to her. We hurried across the street and hung over the edge of the bridge as the splashing came closer. There was a group of drunk tourist-boat captains on a dock looking toward the tunnel and cheering. Boats were moored to the dock in a chain stretching across the canal.

A swimmer appeared, moving at tremendous speed under Nevsky Prospekt. He passed between two of the moored boats and in one motion emerged out of the black water onto the dock, where the ship captains cheered. The men patted him on the back and passed him a bottle of beer. Just fifty metres beyond him, the golden domes of the kaleidoscopic Church of the Saviour on the Spilt Blood reflected the skink-back light of the night sky.

Jennifer was entranced by him. I was too. The mere fact that he was brave enough to swim in that water impressed me. We had heard that the Russian mafia disposed of bodies in the canals. Raskolnikov wandered the banks of this canal in *Crime and Punishment*, contemplating the murder of the pawnbroker in water the colour and depth of the pupil of an eye. This canal in particular repulsed Dostoevsky, and he referred to it as a ditch.

Later, Igor would tell me that, before jumping in, he had been drinking with the captains: "I wanted to be sober, and thought to swim a little bit. I thought, like, it would help. Basically, I didn't realize I was under Nevsky Prospekt. But then I realized it and swam back."

Jennifer and I walked around the corner to what had quickly become our favourite late night haunt, the 24-hour fast-food joint Laima. Gaudy orange paint on the walls clashed with the blue neon glow of the cursive *Laima* signage. A chandelier not unlike one I'd seen earlier that day in the Hermitage hung from the vaulted white ceiling. The waitresses wore *Alice*-era diner uniforms complete with nurse hats. The service industry in Russia was still in its embryonic stage, and a foreigner, especially one who didn't speak a word of Russian, could be sure to absorb only abuse and indifference. But I had inscribed on a piece of paper the phonetic approximation of the words that conjured up my default meal: *kartoshka s gribami* (potatoes with mushrooms). I read them out loud. I mangled them. The waitress balked. She left the counter for a while and talked with one of her colleagues, leaning against the kitchen wall and chewing gum like cud. After a while she returned to give me another shot.

Jennifer and I sat on the patio to wait for our food and have beers.

It was three-thirty in the morning. The twenty-however-many hours of light in the city had short-circuited my circadian rhythms. My body no longer required sleep, only vodka and potatoes with mushrooms. The locals experience something similar this time of year. Giddiness reigns. Russian Ladas—muscular Pintos—screamed by on Nevsky Prospekt blasting techno. The Nevsky Prospekt sidewalks were packed, everyone hailing gypsy cabs and making out and ordering sausages from the food vendors and taking photos in front of the Kazansky Cathedral—where the nose in Nikolai Gogol's nineteenth-century short story "The Nose" stopped in for a morning service, where the czars used to marry before the Soviets turned it into the Museum of Atheism, and which is now, after the fall of the Soviet Union, an important Orthodox church again. Prostitutes left the bar Marstal, where the czars used to stable their horses, arm in arm with foreigners and Russia's new rich. Armour-plated police cars trolled the side streets looking for drunken foreigners to whom they could charge "fines." Bands of military men who looked like fourteen-year-old boys marched in their blue berets and epaulettes and striped navy shirts. Teenage girls galloped their horses along the Griboyedov, swigging from bottles of beer and offering rides to children in the square in front of the otherworldly onion-domed Church of the Saviour on the Spilt Blood, which was built on the spot where Czar Alexander II was assassinated after abolishing serfdom in Russia two years before Abraham Lincoln signed the Emancipation Proclamation. Across the canal from where we sat was the five-storey Singer Sewing Machine building, originally constructed in 1904, home to the American consulate a few years prior to World War II and later home to the Soviet Writers' Union. At the top of the Singer building was a glass globe where, one of the local poets would later tell me, writers used to take their dates to make out, looking down on this whole scene, including what at this particular moment would be a sauced me, a drunk tourist on the Laima patio not knowing any of this.

Before I arrived in St. Petersburg, I didn't know a word of Russian. I had never been outside North America before. I didn't know that Leningrad, after Lenin, had been the name of St. Petersburg before perestroika, and that before the Revolution it had been Petrograd, after Peter the Great. Any points of familiarity with Russia came from the movies *Reds* and *Red October* and *Red Heat* and *Red Dawn*. With regard to Russian politics, I had a mild curiosity about the strange mark on Gorbachev's head. About Russians in general, I knew next to nothing. I have never been one to underestimate my own ignorance, as I have proven to myself time and time again that my capacity in this regard is limitless. My cup runneth over. But by the time I arrived in Russia, I did have some vague expectations of the place, gleaned almost completely from Gogol's "The Nose" and Turgenev's "First Love" and a couple of other stories. At least I'd gleaned something about the scenery and about a certain kind of character that I might expect to meet there—a sadistic barber . . .

But I didn't have anyone like Igor even remotely in mind.

I'd discovered Russian billiards, and I was babbling about the game to Jennifer, who clearly didn't care. "And the balls," I said, "are literally the size of grapefruits. And they're all white. And they barely fit in the pockets, and the table, the goddamn table, it's like the size of the former Soviet Union itself . . ."

She was using the side of her fork to scrape the mushroom sauce off her plate and nodding her head when a voice behind her said, "You like Russian billiards?" The voice belonged to the guy whom we'd seen climb out of the Griboyedov canal. He was sitting at the table behind us, still damp, drinking a beer, a black cylindrical case propped against the wall next to him.

"I do," I said. "I mean, I haven't played. But I saw it. I've seen some people play it. I have no idea. I haven't played. I don't . . ."

He smiled. "This is real pool game," he said. He extended his hand to Jennifer. Then, reaching across the table to shake mine, he said, "Igor." No matter what cultural sensitivity program you graduated from, it's impossible to suppress amusement when this name is said with this accent by a dude like this.

He invited us to a nearby pool hall, and while I was apprehensive, Jennifer immediately agreed. We walked down the canal to a place called Panda, just at the other end of the block by the short Bank Bridge, which was guarded by four massive griffin statues, two on each side.

Inside, the scene was part David Lynch and part Jean-Luc Godard: A stunning bartender surrounded by some other stunning women. Some gangster-looking guys cracking these huge white balls back and forth with sticks the size of cane poles on massive green billiard tables. There was a claw machine with stuffed-animal prizes for ten rubles. A small TV mounted on the wall pumped out music videos, and we had to shout to hear one another. We heard Ricky Martin's "Livin' la Vida Loca" in English, followed by Ricky Martin's "Livin' la Vida Loca" in Spanish, followed by Ricky Martin's "Livin' la Vida Loca" in Ukrainian, which I think was supposed to be a joke. This was the song you heard all over St. Petersburg in the summer of 1999, one version or another, no matter if you were in a club or at a beer garden or in a gypsy cab driven by a sixty-year-old man.

We had some beers, and I peeked into a side room lined with electronic slot machines. A cleaning lady stood there, and it took a moment to realize that she was asleep, propped up by her mop, which was a rag wrapped around a two-by-four attached to a broomstick.

Igor had a little black nylon glove that fit over his index finger and thumb to cut friction. He schooled me for a few games. When it comes to Russian billiards, most people play either Moscow Pyramid or Amerikanka (which means "American girl"). The balls are sixty-two millimetres in diameter and the pockets are sixty-four millimetres. It means you're either dead-on or the ball bounces out. Igor tried to teach me an essential Russian billiards shot in which you carom the cue ball into the pocket off another ball. It required completely counterintuitive angle and spin, and I couldn't make it happen.

A guy wearing a black leather jacket came in with a group of four beggars. Igor nodded at the guy and they shook hands. Then the guy went to the bar and negotiated with the stunning bartender for a moment. He bought the beggars beer and left them.

Igor told me that each beggar on Nevsky Prospekt owes a cut to some mafia, and this is their reward for a good day.

"Now, we will have our reward for good day," he said.

We all went to the bar, where the stunning bartender and her two stunning friends were sitting. Igor ordered three hundred grams of vodka (fifty grams, a shot, for each of us) and six glasses. The bartender filled a carafe of vodka. Igor tapped a glass each in front of me, Jennifer, the stunning bartender, her two stunning friends, and, finally, himself.

The vodka, straight from the freezer, poured thick as syrup. It was nearly six in the morning, and Igor showed no signs of slowing. So I was relieved when he said, "I'm sorry, guys. After this I must sleep for work tomorrow." He turned to me: "I will call you in two days and show you Russian *banya*."

We did the shots. We thanked him. I doubted I'd ever hear from him again after this. The white sun blazed in through the Panda windows.

I.

CONFLICT & CORRUPTION

||||||||||||||||||||||||||||||||||||||||||||||||||||

"If you want to be very high, you had to be at the bottom."
—Igor, Summer 2009

CHAPTER 1

I had been living my whole life in pursuit of something that would blow my mind. And I had burned through some prefatory material—skateboarding, drugs, Bukowksi, grad school—when I stumbled across the short story "The Nose" by Nikolai Gogol.

In the story, a bureaucrat named Kovalyov wakes up one morning without his nose, just a smooth, flat patch of skin where the nose should be. He pursues it around St. Petersburg, but the nose has grown considerably and attained a higher rank than Kovalyov himself—giving it (though "it" seems to be a "him" by that point) the right to flat-out refuse a return to the face of the lowly clerk. Across town, a barber finds a nose that he recognizes as Kovalyov's in a loaf of bread and tries to covertly dispose of it in the Moika canal, but he's apprehended by a policeman ... That's just the beginning.

Looking back, I realize that I was primed in a certain sense by that story. That I would one day travel to Russia and become enthralled by the country was foretold from the moment I read it.

I had never read anything like it. Not much is explained in "The Nose"—neither how the nose disappeared from Kovalyov's face, nor how the nose grew to such proportions and reached its elevated rank, nor how it appeared in the barber's loaf of bread— and even now I'm as taken and flummoxed by it as I ever was. And I'm as taken and flummoxed by Russia as I ever was. My reaction to the story and my reaction to the Russia that it led me to were one and the same.

I used my last student loan to pay for the trip. As far as I recall, my reasons were threefold—two literary and one personal. I wanted to see the place where "The Nose" was set, and I wanted to meet the Russian writer Victor Pelevin, who was going to be a guest at the writers' festival. I would also travel to Siberia to meet my then-girlfriend Yulia's parents and see the city she was from.

I had grown up in north Florida (an area of the United States sometimes referred to as the Redneck Riviera) on a dirt road once known as Old Pig Trail. No one around me was particularly tuned in politically. It was the Reagan era, the waning days of the Cold War, and I didn't pay much attention to anything. Occasionally we had drills in elementary school that did double duty as both hurricane and nuclear attack preparation. After seeing the movie *The Day After*, which solidified in me the understanding that Russians were my enemy, I asked my mom if we could put in a below-ground fallout shelter, and I remember experiencing no small amount of anxiety when she explained to me that in Florida the aquifer was too high for any below-ground fallout shelter. The Berlin Wall fell during my junior year of high school, but I don't even remember it. I started working in restaurants as soon as I turned sixteen, and went to college in Gainesville, where I majored in journalism and served time as an inept cub reporter before lucking into a creative writing program that offered to pay me a very small amount of money to write for three years. Upstate New York might as well have been New York City when I left Gainesville for Syracuse in my '84 Volkswagen Vanagon. There I read Gogol and first got an inkling about Russia. Just a few years later, I used that last student loan cheque to pay my way to St. Petersburg.

And under the category of mind-blowing, Russia was the best thing going. The first time I turned from Kazanskaya onto the Nevsky Prospekt sidewalk at midday, I could not find a way to move through the chaotically shifting wall of people. Russians observed neither the right-left directional rules nor any other peripatetic conventions, and I was shoulder-, elbow-, hip-, and knee-checked before I'd gone half a block to the Subway restaurant I was aiming for. I liked to think that I knew and understood some things, yet here I didn't even understand how to walk down the sidewalk.

Being in Russia was like downloading a new operating system for my brain, or like being on acid: everything was recognizable and familiar on one level, but strange and unpredictable on the other. I wandered in a kind of fairy-tale fugue, unable to read or understand anything, relying on nuance and detail. I might as well have been pursuing my own nose around the city.

One thing was clear: I wanted to figure out everything there was to know about it. I wanted to understand the explicit things, such as how to read Cyrillic and speak Russian, and especially how to curse properly in the Russian slang dialect known as *mat*. And I wanted to learn the more nuanced things. I wanted to learn how to hit that counterintuitive Russian billiards shot in which you carom the cue ball into the pocket off another ball.

I wanted to learn the special *banya* birch-branch beating technique that Igor had learned from his uncle. I wanted to learn how to walk down the sidewalk and how to stand in line, the great twentieth-century Russian tradition.

In this quest of sorts, I read countless books on Russian culture—many of them interesting and enlightening, many of them not. Yet between the interesting and enlightening and my experience of the place, there was a massive cognitive gap: none of those books—even those that seemed to be getting it right—depicted the world I saw in front of my face.

At some point, I stumbled across a travel and photo book by John Steinbeck and Robert Capa chronicling their trip to Russia in 1948, entitled *A Russian Journal.* "It occurred to us that there were some things that nobody wrote about Russia," Steinbeck wrote, "and they were the things that interested us most of all . . . What do people wear there? What do they serve at dinner? Do they have parties? What food is there? How do they make love and how do they die?"

Unfortunately, theirs is not a great Russia book. As they travelled across the former Soviet Union, escorted to one formal dinner after another—most seemingly staged by Stalin's handlers—Steinbeck wrote more about Capa's bathroom habits than about what life was like for the country's citizens. But it seemed to me their intentions were noble. The dominant Western idea of Russia pegs it as the land of the gulags or a place where bears roam the streets. Every Russia story tends to fall into the stereotype of *Russians are crazy!* or *Russians are scary!* Once you'd spent time there, you could feel that these stereotypes were inadequate, but it was harder to say what it was about the place that made it so singular, that had fascinated centuries of Westerners, that had defined us in the West by being the opposite of whatever idea we had of ourselves. If you hoped to peel back the opaque layer of foreignness that cloaked the place, the questions that Steinbeck had asked fifty years ago were the types of questions you had to try to answer.

The writing festival hired me to do some work in exchange for free annual trips, and I returned every summer (as well as a few winters) after that. I spent two, three, four months there every year, and somehow, over time, that surreality became my reality. The however-many months I spent back home were like the temporary, irrelevant period of my year. I moved from Syracuse to New York City to Phoenix to LA to Columbus, Ohio, to Ann Arbor, Michigan, and then to Toronto in 2007. All that moving might seem chaotic, but it didn't faze me because, I think, my mind was somewhere else. It was set on and in the white nights of St. Petersburg.

After the writers' festival was cancelled in 2008, I returned for even longer stretches. The one life philosophy that I felt I could stand by was to move toward what interests you. And Russia drew me; it would not let up.

And gradually I began, in a weird way, to feel more at home on the streets of St. Petersburg than I did walking down Central Avenue in St. Petersburg, Florida, or on Old Pig Trail when I visited my parents, or on the Danforth in the east end of Toronto, where I lived.

Then there was Igor. Despite my hunch that I'd never hear from him again after that night at the Panda pool hall, he called and invited me to the Russian *banya* (bathhouse), and I went.

We didn't have much in common beyond the fact that we liked to play pool and we both spent chunks of our lives working in restaurants. (I wrote a novel, a glorified soap opera, about restaurant workers in Florida, and after Igor read it, he nodded his head and assured me: "The exact same shit happens in our restaurants, man. Exactly the same.") Growing up, neither of us had known our biological fathers. And though I'm a few years older than him, when we were kids, we were both terrified— he of Americans, me of Russians. I pictured Russians as the evil, vodka-swilling brutes we see in the movies. He pictured Americans as privileged, overweight fakes exploiting the world to their advantage in the name of freedom and justice for all.

But that first trip to the banya together put us on the level.

From then on, when I tired of hanging around with artists, intellectuals, and writers at the literary festival, I hung out with Igor at the nearby café where he worked as a barman, and he made for a fine antidote to hanging out with artists, intellectuals, and writers. Igor and I went fishing and played paintball and camped and drank at the Russian banya, talking for hours and sweating our asses off.

In the summer of 2008, I came to Russia intending to write a book about the country's resurgence as a major global superpower under president and then prime minister (and now president again) Vladimir Putin, about the emergence, for maybe the first time in history, of a Russian middle class, and about the sacrifices that had been made. But before that summer ended, Russia was locked in armed conflict with Georgia—its first proxy brouhaha with the West, which backed Georgia, since the fall of the Soviet

Union—and soon afterward, the entire world plummeted into the global economic crisis started in the United States.

By the time I returned in the summer of 2009, the storyline of Russian resurgence had fuzzed out. And the crisis, which looked bad enough in the West, looked even worse in Russia, where stability was more recent, more fragile. Would this crisis end like the crisis of 1998? With a major currency devaluation that wiped out the nation's collective life savings overnight? With the stores emptied of food? Or would the price of oil stabilize and the treasury's foreign currency reserves hold, allowing Prime Minister Vladimir Putin to save the day and paving the way for his return to the presidency in 2012?

The more I sought answers, the more the questions kept coming;

What was Russia? How did it work? How *did* people live? How could they eat *kholodets* (meat gelatin)? Did love mean something different to them than it meant to us? Why did so many women leave the country to marry strangers? What good did it do them to know Pushkin by heart? Where did their collective stoicism come from? Why did the police keep robbing me? Were their soldiers' sacrifices honoured when they returned from Chechnya? How *did* they live and die? Was it true, as a friend from Moscow had told me, that Russians flourish in times of crisis?

While we take stability for granted in the West, this crisis was different. Major global financial corporations were failing. In the United States, whole cities were going bankrupt. And people across the States and Canada and Europe were shaken.

For Igor, the past twenty years—most of his life—had been a steady series of crises. "In Russia," Igor told me, "everyone knows that tomorrow all the rules may change." I had been wondering about the story of Russia today and asking all these questions, and before I even realized it, Igor began answering them for me.

In 2008, Igor was twenty-nine years old, which was, at the time, exactly middle-aged for Russian men, for whom the average life expectancy was fifty-eight. (It has since gone up to sixty-two.)

He spent his early years in the Soviet Union as a Young Pioneer (think Leninist Cub Scouts) and came of age in a country called the Russian Federation, a supposed capitalist democracy, during the Wild West nineties. He grew up at the centre of maybe the most wrenching socio-political transformation of the twentieth century. Throughout his life, the rules kept being changed on him. He kept having the socio-economic rug pulled out from under his feet. He tried out all the possibilities perestroika had to offer him, and as he approached thirty he was working as a manager who doubled as barman in a downtown St. Petersburg café.

But the crisis took care of that. By the time I arrived in St. Petersburg in the summer of 2009, Igor was among the 10 percent of the country unemployed, with little to no prospects.

Complicating matters, my wife had just asked for a separation and my own life had been thrown into limbo. As Igor's world—his job, his relationship, his belief and pride in himself and his country—fell apart, I became, in a weird way, caught up in the collapse. Beyond the fact that Russia continued to compel and flummox me—to be a place where I felt more alive than anywhere else—I didn't know what I was doing there.

On a lark, Igor and I lit off together, first to the Russian resort town Gelendzhik in the south and then to Lake Baikal in Siberia, on a tear of downshifting across a country in crisis.

It's said that a story always involves either a stranger who comes to town or a person who goes on a journey—which, if you think about it, is the same story from different perspectives. All right. So it starts like this: Once upon a time, two strangers came to town and went on a journey . . .

CHAPTER 2
SUMMER 2009

Early, much too early the morning after my arrival in St. Petersburg, Igor bangs on the door of the apartment he had arranged for me near the metro stop Bolshevikov. I nearly sleep through the din, mistaking his knock for the sound of the crows landing on the tin roof over the apartment balcony.

"Don't say any words," Igor says when I open the door. "I am tired also. Just want to fall down."

His T-shirt reads *Soul Survivor*. He looks about like I feel.

I have a dim recollection of the night before: arriving in Petersburg from Toronto, Igor greeting me with a bottle of vodka (brand: Green Mark; slogan: Fresh Vodka!), going to eat at the nearby restaurant Peking/Tokyo in a building called Jewelry Karat (where Igor ate spoonfuls of wasabi as chasers), stumbling back to the apartment, finishing the vodka, Igor leaving at some point in the night to retrieve his stuff for our trip to the Black Sea . . .

"Make way for the Red Dog," he says. He leads in a rolling red suitcase that he bought for ten dollars in Egypt. It has a compass in the handle. The suitcase clunks onto the floor and he throws open the zipper. I pack my things on top of his things: diving fins, a volleyball signed by all the guys he played beach volleyball with in Egypt, two pairs of footwear, namely his white leather wingtips and flip-flops.

Another bag is stuffed with food that Igor's mom cooked for us. I peel away the aluminum foil from a chicken breast and breakfast.

"I need to get sunscreen," I say after adding my stuff to the Red Dog.

"Goddamn it," he says. As we will see, Igor would prefer sunburn blistering his entire body, skin irradiated, to broadcasting the weakness that is the wearing of sunscreen.

In St. Petersburg, the weather is seven degrees Celsius and raining. The sky is white with low grey clouds. The Black Sea coast we're heading to promises thirty degrees in the shade. This is the start of the busy Russian resort season, and the train should be packed. For now, we wear fall jackets and carry umbrellas. In terms of weather, there is very little differentiating this June morning in Russia from, say, a March one in Toronto.

The idea for the trip came together on the spur of the moment.

The world was in a global economic crisis. Igor and I were both in crisis too.

Six months ago, Igor had been the manager in an upscale downtown café called the Atrium, where he'd worked for several years and where he made a decent paycheque. But the economic crisis put the Atrium out of business. Unemployment in Russia was skyrocketing. No one was hiring in St. Petersburg at all, especially in the service sector. Restaurant after restaurant, café after café, bar after bar—empty and going out of business. His engagement to his fiancée was on again and off again, sometimes his call, sometimes hers.

While I had a job teaching creative writing at the University of Toronto, Yulia, who was then my wife, had asked for a separation. She was visiting her family in the Siberian city of Krasnoyarsk this summer. For the first time in ten years of travelling to Russia, I arrived there unmoored. The writing program I had worked with since 1999, the same one that led me to Igor, had ceased operation the summer before the crisis; the ever-increasing bribes and the strengthening ruble had finally made it unviable.

Igor's uncle Vova lived in the resort town of Gelendzhik. Uncle Vova was the identical twin brother of the biological father that Igor had never met. Uncle Vova agreed that we could stay with him, so we decided to go there together for a week, relax, collect our wits. When we returned, so the plan went, I would sit in the apartment at metro Bolshevikov and write while Igor would restart his job search. Surely the unemployment situation, our relationships, the economy, Russia, the world, would get better again soon . . .

At the nearest grocery store, we pick up sunscreen and Ferrero Rocher chocolates, a gift for Igor's aunt. (For Igor's uncle, I have brought along a bottle of Canadian rye from Pearson duty-free.) In North America, the sunscreen would price out around five bucks, the big, decorative box of Rocher, twenty. Here, the sunscreen is twenty and the Rocher dirt cheap. An inversion, I assume, of supply and demand.

We stop at Bar Bunker for hair of the dog. The bar is full by ten a.m. on this Saturday morning. Everyone seems pretty drunk already, but this is to be expected of the ten a.m. Bar Bunker set. We order two shots of vodka and two beers. An old man comes in, and since there are no spots on the benches, he wrestles with a folding chair, but he cannot seem to open it. Finally he gives up and leans against the wall, sipping from a glass of vodka in one hand, eating a piece of black bread with the other.

We take the metro to the Moskovsky train station.

At the station, we sit in the café. We order chicken kebabs with prunes and buckwheat. Then we stock up on the final necessities: ten beers, bread, bananas.

Igor briefs me on the most important aspect of Russian train travel. "On the train, everyone is turning on the imagination. A lot of shit, man. How cool they are. This is the train. Everyone is always lying in the train. It's like, when you want to get away from yourself, try out a new reality."

Trying out a new reality sounds pretty good to both of us right about now.

We board and squeeze down the tight corridor to our *coupe*. For a couple of middle-class dudes, we have middle-class seats. That is, we're not in the *platzkart*, the communal, open sleeper car, and we're not in the "lux" singles, but we have a coupe with four beds, two upper and two lower, that we'll share with two other passengers. The coupe is essentially a walk-in closet with two sets of bunk-style, person-sized shelves, a window, and a small table in the middle.

Igor is hoping that our coupe-mates aren't children or old ladies. "If it's going to be old ladies, they are going to fuck our brains out," he says. "They are going to look at us while we drink the beers. 'Bad boys! Bad boys!' If kids, the same shit."

Igor intentionally bought lower-bunk tickets as a strategy to avoid children. Parents won't buy the higher beds for kids, he says, in case they roll out. So you occupy the two lower bunks and it's an automatic no-kid coupe. Once, riding the train to Abkhazia to spend the summer with his grandparents, a young Igor rolled out of a top bunk, smacking his head on the table.

"The only problem with the lower place is that people are sitting on our seats in the beginning," he explains. "If you get lower seats, it means that it's not your own. It means the guy from higher up has the right to sit on your place. It's so funny to explain all this shit to you. And it's funny for me too, because as I'm explaining, I am understanding, this is real bullshit."

Each car has its own attendant. Our attendant brings linens, mattress pads, and pillows. The train has a built-in radio. Igor reaches for a white plastic knob above the window and turns up the volume. A crackling speaker plays, "I am leaving for the B-B-B-B-B-Black Sea . . ."

I lie across my person-sized shelf, thinking I might sleep. We have a 48-hour train ride there, a week in Gelendzhik, and a 48-hour train ride back.

"*My yedem za positivom!*" Igor cries. Creative translation: "We're going to get our positive on!"

"*My yedem za positivom!*" I repeat.

Ten years earlier, Igor had taught me the first Russian phrase that I ever learned by heart. We were hanging out at an outdoor beer garden with his friend Big Al, a cook at the time in a fashionable downtown restaurant decorated like the inside of a submarine, complete with porthole windows looking out on fish-filled aquariums. The beer garden was in a little semicircular park on Kazanskaya across from the Kazansky Cathedral. By "beer garden," I mean that there were a few plastic chairs, a rickety plywood kiosk around a keg of Baltika—the Russian Budweiser—and an unhappy-looking twenty-something girl serving plastic cups of beer and squid jerky.

We sat there for hours every night. The only problem was that there wasn't a bathroom. Some Russian men had begun improvising, going in the space behind the plywood kiosk. For a day or two, I walked back to my dorm down the street when I had to go, but it took a long time, and eventually I figured, well, all the Russian men pee back there, so I will too. But—and this is an important lesson to learn about Russia—some things are okay for Russians and not so okay for foreigners.

One night, unhappy-looking twenty-something girl serving plastic cups of beer and squid jerky shouted at me when I returned from a pit stop behind the kiosk to our lawn furniture, where Igor and Big Al were cracking up.

"What did she say?" I asked.

"She said, 'This fucking foreigner pees behind my kiosk every night, and he doesn't understand a word of Russian,'" Igor said.

"I can say some words," I said. "Hello. *Privet.* Thank you. *Spasibo.* Goodbye. *Poka.* Excuse me. *Izvinitye.* Beer. *Pivo.* Potato with mushrooms. *Kartoshka s gribami.*"

"Next time you go, she will yell at you again. Don't worry what it means—it's not a compliment, for sure. Just tell her back," Igor whispered, "'*Ty ochen krasivaya.*'"

I repeated it. They corrected me. We spoke in low voices and drank more Baltika. "What does it mean?"

"Just say it," Igor said.

"No way I'm saying it without knowing what it means."

"It's nothing bad, just, 'You're very beautiful.'"

"You're very beautiful?"

As I refilled my bladder, I repeated the sounds of the phrase to myself, and I considered that I had no way of verifying if in fact *Ty ochen krasivaya* meant "You're very beautiful." It could mean something terrible, but the sound was crisp and clean. I watched several Russian men disappear behind the kiosk, and she didn't say anything to them. And so I became slightly, drunkenly indignant.

I went behind the box, and as I returned, she shouted at me again. I turned and calmly delivered my line. She went silent. I could see her confusion as she wondered whether she'd heard me correctly. I repeated, *"Ty ochen krasivaya."* She blushed and smiled. Igor and Big Al fell out of their plastic chairs. And from then on, I could pee behind the kiosk without getting yelled at.

When I returned to the United States after that summer, I immediately enrolled in Russian classes. And now, after many years, I read well enough but still speak poorly. Igor cringes. "Your Russian hurts my ears," he cries. So we mostly speak Ruslish.

Blue, ruffled curtains shade the train window and a little net is attached to the wall over each bed for pocket stuff. Igor throws open the Red Dog. He strips down to his underwear and changes into a navy-striped wife-beater, shorts, and flip-flops. Then he pops out to smoke. I peer into the hallway and note that everyone on the train has, like Igor, instantly changed into house wear. People crowd the corridor in slippers and pyjamas or nightgowns, lining up for tea at the end of the car in front of a massive steel samovar built into the wall.

Igor returns and a waitress comes through selling hot dogs from a cart. Igor talks with her for a while. I don't really catch it all. She smiles and flirts and he flirts back. She has long black hair and heavy blue eyeshadow.

I ask him, "Does it take so long to decline a hot dog?"

"The problem," he says, "in Russian, if you are saying no, you need to say a lot of words."

We wait for our coupe-mates to show up. But they never do, and suddenly the train is rolling, half empty.

Before we boarded, Igor kept saying, "I am waiting only to fall on the train and sleep." But now he says, "We were drinking a lot and not sleeping, and still I have some spryness." *Spry* is one of his favourite English words, picked up from one of his favourite English-language films, *Bad Santa*.

So instead of falling down, he invites his new friend, Sergey, whom he met just a few moments ago smoking between the train cars and whom he already calls by the diminutive Seryozha, to join us.

"This is the theme, as I told you," Igor says. "In the train, you are becoming friends and all this shit."

Before we are even out of the station, Seryozha and his wife, Masha, are drinking beer in our coupe. Seryozha brings a bottle of Golden Pheasant and Masha a plastic Baggie of smoked string cheese. We finish the first beers and pop open seconds and then thirds. I devour Masha's string cheese, a fatty, processed Gouda-type product called *chechil*.

Seryozha and Masha are vague about what they do. They tell us they work in security and that they both served in the military. They do not look like security services types. Seryozha is missing his left front tooth and the right front tooth is mostly black. He is a tall, stocky dude, with one of those broad but firm beer bellies some Russian men cultivate. He wears a shirt that reads *Don't fuck my brain. Violators will be shot. Survivors will be shot again.* Both are probably in their early forties. Masha has thick curly hair. She is squat and doe-eyed with freckles. We ascertain that we are on the same train with Sergey and Masha coming back from Gelendzhik in nine days.

"Jeff is a famous Canadian actor," Igor tells them. "And I am his translator. Maybe you've seen some of his movies." He enumerates a list of made-up and real titles that I have supposedly appeared in, including *Bad Santa.* Seryozha and Masha are impressed, but they're sorry, they have not seen any of my movies.

We are having a good little party when, at the first stop, a troika of policemen—the train police, a particularly menacing sort—appear in the doorway to our coupe.

"Aha! What kind of holiday are you celebrating here, people? Passports and tickets."

Masha and Sergey scurry away. Igor and I hand over our passports. We are both already a little drunk. The cop reading my passport turns it upside down and then hands it to his partner, who looks at me. Clearly neither of them read English.

When they talk, they address only Igor. It is the first time in the ten years I have known him that I have heard him addressed in the formal manner, by his first name and patronymic: "Igor Yurievitch, you are of course aware that it is illegal in the Russian Federation to be drunk in a public place." Igor blinks. He nods condescendingly. If we piss them off, they might fine us. "This one time we are willing to let you go, but if it happens again, we'll haul you off the train."

Igor hangs his head. "Thank you," he says. He reaches over and slams shut the door of our coupe.

Igor says that beer is not alcohol under Russian law. He says that under Russian law, beer is a foodstuff, and he is right. (This designation has since changed; beer is considered alcohol since 2011.) And furthermore, they didn't wear their hats, in correspondence with the strict uniform requirements, and they didn't identify themselves by name as transport police, as they are supposed to, and they didn't salute, which is also required of them. Lots of people are drunk in public places in Russia. "But you can't say anything to cops," Igor says. What we learned is that we need to keep the door to our coupe closed. "If they can't see us drinking, we are not drinking," he says.

Sergey and Masha do not return. Igor sulks while staring out the window as the train rolls toward the getting on of our positive.

CHAPTER 3

Just one year before Igor and I began our trip across a country in crisis, things looked very different in Russia. In the summer of 2008, nearly twenty tumultuous years after the fall of the Soviet Union, Russia was again a global superpower. The 2000s had seen the emergence of a bona fide middle class, maybe for the first time in Russian history. For this, there were oil prices and Putin to thank. Mostly oil prices. The price of a barrel of oil, the linchpin of the Russian economy, hit a twenty-year high at US$147 that year.

Igor wasn't by any stretch the poster child for the new Russian middle class. He wasn't an IT consultant or banker. But in practical lifestyle terms, he wasn't so far off. He made, as manager of a fashionable downtown St. Petersburg café, a decent salary. And even though Moscow was then *Money* magazine's most expensive city in the world and St. Petersburg sat in twelfth place, the fact was that one could live quite cheaply amid the opulence.

Igor had helped his long-time girlfriend Anya buy a car, and they regularly went on all-inclusive vacations to Tunisia and

Egypt, where Igor scuba dived and Anya sunned on the beach. Igor still lived with his mother, but so do many single Russian men, and even some married ones. He had saved a lot of money over the years, which he kept in cash and stocks. He planned to buy his mother a retirement home in Abkhazia in the coming years so that he could take over her apartment. He held his cash mostly in dollars and euros, but the ruble was now so strong that he was considering, partly out of national pride, converting to Russian currency.

Oil and the improved economy weren't everything, of course.

Global Russian sports dominance had been restored to the glorious Soviet-era levels. Moscow's CSKA basketball team had won a Euroleague championship. The St. Petersburg soccer club Zenit took the 2008 UEFA Cup. Russia beat Canada at the World Hockey Championships. Women's tennis was dominated by Russians, and all three owners of heavyweight boxing belts in North America were citizens of the former Soviet Union.

Russians even had a piece of global popular culture, something beyond the scope of the former Soviet empire. Universal Pictures released Russian-Kazakh film director Timur Bekmambetov's *Wanted* (known as *Extreme Danger* in Russian), in which Russian heartthrob Konstantin Khabenskiy smooches Angelina Jolie. (Technically, the interaction described in the Russian media as a "kiss" is more like this: Khabenskiy's character, who has just been shot in the chest and is actively spitting up blood, receives mouth-to-mouth from Jolie's character. But still, there was a Russian actor making lip contact with Angelina Jolie, directed by a Russian director in a Hollywood production.)

Russia had been a wreck in the nineties. A small number of businessmen, known as oligarchs, had privatized the country's immense resources for their personal gain. President Boris Yeltsin drunkenly bumbled and stumbled across the world stage, to the country's collective national humiliation. The nineties saw the degeneration of the Russian educational system and a devaluation of the ruble that overnight turned many a person's life savings into pocket change. It all must have seemed like an embarrassing and cruel joke to the citizens of what had recently been one of the world's superpowers.

Then Putin, a former KGB bureaucrat from St. Petersburg, came to power and things began to change, for the better and for the worse. Putin looked different, almost like the young reformer some believed him to be, and he behaved differently. A biography intended to introduce Putin to the world depicted him as the product of a hardscrabble youth in St. Petersburg, a man who had followed his dream of becoming a KGB officer against all odds.

Igor too had grown up in St. Petersburg courtyards, the spaces between apartment buildings where there's often a playground for kids and benches for the adults to sit together and talk. The courtyards are where much of the social life in Russian cities takes place. While Igor wasn't the tough that Putin was portrayed as, he had to fight when fights came to him. Igor, like many, could relate to this romantic story of fighting one's way out of the St. Petersburg courtyards to the highest office in the land.

Putin played to nationalist pride by reinstating the Soviet national anthem, albeit with new lyrics (this was the second time in the anthem's history that it had been rewritten; the first was during Khrushchev's thaw to edit out a reference to Stalin), and he stood up to the Western powers where Yeltsin and Gorbachev before him had only seemed to bow down. He corralled the oligarchs: the result of his showdown with oil magnate Mikhail Khodorkovsky (who defied Putin by, among other things, funding the parliamentary opposition) was that Khodorkovsky, once sixteenth on the *Forbes* list of billionaires, sat in a prison cell in Siberia for a decade. And he secured his power base. Less than a year into Putin's presidency, the state controlled the three major television networks. Putin installed his former cronies and their cronies' cronies from the KGB and its successor organization, the FSB, throughout every layer of government. He decreed that the country's regional governors would be appointed by the Kremlin, consolidating power in his tightly controlled circle.

He missed no opportunity to show that he was a macho badass, the iron-fisted leader that some believed Russians needed. Long before he hunted Siberian tigers and wild bears and flew with cranes, he landed a fighter jet in Chechnya and fought as a black belt in judo competitions.

And these shows of strength had powerful effects. An all-girl pop group had a hit song entitled "A Man Like Putin," with lines such as "I want a man like Putin, who's full of strength / I want a man like Putin, who doesn't drink / I want a man like Putin, who won't make me sad." Opinion polls routinely asserted that Putin was the sexiest man in Russia—proving that, like the citizens of many other nations, Russians confuse power with sexiness.

The quid pro quo of the stability Putin offered soon became clear: the citizenry would support him, often vociferously, overlooking the corruption, the curbing of civil liberties, the state control of the media, the suppression of the opposition, the small group of former security service operatives who now held the country's reins.

In March 2008, Putin's hand-picked successor (term limits prohibited Putin's running for a third consecutive term) Dmitry Medvedev, a technocrat who had never held elected office and had no political base beyond Putin's support, won the presidency of Russia with more than 70 percent of the vote. Medvedev immediately appointed Putin as prime minister. Anyone on the streets of Russia at the time could have told you what Medvedev and Putin admitted four years later: they arranged the temporary power switch so that Putin could run for president again in 2012. Putin was the boss all along. It was his show. And everyone knew it.

But stability was less than perfect. One result of Putin's quid pro quo was that corruption was institutionalized in almost every aspect of society. Today, Russia generally occupies the upper percentiles of Transparency International's list of the world's most corrupt nations, in the company of the Republic of Congo, Laos, and Tajikistan.

In a survey by the Foundation for Public Opinion Reports on attitudes toward corruption, 50 percent of Russians said they were certain they would have to bribe someone in the event they needed to address the authorities. However, when asked what seemed to be the biggest social ill in Russia, "corruption and bribery in organs of power" ranked only eleventh. In part, corruption ranks so far down the list because everyone is used to it. The study projected the total cost of day-to-day corruption in Russia for 2010 at 160 billion rubles, or around US$5.3 billion.

In the survey's comments section, respondents detailed their various experiences with corruption: *I paid off the police when I beat up a bastard; We bought our son out of court so that he didn't go to jail; I needed to build a garage in my dacha and I had to bribe the chief of the garden settlement otherwise he wouldn't allow it;* and *I have to bribe somebody every day.*

Igor, like many, got a taste of this way of life early in the Wild West nineties when Putin was still building his political base in the St. Petersburg city government.

Three boarders lived with Igor and his mother in the spring of 1995. The boarders, one Russian and two Chinese, occupied the second room of the small flat, and they founded what Igor believes to have been the very first Western-style potato chip company in St. Petersburg.

Despite the strong presence of potatoes in eastern European cuisine, potato chips were a rarity in the Soviet Union and in post-perestroika Russia. What passed for potato chips during Soviet times were rectangular, unsalted wafer-like snacks flavoured with dill. The potential demand made American companies salivate, and several of them attempted import operations during the period of glasnost. History supported the move. Potatoes didn't even exist in Russia until Czar Peter the Great, the founder of St. Petersburg, sent a sack of them back home during his seventeenth-century travels in the West. At first the unfamiliar tuber was rejected. According to the *Cambridge World History of Food*, conservative religious factions and pagans called them the "devil's apples," and the empire's eventual decree that they be grown on common land was met with the so-called potato riots of 1843. Today, over 150 years later, it's hard to imagine Russian cuisine without the potato. It's a staple in almost everything, from the ubiquitous New Year's potato salad Olivier to vodka to the wonderful concoction *pirozhki s kartoshkoi*, which is essentially mashed potatoes baked into a soft, flaky bun, a delicious carb overdose that's nearly as popular in Russia as sandwiches are in the West.

The Russian and Chinese entrepreneurs renting Igor's room spent their days in a little warehouse slicing and frying potatoes, and they returned home smelling of salt and grease. There were only two beds in the flat's second bedroom, and they alternated: one of them got a bed to himself for the night while the other two slept *valetom*, "top to tail."

Igor knew whether or not the chip makers were home as soon as he stepped through the door. If he heard the chomping of chips, they were there. They constantly ate chips. That was the sound of the apartment after they moved in, and to Igor it was a comforting sound. Crumbs littered the flat. The crumbs ground under his slippers when he went to the bathroom. They spread throughout the apartment, down the hall, into the kitchen, somehow finding their way under the bed in the room Igor shared with his mother. Igor's cats, Russian blues, licked the crumbs off the floor whenever they needed a salt fix.

Late one night, Igor remembers peeking into their room. The three of them reclined on the beds—one of the Chinese guys alone on one bed and one with his head by the Russian guy's feet on the other. They held books over their faces and spoke stiltingly in the constructed international auxiliary language Esperanto. When they saw him, they welcomed him in and handed him a bowl of chips.

"Teach me that language," Igor said.

"Do you know what Esperanto means, Igor?" the Russian guy asked.

"No."

"One who hopes," he said. "We four men here, us and you, we're all Esperantos!"

Igor mouthed the word. It reminded him of an English word he'd picked up from a Western movie: *desperado*.

Igor had never known his real father. Igor's mom and his biological father, Uncle Vova's twin brother, divorced one month after Igor was born. Igor was sent to Abkhazia to live with his grandmother. Around the same time, Valiko, a Georgian, married his grandma. Igor lived with them for five years (and afterward spent every summer there until he was thirteen).

In that time, his mother had married a policeman who turned out to be an alcoholic and an abuser. One night when Igor was twelve, he'd had enough. He was still way too small to stand up to his stepfather, and he didn't know there was not—and still is not—any Russian law specifically prohibiting domestic abuse. As his mother and stepfather fought, Igor called the police. He gave the officer his name and address and said that his father was beating his mother. The officer told him he'd send someone right over.

Twenty minutes later, the police knocked at the door. Igor stayed in his room. He could hear his mother crying. The police didn't come inside. His stepfather left the apartment. Igor could hear them talking and laughing in the hall. He crawled under the bed. They talked and laughed for a long time. When the door opened again, he heard his stepfather coming down the hall and into the bedroom. He snatched Igor's foot and pulled him out from underneath the bed and kicked him a few times.

"Don't call the cops on the cops, idiot," he said.

The next day, after his stepfather went to work, Igor and his mother packed up their stuff and moved in with her brother, who at the time was living in a single room in a dormitory.

"We had nothing," Igor says. "No TV. I was hanging out reading books. Uncle was taking me to the bathhouse. I was going to school. Well, basically, man, I was happy."

Igor has a way of reducing a whole, rather shitty-sounding period of his life to one surprise emotion with the phrase, "basically, man . . ." It doesn't cross his mind to characterize his childhood as anything but pretty happy.

The three of them lived in his uncle's dorm room for a year and a half. His grandfather Valiko used to send money when they needed it. Then one day his mother received a call informing her that her husband had been convicted of a crime called *prevysheniye polnomochiy* and sentenced to prison. His mother didn't know exactly what he did, but it must have been pretty serious. He was a low-ranking cop, and minor indiscretions, such as taking bribes, are the norm. The name of his crime translates as "going beyond one's commission."

The apartment was still registered in both their names, so Igor and his mother moved back in and started renting out the extra room. She didn't tell Igor that his stepfather was in prison; she said he was away on a long business trip. At this point Igor was fourteen, and he understood that something was wrong, because his stepfather never even called.

His friend Oleg, whose father was a high-ranking police officer, found out about Igor's stepfather's situation and passed the news along to him. He was living in Kresty prison, a notoriously overcrowded prison in St. Petersburg. Oleg told him that his stepfather had a nickname in jail: Archimandrite. In the Russian Orthodox tradition, it's a term used for the highest-ranking abbots, from among whose ranks the Church selects its bishops.

"He was believing in God very much," Igor says. "He was there for two years."

In the meantime, Igor's mother finalized the divorce, and because her ex-husband was in prison, she'd been able to take registration of the apartment on her own. He came over a couple of times after that. Igor was much bigger now and already lifting weights after school. He could stand and look him in the eye and squeeze his hand when they shook. His stepfather couldn't go back to work for the police, so he started working for a security company and trying in vain to win back Igor's mother.

"He was saying how much he was earning, and it was a lot," Igor says. "I understood it was some criminal company. He was calling for a while and then, I don't know the reason, he left for his native city and there he became a drunkard living on the street. This is the end of the story with him. Maybe he is dead."

While Igor told me many of the stories in this book over and over again, he only mentioned this one once.

Had his stepfather the cop, who had connections with gangsters, been around during the school fiasco, he might have had some leverage in negotiating with the school director. But he wasn't.

Igor had only his mother, who rarely made it to the annual parent days in Russian schools. She worked around the clock to make what they lived on. "Mom was always working in state tax department," Igor says, "always very tired, always like, 'Do everything by yourself.' She wasn't helping with homework or school. Basically, I was on my own. I was thinking myself, studying myself, and, sometimes, copying off someone else."

During that last week of ninth grade in 1995, he should have been thinking about his summer plans to visit his grandparents in Abkhazia. But word had circulated among the students that any of them intending to continue to the tenth and eleventh grades should schedule one-on-one meetings between their parents and the school director. Igor's school had a focus on English language learning, and Igor had solid marks. From a purely academic standpoint, there was no reason for him not to continue at the school.

Igor was sixteen years old. He'd recently been called to the Military Registration and Enlistment Office, where he'd gone through a medical exam to assess his preparedness for the armed forces. He'd been asked for his preferred division and he'd announced Paratroopers, Special Forces. The idea seemed romantic to him at the time.

It was clear even to him and his teenage peers what these parent meetings with the school director were all about: those who could meet her price would see their kids attend the tenth and eleventh grades; the children of those who couldn't pay would take "early graduation."

Igor waited with two of his classmates, two brothers, Mitya and Kostya, in the hall outside the director's office. The brothers' father was inside having his meeting with the director. When he emerged, he had his hat in his hand and a weary look on his face. He closed the door quietly behind him.

"No, children," he said, "you won't be here for tenth grade."

"It was difficult times at this period," Igor remembers. "I

was standing with my classmates after this, saying nothing. Then we realized it's time to say goodbye."

Igor understood that the kids whose parents managed to pay didn't have to say goodbye to each other. This new insight went a long way toward helping him make sense of those strange, unknowable ideological terms in his head and on the lips—sometimes hopeful and sometimes derisive—of the adults: *glasnost, perestroika, capitalism, democracy* . . . He now had an inkling of what it took to live in the new country he and the rest of the population found themselves in. The Russian Federation was only four years old; its market economy was a colicky infant. By some estimates, 50 percent of the country was living in poverty.

Igor and his mother decided that he would enrol in a vocational program. He wanted to continue at his current school, but they had no choice. She could not afford the bribe.

When the potato chip makers came home late at night, Igor woke up. Usually he heard three quick, consecutive bathroom trips, and then they retreated to their bedroom. What followed was the comforting sound of Esperanto recitations and chip munching. On the night before his last day of school, though, they scuttled loudly into the bedroom, banging drawers and speaking in hushed and frantic voices. Then they left again, slamming the door. That was the last time he ever heard them.

When he came home the next afternoon, he found the apartment uncomfortably quiet. His mother was working late in the tax office. Igor knocked on the renters' door and stepped in. There was one table in the room, and Igor noticed that their books, which usually occupied the shelf, were missing. He opened the top drawer of the dresser, where they kept their documents. It was empty except for a constellation of potato chip crumbs.

They had left without their clothes, which were strewn all over the room, taking only their documents and the textbooks on the constructed international auxiliary language. They never returned to the apartment. *Probably owed a gangster some money,* Igor thought.

He surveyed the room. It would take three years to finish the vocational program. Only at that point would he be able to get a job and support himself and his mother so they wouldn't have to rent out the room. Until then, he would sleep in the other room with her. But he began thinking about the room as his at that moment, and he liked the idea.

Igor had plans to meet his former classmates later that day. Right now, he wanted to have a pre-celebration dinner to mark his graduation. ("Well," he says in retrospect, "it wasn't technically a graduation. More like, 'Sayonara, baby.'") He opened the fridge and found it completely empty except for one beet. "At that time, I fucking don't care what to eat," Igor says. He took the beet from the fridge. It was about the size of a softball. It fit perfectly in his large palm. He peeled it and tried to bite into it like an apple, but it was too hard. He took out a small cutting board. He cut it in half and then chopped each half into little cubes. He ate the cubes one by one with his fingers, feeling strangely free and happy.

He left the apartment and took the path past his childhood playground, past the brick wall at the technical university that he used to scale as a kid, across the train tracks with their memorial signs marking Doroga Zhizni (the Road of Life), which provided the only access to the city of Leningrad during the 900-day siege of World War II. He climbed through the iron bars of the fence into the courtyard of his now former school, Gymnasium 192, Bruzovskaya Shkola, named for the symbolist poet Bryuzov. He looked up at the fourth-floor classroom that had been his.

Mitya and Kostya showed up. He had given them some rubles to buy a couple of bottles of port wine. The labels had three sevens, but they called it Triple X. They sat on a bench in a courtyard and drank it.

He often went fishing with Mitya and Kostya on the weekends. Before dawn, they would get up and take the suburban train as "rabbits," the nickname for passengers sneaking rides before the ticket takers started checking. They'd get off at a military base and climb through the barbed wire. They always caught a lot of fish there. They didn't start a fire because the military helicopters might see them. It was exciting to be where you weren't supposed to be. And they'd fish all day. They'd catch *plotva* and *karas* and *okun*, and Igor would bring them home to feed his cats, his two beloved Russian blues.

They had all expected to be in school two more years. Their sudden freedom came as a complete surprise.

Kostya said, "The school director is a fucker."

"Fat ass," Mitya said.

"I heard a joke about her," Igor said. "She leaves the office going down the narrow corridor and then remembers that she forgot her bun in the office. She tries to turn, but her ass keeps hitting the wall. Finally she understands: like a truck, she has to make a three-point turn."

They laughed. He repeated, "Three-point turn."

At the time, Igor was a tall, skinny kid. He wore his hair long. He liked listening to punk and heavy metal. The Triple X reminded him of a famous Russian punk song by the band Kino, fronted by Viktor Tsoy (a sort of cross between Jim Morrison and Sid Vicious). The chorus went, "Mama is anarchy / Father is a glass of port wine."

They talked for a long time, drank all the wine, did some pull-ups on the courtyard monkey bars. After a couple of sets, Igor felt woozy. He shook hands with his former classmates and stumbled home. He wobbled down the street and tried to feel happy, as if he had had a celebration. He fumbled the keys in the apartment door and entered to the same silence he'd come upon earlier. His head was spinning. He ran to the bathroom . . .

"I remember this moment," Igor says, "head spinning, puking up beet, groaned, and went to sleep." He went to sleep on one of the beds in the rented room that would one day be his, amidst the heavy smell of grease and salt and potatoes.

Corruption could occasion your "early graduation," but it could also save your life if you knew how to play the game. Just a few months before Igor and I met in 1999, he had received a notice to appear before the local military recruiter for the spring draft. He went through the medical commission and proved himself, unfortunately, after years of daily workouts and his vocational training in electronics and truck driving, to be an ideal specimen for war.

When he received the dreaded three-day notice requiring him to report for duty, it was all but certain that he would be shipped to Chechnya, where a cruel and bloody war was brewing.

"The first day, I was sitting and thinking, *What the fuck is going on?*" he says. "I remember it was a sunny day, very hot in the *marshrutka* [shuttle bus]. And I was sweating. In my mind, I was three days from a date with Chechnya. I was thinking, *What can save me?* I was thinking about it. I thought, *I will go there and die.* Three days of life. How to spend it? I already forgot how nervous I was."

Two of the most common techniques for evading military service were paying a bribe to a doctor for a false medical report and enrolment in a college, which would bring about a deferment. Ultimately, Igor utilized both.

With three days to go, it was too late to organize a bribe to a doctor, even if he'd had money, which he didn't. He had just started his first real job, serving draft beer and shashlik at Chaika, one of the city's upscale restaurants catering to foreign businessmen, governmental officials, and prostitutes, on the same dock where I'd later see him swimming. His only hope was to convince the recruitment officer that he had enlisted in a military or police academy, which would land him an automatic deferral. So the next day, first thing in the morning, slightly recovered from the shock and feeding off adrenaline, he called a friend who was studying at a military and space university. He asked how one went about entering, and followed his instructions. He went to the registrar, picked up the applications, and filled them out. He pleaded with the secretaries to process them on the spot. He showed them his draft notice. And they took pity on him. On the third day, he returned to the recruiting office with proof that he had filed enrolment papers.

The recruiter looked at him blankly. Igor recognized this look from the face of the school director who had him kicked out of school.

The recruiter at first said nothing as he scanned the documents.

"Okay," he said finally. "If you don't enter the university, you will be drafted in three months." He tore up the draft notice and made some notes in his file.

"I felt like I was reborn," Igor says.

Reborn, Igor had no intentions of entering the military space university. He decided to enrol at the shipbuilding university, not so much because he wanted to be a maritime engineer as because it had the easiest entrance exam, testing only one subject: mathematics. He signed up, and this bought him the summer, three months to prepare for one entrance exam in math.

Then he promptly forgot about it.

Working as a barman on the dock run by the restaurant Chaika, right there on the Griboyedov canal, Igor sold beer to tourists taking trips along the city's canals. He partied every night with the ship captains.

One morning he awoke with a mind-numbing hangover and the realization that his entrance exam was three days away, and if he missed it, the likelihood that the recruiter would approve another educational deferment was slim. He had, in effect, another three-day notice. He hadn't prepared for the exam at all. And math was not his thing.

"Then," he says, "it came to me. I remembered: I've got my old pal Tarasov." While Igor had attended a secondary school with special emphasis on English, Tarasov had attended a secondary school with special emphasis on mathematics.

He called up Tarasov and offered him a bottle of cheap Russian vodka in exchange for taking his entrance exam, and Tarasov happily agreed to come right over to prepare.

At first, Igor thought about switching the photo from Tarasov's passport to his. He tried, but it didn't look convincing. "I thought about chancing it, then thought, *Fuck it. We will burn.* I said, 'Okay, Tarasov, don't shave.' And he has a heavy beard. I said, 'Don't wash hair.' He had long hair like me at the time." He put the passports back together and they parted ways.

After just three days, when Igor saw him outside the university on test day, he barely recognized him. Tarasov looked like a bum. He had a thick beard, and his hair was scraggly and greasy. Igor was impressed. Igor mussed Tarasov's hair, gave him his passport, and administered the sign of the cross over him. "Go," he said. Tarasov went. Igor watched through the crack of the door as he showed the passport to the proctor. The proctor made a notation, and Tarasov sat down to take the exam.

Igor went to the second floor, where there were two Russian billiards tables, and started shooting by himself. He was practising that shot where you carom the cue ball off the object ball and into the pocket. The exam took two hours. Igor thought, *By the end of two hours, I will make the carom every time.*

But after only thirty minutes, Tarasov strolled in. He approached the pool table and handed back Igor's passport.

"What the fuck?" Igor said. "It's a two-hour exam."

"I'm finished," Tarasov said. "Also, I helped a couple other guys. Then I left."

"Okay," Igor tells me. "I knew I had the right man. And that's how I got into the shipbuilding university, and out of the army for the second time."

In a redemptive story, Igor would learn his lesson. He'd focus on his studies, apply himself, maintain good standing, and stay out of the army. But his intentions at the university were far from academic. He hardly showed up except for biweekly badminton classes. He was there for one reason: to stay out of the army. His marks showed it. Within a year, he was on academic probation, and then he found himself facing expulsion. By that time, he had learned something about how Russia works. Now, he decided, with the salary from his work at Chaika—he would soon graduate from working the canal dock to being head barman, with a good salary and tips—he could put Russia to work for him.

"Then began my search," he tells me, "who to bribe to get rid of fucking army for good. I began to save money." The highest rate Igor came across for a medical certificate that would declare him unfit for military service in 2001 was five thousand dollars. But even in matters of such delicacy, Igor considers himself a master negotiator. "So I was calling to all my pals to get this info. Then found through some guys the real price: six hundred dollars."

Igor called the doctor who charged six hundred. She lived nearby. He brought her the money.

She took the cash and looked him over. At that point, Igor had been lifting weights for almost six years. "Oh, you are a huge guy," she said. She thought. "Let's say you broke your back training." She told him which X-ray clinic to go to. "I will call ahead," she said. "Everybody will know about you."

The next day, he went to the clinic. He gave his name and waited. Shortly, an attendant called him into the back and hung a set of X-rays on a light box. The X-rays had his surname printed on them. The attendant pointed to a small line in the spinal column—a clear fracture.

Armed with his independent medical analysis and fraudulent X-rays, the next step was to go through the medical screening at the commission with the military doctors. His doctor had connections there too. She said, "Go. Doctors over there know everything. When you're seeing the specialist, he will ask you to make push-ups. You need to say, 'Oh oh, my back! I can't!' And he will look at your X-ray and say, 'Aha, I see.'"

"And that's what happened," Igor says. "I also went to the psychologist that day. He asked me, 'What do you think about the army?' I said, 'I don't like when someone is commanding me.' He was writing in notebook."

After the medical screening, Igor returned to the recruitment officer who'd given him his three-day notice two years earlier. It was the final step. He was nervous. If it didn't work, there'd be no more options.

"Well, Igor Yurievitch," he said. "We can't take you in the army." He stamped Igor's file.

In two days, Igor got what they call his "military pass," declaring him ineligible for service in the Russian armed forces. "Whole process took four days," Igor says. "And when I've got it, I remember the air was so fresh. Like a breath of freedom or something."

CHAPTER 4
SUMMER 2009

Six or seven hours into the train ride, Igor and I decide to check out the dining car. The tight corridors of the train remind me of the cramped, stuffy hallways common in St. Petersburg apartments. The sliding, wood-panelled doors to each coupe look like the doors to wardrobes.

A trio of little girls block our way. Igor doesn't take kindly to having his way blocked by little girls. *"Blin, devochki,"* he mutters. One of the girls puts her hand on her hip and glares at him. *"Blin sam,"* she says. (The literal translation of this exchange is wonderful. The light curse *blin* means "pancake," and is also a euphemism for the stronger Russian swear word *blyad,* "whore." In literal translation, then: "Pancake, girls," Igor says. "Pancake, yourself!" the little girl replies.)

The waitress in the dining car, the same one Igor flirted with earlier, says to us, "Buy me a bottle of champagne." Igor asks how much. She tells us it costs nine hundred rubles. "No," Igor says. Instead, we buy her a juice box and one hundred grams of cognac. Russians bartenders measure alcohol in the units North Americans reserve for cocaine and saturated fat. Lena accepts the juice box and cognac—she sits down to drink with us—but does not hide her disappointment.

Lena and Igor step between the cars to smoke. I glance around. There are Orthodox icons taped to the windows and TVs mounted on the ceilings. Three girls in their early thirties dressed in bright sleeping outfits occupy one booth. The table at each booth is set for four. Each table has a little vase of flowers and a tall glass with a silverware set wrapped in a pink napkin. The place settings vibrate with the train's movement. The crackling speakers play a song by Pink.

When they return, Igor refers to Lena as Lenochka. We order two more beers. Lenochka combs through receipts at one of the booths with a Cruella De Vil type more than six feet tall. The table is essentially their office: cash register and folders, calculator, pencil holder.

Periodically, Lenochka gets up and runs to one side of the car or the other. "Buy me champagne. Buy me champagne," she implores when she passes us.

Igor explains to me the ploy with the champagne. She buys a couple of bottles for ninety rubles before each shift. Then she flirts with guys on the train, asking them to buy one for her for nine hundred rubles. She makes a tidy profit, which she splits with her director, and drinks the champagne to boot. This type of scam may be familiar from Western strip joints and escort clubs, but in Russia it comes into play anywhere a service worker wants to make an extra buck. Corruption on the micro level.

I'm a bit loopy from last night's hangover, the lingering jet lag, the constant movement of the train, and the continuous drinking.

"I have never been so drunk on a train," I announce to Igor, and we return to the coupe.

Igor passes out by 8:38 p.m. I lie there on my sleeping shelf listening to the rhythm of the train in the spaces between Igor's profound snoring. Sometimes the train goes *thump-a-thump, thump-a-thump* and sometimes it goes *clack-clack-clack-clack-clack-clack-clack*.

I read from John Steinbeck's *A Russia Journal.* "What do people wear there? What do they serve at dinner? Do they have parties? What food is there? How do they make love and how do they die?" At one time or another, I have put all of these questions to Igor.

What do people wear there? Igor wears jeans and New Balance sneakers and button-up shirts with English sayings such as *You may think you are free but you are already hooked on me.* What do they serve at dinner? What food is there? At dinner, Igor's mother often serves his favourite, pasta with chicken hearts. Other foods there include *kholodets* (meat jelly), pickled herring, salads (many with beets and potatoes), *pirozhki* (the aforementioned mashed potatoes baked into bread), and pancakes. Do they have parties? Yes, they have parties. They party, Mr. Steinbeck. Igor and his friends have parties in the woods near his St. Petersburg neighbourhood known as Piskaryovka on the edge of the infamous Piskaryovskoye Memorial Cemetery, where around half a million who died in the siege of Leningrad are buried. The parties of Igor and his friends involve drinking vodka around a campfire in which they later explode the empty bottles. How do they make love and how do they die? No comment on the former, but on the fortieth day after a loved one's death, many Russians visit the grave to see the soul off into the afterlife.

And then there are Igor's sleeping habits. He snores like, I'm sorry, a bear. The sounds he produces drown out those produced by thousands of tons of train rolling across the Russian countryside. It's impossible to sleep. I punch his arm and tell him to shut up. He barely stirs to consciousness and immediately falls out again. I climb to the top bunk to put as much distance between us as possible.

And just as I begin to fall asleep, around three a.m., the bear roars back to life. He opens a bottle of beer and says, "I am just wondering, why is it this samovar on the train is called *titan*?"

"How should I know?" I say.

He fidgets around with my laptop. Then he watches *Waiting*, a medium-crappy film about American kids working in an Applebee's-style restaurant. He laughs hysterically when one of the kitchen workers refers to the technique of pulling taut the skin of his scrotum as the "batwing."

"Jeff, you remember this part?" he says. "It's exactly how it is. Restaurant life. Truth, man, truth. Excellent."

He plays Frank Sinatra on his phone and sings along with "Fly Me to the Moon." I lapse in and out of consciousness, half dreaming for millisecond bursts. A little later I hear some shutter clicks. I peer over the edge of the bed and see that he is taking photos of the coupe and of me sleeping, and he is laughing loudly at the photos. He shows me a photo with my foot hanging off the bed and another of me with my bare chest covered by a small pink kitchen towel placed there, apparently, as a prop.

So it is impossible to sleep when Igor is asleep and impossible to sleep when he is awake. I remember that, for most of my life, he was my enemy. And now, seventeen years later, he attacks via sleep deprivation.

"Stop fucking my brain," I say in Russian, and he applauds. "Goodie!" he says. "Excellent one."

"Fucking my brain" is the literal translation of a not-uncommon expression in Igor's circles. One might back-translate it as "Screwing with me," but that doesn't quite match the imagery of the original, does it? To be screwed, even to be fucked, and to have one's brain either screwed or fucked— these are very different things.

I give in, sit up and eat half a chicken with his mom's home-made spicy sauce and bread, and listen to him. He wants to talk to someone. It's almost four in the morning.

"Man, it's pity I slept through Moscow," he says. The mutual loathing between Muscovites and Petersburgers is legendary. "When I am on the train," he says, "I get out there just to spit on it."

In the morning, Lenochka pushes her cart of chips and drinks through our train car, demanding again that we buy her a bottle of champagne. She invites us to the restaurant car for breakfast. It's clear she is bored to tears with her job as dining car bait. Igor asks when we will get coupe-mates. At every stop, we've expected the pensioners and their legions of grandchildren to invade our coupe. But no one. She tells us the train is barely half full. Crisis.

She asks Igor where he is from. He says from Peter. She says she knew it, she can tell by the accent. She is returning a few days after our return. "Change the ticket," she says to Igor. "Ride back with me."

"Can't. Have two cats," Igor says. "Stop playing with us."

We sit in the coupe and look out the window. *Thump-a-thump, thump-a-thump.* It's sunny outside, maybe twenty-five degrees, nothing like the rainy dreariness of Petersburg. Birch and pine tree forests, blue sky with not a cloud in it. Today is a holiday.

It seems that it's a rare day that is not a holiday of one type or another in Russia. There are the big public holidays: New Year's Day on January 1 and Christmas on January 7 (the date of Christ's birth according to the Julian calendar, a holiday that was instituted in 1991 after the demise of the atheistic Soviet state). There's the Defender of the Fatherland Day on February 23, when the country honours the armed forces; International Women's Day on March 8; Labour Day on May 1, formerly International Worker's Day; Victory Day on May 9, one of the biggest Russian holidays, which celebrates the victory over Nazi Germany in World War II; Russia Day on June 12, Russian independence day; and National Flag Day on August 22, celebrating the 1991 defeat of the putschists. Then there are unofficial holidays, such as the Old New Year (according to the Julian calendar) on January 14; Tatiana Day (or Russian Students Day) on January 25, when all students get drunk; Cosmonautics Day on April 12, to celebrate the first manned space flight on April 12, 1961, when Yuri Gagarin circled the Earth; Ivan Kupala Day on July 7, the pagan celebration when miscreants throughout Siberian cities douse each other with buckets of water and wander around in the woods looking for ferns; Paratroopers Day on August 2, when members of the military unit the VDV get drunk in the streets and make sport of terrorizing non-white Russians or immigrant workers; Saviour of the Apple Feast Day on August 19; the Day of the

Great October Socialist Revolution on November 7 (October 25 by the Julian calendar), when Bolsheviks seized power in St. Petersburg; and many others. On top of all that, there are commemorative days such as the Memorial Day of Radiation Accidents and Catastrophes on April 26, the Day of the Russian Language on June 6, the Day of Remembrance of the Victims of Political Repressions on October 30, and the Day of the Detention Centres and Prison Workers on October 31. And so on and so on.

In Igor's words: "People cannot track all these holidays. People cannot even remember them all. Just okay, day off. Or not. Whatever."

Today is Holy Trinity Day, fifty days after Easter. All the cemeteries we pass are decked out with flowers and arrangements.

The railway radio station plays a constant mix of old Russian rock and pop contemporary through the crackling coupe speaker. It's seven a.m. Only twenty-four hours to go.

"You have to understand," Igor says, "on the train either you are drinking or you are looking out the window, sometime sleeping."

"It would be nice to sleep," I say.

The attendants have brought each of us a metal goblet called a *podstakannik*. Literally, this word means "under the glass." It is metal and is designed to hold a small glass. We go to the titan, the mysteriously named train samovar, and fill the glasses with hot water. At this moment, Lenochka passes by again. Igor asks her why the titan is called *titan* and she says, "Why are you called Igor Yurievitch? That's how it is."

"No one knows," he says to me.

We put the goblets on the little table dividing our coupe and dip cheap black tea bags into the hot water. The metal *podsta-kannik* instantly transmits the temperature of whatever you're drinking to your hand. The metal handle of the *podstakannik* is scalding.

At a stop in a town called Liski, fleets of peddlers swarm the platform, selling strawberries, cherries, cigarettes, clothes, beer, water, chicken, potatoes, sweaters, toys. They jump on and off the train car and the attendants yell at them, mostly old women in sandals and head scarves. They seem bitterly disappointed by the lack of passengers.

Igor jumps out of the train and rolls his ankle on the stones. He is the big, gregarious drunk guy on vacation. He seems to instantaneously inspire in people either genuine fondness or emphatic loathing. He negotiates with one of the old-woman peddlers for some perogies, which Russians call varenyky, that he has no intention of buying. He just likes engaging in the negotiation. After he establishes how little he could get them for, he says, "No thanks."

We hang out—Igor smokes—for about ten minutes under a federal billboard that reads *An honest taxpayer makes a rich country*. Then everyone boards the train again.

One of the peddlers curses us. "I've sold more eggs to trains of ghosts," she says.

Igor plugs his phone charger into the outlet above our table. It doesn't work. He tries to switch on the train radio. It also doesn't work anymore. "Man, I don't know where we are at," he says. "I have no fucking clue."

"We're leaving Liski," I say.

"Where the fuck is it? GPS not working, electricity not working, nothing is working."

A little while later, we stop in Rossosh. Peddlers here offer huge platters of crawfish and dangle smoked fish strung through the eyeballs. There are stands selling honey and kvass, malted black bread, in clear plastic bottles.

As we've travelled farther and farther south, it's begun to get hot outside and hot in the train. Igor seems able to absorb any amount of beer. With the exception of a cup of hot tea here and there, it's all he drinks. The train radio crackles again. I drift in and out of sleep.

"You are not spry!" Igor shouts at me. "You are like a bacteria. An amoeba. I am filled with enthusiasm. I know where I'm going. You don't. On the way back, you will understand." He slams the coupe door.

Other men who love to talk immediately identify Igor as one of their own, as he does them. Not long after dark—I have yet to sleep—there's a knock. Seryozha again, but not the security services Seryozha whom the train cops busted us with. Another Seryozha, this one from Murmansk, is here to chat. Igor met him on the platform. I realize that it's possible on any given train trip for Igor to befriend an infinite number of Seryozhas. This Seryozha is in his fifties and has lots of recommendations for our travels.

Seryozha says to me, *"Russky mat?"* Do I understand Russian cursing?

"I am studying with the best," I say, indicating Igor.

When Sergey leaves, he and Igor embrace like old friends.

A little later, Seryozha's (the other Sergey's) daughter Katya comes to hang out with us. She is maybe fifteen. Her parents are boring, she says. She talks to us for an hour. She and Igor sing along with ABBA's "SOS" from the crackling train speaker.

I lie on my person-sized shelf listening to them and thinking about the train trip described in a Russian novel I'd given Igor about a year ago.

It takes me forever to read a book in Russian, but Igor burns through them. He consumed a book a day at work as he sat behind the bar of the Atrium ignoring cappuccino-seeking tourists. So at some point we had arranged for him to read those that interested me, or those that I'd heard good things about, and report back. Then I'd have at least a suspect opinion as to whether or not they were worth it.

Like most Russians, and for that matter like most North Americans, he reads pure unadulterated crap. I had passed along to him the Mikhail Zoshchenko short story about the Russian bathhouse—in which he ridiculed the ubiquitous Soviet bureaucracy requiring a naked man in the bathhouse to tie a ticket to his leg in order to reclaim his clothes after washing—thinking he would find it funny (he did not) and the comic absurdist Daniil Kharms (he didn't like that either) and even the Russian drinking novel *Moscow to the End of the Line* by Venedikt Erofeev (nope—at least not until some time later, when he listened to it on audiobook and finally appreciated it).

I'd had more success passing him novels by American writers who had attended the writers' festival I was working for—we brought established North American writers to St. Petersburg to teach workshops to younger writers and meet with their Russian counterparts—and this impressed me the most. The fact that this guy, who wasn't by any stretch of the imagination an intellectual, who'd been booted from school in ninth grade and had mostly refined his English on his own since then, working in foreigners' bars—that he could read and *get* contemporary American fiction was astonishing to me. It helped that he had the personal connections. He'd met a lot of the writers. They tended to frequent the Atrium, and he gave them all discounts on their cappuccinos.

His enthusiastic reaction to the train novel I was thinking about had surprised me too. The novel was called *Rossiya: Obshchy Vagon* by Natalya Klyucharyova, a young writer from the Moscow region. The title is tricky to translate. It's been called, in literary circles, *Russia on Wheels*. But that's too goofy. *Obshchy vagon* translates as "common wagon," and refers to the lowest class on Russian trains. So the idea is something like *Russia by Common Wagon* or *All of Russia is a Common Wagon . . .*

I gave it to him one morning, and that evening, near the end of his shift, he handed it back to me. There was an Atrium receipt in the book, on the back of which he'd written his report. "Read it while I clean up," he said.

> *Story about lost love. Nikita is trying to fill emptiness in his soul by travelling and talking with people he is meeting with. Trying to help and understand. He found the advantages in downshifting. At last he found the reason of living (while he was in fever) and going in village forever. Story made like puzzle with pieces from different times of Nikita's life, which in the end becoming one long story. While reading some episodes there is feeling that there is a lack of something, but in common I recommending it to read. Fucking good emotional transmission.*

Igor's summary is much more eloquent than anything I could do. But there was one word in particular that I didn't get. "What does 'downshifting' mean?" I asked.

"It means when the man is tired to live in big city, he is going fucking far away from that place," Igor shouted as he mopped the area behind the bar. "While I was reading this book, I was crying. Like I wrote you, fucking good emotional transmission."

Later, I read it and even had occasion to speak with the author. She said something that stuck with me: "The plot of the road is the plot of the road in my life, both actual and allegorical—in fact, we are all on the road."

The novel's hero, Nikita, found that he had lost part of his soul living in post-Soviet urban Russia, a recurring theme among contemporary writers. Nikita's train trip into the "real Russia" was undertaken to restore himself.

As Igor and Seryozha's daughter Katya jubilantly howl along with ABBA, I understand that Igor, unemployed in the middle of Crisis Russia, has embarked on a similar downshifting mission. I understand why the book had such powerful fucking emotional transmission for him.

Because he felt that he'd lost part of his soul as well.

CHAPTER 5

During the 1990s and the early 2000s, love was the ticket out of Russia for many Russian women. But Russian men didn't have the currency on the foreign spouse market that their female counterparts had.

The only escape route Igor ever flirted with involved cereal production.

This was in 2002. Igor and his friend Rafik were tapped to be managers at a new British muesli plant set to open in St. Petersburg. The owner of the British plant was a regular at the restaurant, Chaika, where Igor and Rafik were both barmen. The St. Petersburg muesli plant promised to be a good job, but the big perk was the practicum: a month in the UK studying the muesli production facilities there. A practicum meant standing around taking notes, essentially doing nothing—a month's free vacation abroad. The question of whether to return once he was out of the country was one to be answered later.

The word *lovely* was the first thing Igor came to hate about the UK. It sounded so beautiful. It had the word *love* in it. But really, it just meant okay, at best. It meant, in Russian, *normalno*. And he felt, by the end of the trip, that its overuse in Peterborough said everything that needed saying about the place.

The Sleep Inn sat on the highway next to a gas station with a convenience store. It had a small restaurant serving a daily buffet, but it did not have a bar. From the Sleep Inn, their handler drove them ten minutes along a highway with no shoulder, a route Igor and Rafik understood they'd have to walk from now on, past wide open fields, to the muesli plant.

The director shook their hands, welcomed them, and said, "Okay, who will take the first shift?"

He handed them white coats and white shower caps. "I asked, 'What for? I don't have hair,'" Igor recalls. He wears a perpetual crewcut. "They said, 'Anyway, put it on.'" The director asked their shoe sizes and brought a pair of special white boots, steel-toed with non-slip tread, for Rafik.

"We don't have your size," the director said to Igor. "I'll see what I can come up with tomorrow."

He walked them around the plant. Introduced them to the guys, Abdul, Jammy, and John, who in turn introduced them to the system. They spent about fifteen minutes studying each position.

Their idea about what they'd come here for and the director's idea, they quickly realized, were vastly different. Igor and Rafik had imagined strolling around in street clothes, looking over the shoulders of the men working. They imagined studying the construction and schematics of the factory and discussing, over cups of tea, possibilities for the factory they were subsequently to manage in St. Petersburg. They imagined a free trip to the UK and fifteen pounds each per day for meals.

Instead, they found themselves scheduled for twelve-hour consecutive shifts (when Igor clocked out, Rafik would clock in, and vice versa), Igor's starting early the next morning. They'd work six days on the line for that fifteen pounds per day, alongside other guys making more than eighty per day. "The first shift, they were showing me how. The next shift, I was working," Igor says. Every three hours they got a twenty-minute break. Then, so they wouldn't get bored, they'd shift stations, from the mixer man to working the line to filling in the batches of individual fruit and flakes to moisture testing . . . They would hardly see each other except during the shift change. Every week, they had one free day: Sunday. For the whole month, then, the entirety of their free vacation to the UK, they'd have four days off.

They left the plant, carrying their shower caps and white coats and Rafik's matching white boots.

They walked back along the highway to the Sleep Inn as the sun was setting on their first full day in the UK. Igor was transfixed by the cars' headlights. "I think we've been trafficked," Igor said.

Rafik left the road and hopped a small fence. "Are those cherry trees?" he said.

Igor hopped the fence after him. A whole field of cherry trees. They picked and ate them and dropped some into a plastic bag for later.

As they ate, they heard a strange shuffling sound. Rafik's arm pointed at something in the grass, and it took Igor a moment to make out that it was a rabbit. A small grey rabbit with its back to them, its nose in the air, sniffing, and alert ears. All around them, small spots of fur darted in the same erratic flurry. The field was infested with rabbits.

At the Sleep Inn, they walked through the restaurant and inspected the buffet. "There was a very, very pretty waitress there. But it cost seven pounds per person," Igor says. They went upstairs to their rooms. Rafik packed two of the four Sleep Inn towels into his suitcase and zipped it up.

"Fuck," he said.

"What?" Igor asked.

"The maid's going to come in here tomorrow and see the towels are missing."

"So take them when we leave."

"I don't want to miss my chance."

Igor thought for a moment. He went to the door and snatched the *Do Not Disturb* sign. He held it up for Rafik to see, then opened the door, hung it on the knob, and lay on the bed. They both laughed. In the standard Russian hotel, such a simple thing as a plastic sign hung on a door could not possibly keep the cleaning ladies out. "It's worth a shot," Rafik said.

When Igor clocked in at nine a.m., there was a pair of cheap black workboots waiting for him. The plastic soles were more slippery on the floor than his sneakers.

Jammy helped him acclimatize to the mixer. "First of all," he said, "when you on mixer, you the Mixer Man. That's usually my spot, but you cool. When you on mixer, you take it."

Mixer Man handled ten-kilo pallets of pure cashews, fifty-kilo bags of coconut, and other obscene volumes of every nut Igor had ever seen (and some he hadn't), raisins, flakes, and so on. The machine did most of the mixing, but Mixer Man oversaw the quantities and made sure the mixture soaked long enough in the bath before sending it down the line.

"You the man, Igor," Jammy said to him. "You keep at it like this, I'm gonna convert you to my religion."

"I am atheist," Igor said.

"Smoke a ganja, shake a woman. That's my religion," he said. "And one other thing: call me Pomi."

He didn't quite know what to make of Jammy, but he liked him. And after being told to call him Pomi, Igor and Rafik from then on referred to him as Pomidor, which means "tomato" in Russian. The director they anointed Greedy Bastard.

One of the other guys on the shift was Dirty Johnny. "He was a strange dude," Igor says. He had thick glasses and hardly spoke, but when he did, Igor couldn't understand him. He sounded like the Russian voice that dubbed Beavis on *Beavis and Butt-Head*.

"Don't mind him," Pomidor said to Igor. "He eat them rabbits from the field. Done fucked him up."

"We saw the rabbits."

"No, man," he said. He explained that the government had employed some chemical pest control that hadn't killed the rabbits off but made them all go blind. The field was infested with blind rabbits. "That lad right there"—he pointed to Dirty Johnny—"he hunt them and eat them."

Rafik showed up about thirty minutes before the shift change and told Igor he needed to consult with him about something. They stepped outside.

"It worked," Rafik said.

"What worked?"

"The cleaning lady didn't come in because of the sign. But—I can't believe it—she left two more towels, and two more rolls of toilet paper."

"You mean to say she left two more rolls of toilet paper today?"

"Yes."

Igor digested it for a moment. "It is strange," he said.

Pomidor suggested that he and Igor get some booze. Igor walked and Pomidor rode his bike alongside him. The Victoria Wine Shop was one of the few places in the city open when Igor's shift broke.

After they bought some Guinness, they sat for a little while drinking in the courtyard by the liquor store. Igor asked him about UK cops. He had yet to see a police officer since he'd arrived.

"This is our cops," Pomidor said. He pointed across the courtyard to an object that Igor thought at first was a light post. It had a conical base covered in anti-climbing paint and rings of barbed wire. It curved at the top and ended in a dark tinted-glass sphere.

"What the fuck?" Igor said.

"They are watching, and when seeing something, they are coming."

Igor smashed his empty Guiness can, dropped it under the bench, and opened another.

"You moving here, then, bro, or what?" Jammy asked.

"I only have four weeks visa," Igor said.

"Only four weeks visa? Shit, for five hundred pounds I can get you a UK passport. The real deal. Welcome home."

Igor looked at him. He seemed to be serious. They were silent. He thought about St. Petersburg and the white nights. He thought about difficult times in Russia. He thought about the hours he was working with only one day off on what was supposed to be a practicum in a country that respected its work-force.

Every morning, Igor trudged up the highway. He stopped in the field and picked cherries to supplement his muesli diet. For a moment, when he startled the rabbits, their clouded eyes would meet his before they began darting erratically around, sometimes running into the cherry tree trunks.

And every evening that week, when he returned home after drinking Guinness with Pomidor in the Victoria Wine Shop courtyard, he discovered two more rolls of toilet paper added to the little two-by-two tower Rafik was erecting in the motel room. Rafik's suitcase had become pregnant with the Sleep Inn towels.

At first, they had assumed that the delivery of two towels and two rolls of toilet paper must be for the whole week, or that someone had made a mistake. After all, they already had two towels—not to mention hand towels and floor mats—and two rolls of toilet paper in the room. But when they switched shifts the next day, Rafik reported that it had happened again: two more towels and two more rolls of toilet paper. They were shocked, and a bit disconcerted. Did the cleaning lady imagine Russian men like them went through two rolls of toilet paper per day? Was it some kind of insult? "Every day, we were sitting and wondering why she is giving us every day two rolls," Igor says. "Like we are shitting all day."

By the morning of their first day off, they ran out of soap. Soap didn't come in near as plentiful a quantity as the towels and toilet paper. They discussed the situation.

"Should we let her in today?" Rafik asked.

"We need the soap," Igor said.

"We could buy soap. The soap is quite cheap. It is cheaper than the towels."

"If we can get it for free *and* get the towels, that is cheaper, though."

There were other compelling reasons to let her in. The room by now was a real mess.

"It is true. But maybe she is not so generous?"

They thought it over and decided. They had no idea what the woman would do when she discovered two towels where fourteen should be. They removed the *Do Not Disturb* sign from the door and quickly left.

They walked an hour along the highway into town. They passed by a junkyard and stopped. A friend of Rafik's in Petersburg who drove a Rover had had the emblem stolen, and he'd asked Rafik to pick him up a new one. The junkyard had one, but they wanted seventy pounds.

The junkyard guy directed them to a bus that would take them around the city. They saw factories and houses. The bus driver told them about a public swimming pool. Two huge pools—one indoor and one outdoor. He told them which stop it was at. When they arrived, they were the only ones there. Just them and lifeguards sitting in the corners. They didn't have suits, so they went in their underwear.

The lifeguards suggested a cinema nearby. They carried plastic bags with their wet underwear. They had some trouble finding the cinema. Each person they met told them to go in a different direction. One guy said for certain it was just right down there. They went and found nothing. They asked another person who told them absolutely, one hundred percent, it was right back where they'd just come from.

When they finally stumbled across it, they were amazed. Twenty-five screens. The kind of thing that is absolutely typical in and around both Petersburg and Moscow nowadays was to them, at the time, an enormous and exotic technological entertainment marvel. They watched Tom Cruise in *Minority Report*. They had already seen it dubbed in Russian before they left, but both of them agreed it was cooler in English. In Russian it had been impossible to understand what it was about.

They tried to make the most of their day off, to forget about muesli for a little while. To forget about the fact that they still hadn't been given their proper food money. To forget about what had become of their great UK vacation. Russians expect to be taken advantage of in their own country, and while it wasn't necessarily a shock that the British were taking advantage of them, it wasn't the promise of freedom and fairness and honesty that Igor had imagined.

They'd hoped to take a bus home, but they found that there was no bus going anywhere near the Sleep Inn. Everyone came to the cinema by car.

When they entered their room, they smelled disinfectant and cleaner. The stack of toilet paper stood by the door, still seven storeys tall. Rafik walked into the bathroom. The tile and mirror had been wiped. And new towels hung from the rack. This was what it meant to be in Europe. It meant that even though she now had confirmation they were stealing towels, even though she now understood that the volume of toilet paper she left daily was too much even for such Russian guys as them, she would continue to bring it.

"Pomidor told me he can make UK passport for five hundred pounds," Igor said.

"You think it's bullshit?"

"Probably it's bullshit. But maybe not."

"Did you get the money for food from the Greedy Bastard?"

"He gave a little."

"Greedy Bastard. We should be taking notes and we are working like this."

They lay in their beds. They thought about how, after only one week, they hated the taste of both muesli and cherries. They thought about the possibility of UK passports. And they started to think about how to get their revenge on the Greedy Bastard.

The next morning, they went to the smorgasbord in the Sleep Inn and the pretty waitress took their order. She had an accent, Igor thought, and he asked if she spoke Russian. She was Lithuanian and spoke Russian pretty well. She was there, she told them, with her husband, who was the dishwasher. A scruffy-looking dude with a dark moustache came out of the kitchen carrying a bus tub. "That is my husband," she said.

Igor drank coffee while Rafik went back to the room for a plastic bag. When he returned, Igor distracted her while Rafik, watching out for her husband, filled the plastic bag with sausages, boiled fish, eggs, and buns. They didn't have a refrigerator in their room, but they could eat off of it at least for the day.

Then Igor went to the muesli factory for his shift. When he arrived, he asked the Greedy Bastard for their food money again.

"Oh, shoot, Igor, I only have credit cards on me right now. Here's enough for a couple days. I'll give you the rest later, okay," he said.

He gives us our due like giving scraps to stray dogs, Igor thought. A few days would pass and Igor would come to him again and the process would be repeated. Igor was certain that if he didn't ask, he wouldn't get anything. He grew more and more pissed off.

He did like the guys he was working with, though. Even Dirty Johnny was okay.

Abdul was very respectable. He had a family, a wife and five kids. He was the shift manager. He drove a Rover. One day during the break, right before shift change, Igor and Rafik were wondering about the price of such a car in the UK. Dirty Johnny, they knew, drove a Ford Fiesta, which he'd bought used for two hundred pounds. Igor rode in Dirty Johnny's Fiesta once. He'd offered him a ride back to the Sleep Inn after a shift, and Igor accepted. He noticed the back seat was filled with trash up to the windows. He opened the passenger door and Johnny swiped soda bottles and cans and chip bags onto the floor so that Igor could sit. The crevices of the seat were thick with muesli crumbs. Igor remembered the ubiquitous potato chip crumbs around his apartment.

Abdul told them how much he'd paid for the Rover. Igor doesn't remember now how much it was, but it was a lot, and he and Rafik agreed that it was a reasonable price for such a car.

On their next day off, Igor and Rafik invited Pomidor to the Sleep Inn to drink real Russian vodka and hang out. Since they didn't have a fridge, they filled the tub with cold water and soaked the bottles for a little while.

Pomidor slammed the door and the tower of toilet paper— two by two and nearly as high as the top of the door jamb—collapsed.

As they drank, they talked about how much they hated the Greedy Bastard. Pomidor also didn't like him. Pomidor told them that they were not the first foreign guys to come in for a "practicum."

They had worked through the Russkiy Standart and most of the Flagman when Jammy noticed the manual on Sleep Inn hotel services. He found out you could order pornos and you wouldn't be billed for them until you checked out. The room was billed to Greedy Bastard.

They ordered up a couple and turned the volume on the TV all the way down. The three of them sprawled across the beds, drinking bathtub-cooled vodka.

Then Rafik said, "I want to call home."

Igor said, "I also want to call home."

And the lightbulbs went on simultaneously for all three of them.

"Yes, my friends," Igor said. "That's it. Call all your friends, call all your enemies, and say to them, 'Fuck off!'"

First Rafik called a couple of girlfriends back home. Igor called a girl in Moscow, then another girl in Germany. He urged her to spend her euros on any breakfast cereal except muesli. He proceeded to call girls he knew in three different regions of St. Petersburg. He said, "Hello, we are in UK. We are conducting an analysis of the regions of St. Petersburg. What's going on with the weather there, baby?" In one part of the city it was seven; in another part, five. He was surprised, and asked the girl in the Leningrad region to double-check when she said it was five. Other than that, neither he nor Rafik had much to say. The story of their UK adventure had been a disappointment. They drank shots, toasting the receiver so the person on the other end could join them. Pomidor rubbed his hands together like a cartoon villain the whole time, repeating, "Greedy Bastard, Greedy Bastard," and drinking vodka from the Flagman bottle. They kept the porno running without paying much attention to it.

At some point, perhaps with one person or another on the line, they passed out.

Igor had to be there in the morning for his shift. Igor was Mixer Man. He stared into the swirling basin and felt his head spin. His stomach turned with each revolution of the mixer. It was as if he himself, his whole body, were a gigantic mechanical mixing machine. And the sensation wasn't at all pleasant. He was staring into the trough when he heard the Greedy Bastard's office door slam shut. He looked up and saw the director storming toward him. His eyes were the size of golf balls and his face was bright red.

"Igor, what the hell? I just got a call from the hotel. Did you call Russia last night? Did you make many calls to Russia last night?" His ears and neck were redder than his face. He was an even-tempered man, and though inside he might have been in a rage, he managed to contain it. "Do you know how expensive it is?" His clenched hands pulsed in front of him.

"Oh, really?" Igor said. His spinning head and woozy stomach facilitated this charade of guilt. "We didn't know. Only, we were missing our families very much." When he said this, he realized that the only person he'd somehow neglected to call was his mother.

"If you want to make calls, and I'll tell Rafik this later too, you can make them from my office. Whatever you do, don't call from the hotel ever again."

"I'm very sorry," Igor said, doing a contrite good boy routine. "We won't do it again."

By their last week, Igor had lost two kilos and Rafik six.

As they stumbled home one day that week, Igor shouted, in Russian: "Fuck the UK! Fuck the Greedy Bastard! Fuck the muesli!"

They decided to inflict damage. They came across a construction pylon in the street, and Igor pounced on it. He rocked. He planted his feet and strained to pull it out of the ground, but bolts fastened it to the asphalt. "Fuck the lovely UK!" he shouted. "Fuck the bloody UK!" There was another one further down the street. He ran to it and kicked it, but it too was bolted down. Then Rafik tried, with the same result.

When they arrived at the bridge that took them to the highway, where one of the police sentinels stood guard, they followed the cable for the camera down the other side. Rafik took his Swiss Army knife and prepared to cut it. Igor swayed back and forth. He was somewhat nervous, but his anger outweighed his nervousness. Then something occurred to him. He said, "Stop, Rafik, stop."

"What?" Rafik said.

"Don't do it. You will get electric shock."

Rafik looked at the cable and at his knife blade. "Probably you're right," he said.

"Fuck the UK," Igor said. "Let's go home."

The prospect of taking Pomidor up on his UK passport idea was no longer conceivable. For that moment, after the aborted UK vandalism, "home" meant the Sleep Inn, but after three weeks there in that life, Igor wanted only to return home to Russia.

During one of their final shift changes, Igor sat drinking tea with Abdul, Pomidor, and Rafik. Abdul seemed upset about something.

"Some asshole took the emblem from my Rover," he said.

"Yes," Rafik said. "We have this problem in Russia also."

Igor asked Rafik later if he had taken Abdul's Rover emblem. He said that he had. He didn't feel good about it, but he planned on selling it back to his friend in Russia for five hundred rubles. Rafik packed his bag full of Sleep Inn towels. He stole the common-use iron from the hall, and he kept the white work-boots from the muesli factory.

Because the Russian airline Aeroflot had very strict weight requirements on baggage and Rafik didn't want to pay the fee, he wore most of his clothes in layers, so that, even though he'd lost weight, he looked puffed up and doughy.

Igor purchased one final souvenir at the airport. The Sleep Inn towels wouldn't do for him; he wanted one with the Union Jack on it. "To dry my ass back home," he says.

When they boarded the plane, Rafik took off his extra layers of clothing and piled them with his hand baggage. Then they sat in silence, thinking how much the Greedy Bastard had made on them: eighty pounds a day times six days per week times four weeks times two Russian suckers.

As the plane touched down, Igor remembered a few lines from *The Igor Tales*, a twelfth-century poem chronicling the battle of Prince Igor against the Polovtsians, the basis for the classic Russian opera *Prince Igor*. Igor and his men are defeated and taken prisoner. He escapes several months later and returns home, and the poem goes:

> *It is difficult for a head to be without shoulders.*
> *It is equally difficult for a body to be without a head.*
> *It is difficult for the Russian land to be without Igor.*
> *The sun shines in the sky.*
> *Prince Igor has returned to the Russian land.*

CHAPTER 6

What Igor would tell you if you asked him for some context regarding his life in Russia is probably something like what he told me one day in the summer of 2008 during a paintball game on the outskirts of St. Petersburg. We had both been given red headbands to wear; our team would be red and our enemy's yellow. He tied the headband around his neck, the way the Soviet Young Pioneers, the youth organization of the USSR, wore red bandanas around their necks. The Soviet Union was the country he grew up in, and he was a proud pioneer. "Before perestroika," he told me, "we were wearing them like this. And after perestroika, we were wearing them like this." He raised the handkerchief so that it covered his nose and mouth, and turned his hands—index fingers and thumbs—into guns.

That summer, one year before our train trip, he had asked me to facilitate his latest obsession—paintball—by bringing him a paintball gun and accessories from Canada. Every year, he asked me to bring him a list of goods, which he repaid me for. Usually it was just a couple of New York Yankees ball caps, maybe some poker chips. This was by far the priciest haul ever. His requests cost well over a thousand dollars, more than five times the average monthly salary of Russians. So I figured he was doing all right.

Picture me, then, clearing Russian customs with the Igor contents of my luggage: the Tippmann X7 automatic paint-ball marker (designed to look exactly like a real assault rifle, either the M-16, H&K G36, or AK-47, depending on the configuration) with magnesium receiver, sixty days' worth of maximum-strength nicotine patches, black Rap4 Strikeforce swat paintball vest, a three-litre bottle of Jack Daniel's, Straightline barrel kit, the BT Designs APEX adjustable barrel (which has a grooved cylinder allowing one to shoot around corners), paperbacks of *The Devil Wears Prada* and *Confessions of a Shopaholic* in English for his fiancée Anya, TechT Paintball "Ludicrous Speed" Cyclone X7 upgrade kit, a Mario Batali cookbook for his friend Alexei, whom we call Small Al, and a tactical laser sight.

The mob in line at McDonald's near the Moskovskaya metro stop was ten people deep at seven a.m. I did this at least once during each of my annual trips to Russia: had an Egg McMuffin in the early morning, when I had grown tired of porridge and buckwheat pancakes. More of those unanswerable questions occurred to me: How can this Egg McMuffin taste exactly the same as those I had as a child in north Florida? What would these fresh-faced young Russian people be doing with their lives if they weren't working for the well-advertised stable wages and regular raises of McDonald's? Why is McDonald's the most popular Western fast-food chain here, when the others, most notably Rostiks (KFC) and Subway, serve draft beer?

A girl in the patio booth next to me left half her flapjacks on the table in the Styrofoam pancake container, making a little party for the pigeons and starlings. No one here buses his own tray, but I felt compelled to. What is this strange compulsion? Does it mean that I am hopelessly fucked?

My cellphone rang. Igor.

"It's a good day," he said, and then paused.

"Yeah," I said. "It's nice out."

"It's a good day to kill somebody. Listen, bring four litres of water, okay?"

"Okay," I said.

Then I bused my own tray and bought four litres of water.

I met Igor and his friend Alexei, the one we call Big Al, in the subway, at Chyornaya Rechka, near where Pushkin took a shot to the spleen and died in a duel.

Igor and Big Al approached, two hulking skinheads. Igor wore torn jeans and a wrinkled button-down plaid shirt; Big Al, sweatpants and a polo.

We took an endless series of streetcars and buses and *marshrutkas*, each bus smaller than the last, until we were beyond the outskirts of the outskirts of St. Petersburg, and the *marshrutka* let us out in front of a gas station on a lonely stretch of highway. We ran across the road, to a gas station parking lot where a group of people had gathered.

The organizer, Misha, another hulking skinhead, wore camo pants, combat boots, and a black T-shirt with a picture of a skull and crossbones and the word *Пейнтбол*. He welcomed me with a firm handshake, and told us to climb into a car, any car that had room, and follow him.

We drove for twenty minutes down narrow dirt roads until we emerged onto the grounds of an abandoned cement factory on the bank of an inlet to the Finnish Gulf, where a pool of brown water oozed toward a bridge and a highway in the distance. Antifreeze bottles bobbed on the surface. Hundreds of spent condoms and smashed bottles of beer littered the ground.

There was a crumbling barn that Misha forbade us to enter; a conveyor with several lookout posts connected to a control tower; and a rusted-out eighteen-wheeler trailer. Behind the barn stood two dilapidated cranes. Bursts of paintball paint spattered every conceivable surface—red, blue, green, and yellow. The trailer facade looked like a giant Jackson Pollock. Surprising bursts of wildflowers matched the paint. Rigid growths of sharp rebar sprouted from the earth and from giant wedges of concrete.

"Seriously, man," Igor said to me. "This crap. And we will play in this crap. This is the worst, most dangerous playground I have ever seen."

An endless line of cars filed in behind us, and more and more men and several women got out. Igor fired the X7 for the first time across the canal. He held down the trigger and the automatic *rat-a-tat-tat* attracted a crowd, all of whom wanted a turn firing it.

One group of men with whom we'd soon be at war were shirtless, their bodies canvases of scars and tattoos and fresh and not so fresh paintball welts. Some also had precision, high-dollar, semi-automatic markers—though not quite as swank as Igor's. Some groups seemed to be organized into teams. They communicated through wireless walkie-talkie headsets and lined up along the banks of the inlet shooting at the antifreeze bottles bobbing in the brown water. To kill time before the games began, they took cellphone pictures of each other blindfolded on their knees with guns held to their heads.

I had never played paintball before. I rented a marker from the organizer, Misha, that fired one paintball at a time, and whereas the others' guns torpedoed a barrage of paintballs across the expanse of the canal, mine lobbed a single paintball about twenty feet before it splooshed into the water.

Igor told me that, with this rental marker, I fell into the category of what the experienced players call "hamsters."

We gathered in a circle as Misha explained the rules and scenarios. If you're hit, you immediately hold the marker in the air, which means you're dead. You return to base. I speak passable everyday Russian, but much of what he said was war- and weapon-specific, and afterward Igor asked him to elaborate on a few things for me.

"The main thing," Misha said, "is not to impale yourself on the rebar." He pointed to a sharp spike of metal sticking out of a hunk of cement.

"Got it," I said.

Misha and his wife handed out the red and yellow bandanas to differentiate the two teams.

Igor and I drank water and some raspberry tea he'd brought in a Thermos. I asked him where the vodka was, and he shook his head disapprovingly. "You can't drink while playing paintball," he said. "Alcohol makes your mask fog." It didn't seem to bother our opponents, the gang of Chechen vets.

The first game was the usual scenario. Our team dispersed into the landscape. We had about two minutes, after which one of the referees in neon vests blew a whistle. The other team charged after us.

Igor and I hid in the thick of the brush around the cement factory barn. The ground crunched under my feet. I crouched along behind Igor, using him as a shield. He climbed onto the roof of the Dumpster and hunkered, mowing down some yellow-team guys trying to stealth by on the other side. He leapt from the Dumpster and rolled through a dusty pile of spent condoms. He came up firing and turned a three-sixty into the cover of a tree before hitting the deck flat.

Because my hamster marker lobbed, I had to aim up if I wanted to get any distance and let the arc take it. Despite his moves, someone pegged Igor on the side of his helmet with a splash of red paint. "Whore," he shouted. I climbed down the back of the Dumpster and utilized Misha as my replacement human shield. We picked our way through thick bushes to the top of a small hill. I fired into the sky in hopes that my bullets might rain down on someone from the yellow team.

Two members of the yellow team wearing slick blue helmets, the walkie-talkie guys, popped up in front of us. They pelted Misha, but I managed to duck back.

Misha slapped at his chest, and his hand came away covered in orange paint. "Avenge my death, Jeff!" he shouted. I avenged his death.

And as I revelled in the pride of my first kill, a green paintball tagged me in the meat of the thigh.

┅┅┅┅┅┅┅┅

I asked our fellow combatants about their attraction to paintball. A few of them, like Igor, seemed to have somehow or other conned their way out of the military.

Most of the guys we were fighting beside and against were former Special Forces guys and veterans of Chechnya.

Vadim, a veteran and neighbour of Igor's in Piskaryovka, told me, paraphrasing (if I've got the origin of this correct) Jesse Ventura: "Once you've hunted men, it's not interesting to hunt animals anymore." Vadim was on the yellow team.

I didn't know exactly what the attraction was for Igor. If I had narrowly avoided conscription in a cruel military and a brutal war, I'd feel for some reason honour bound to not engage in elaborate, pretend dramatizations of combat. I tried to get a bead on Igor's feeling about it, but he kept dodging.

"Did you see my dismount from the Dumpster?" he said, changing the subject. He smiled at the aesthetics of it. And I have to admit, at least as far as simulated combat goes, he looked pretty good doing it.

Later, in the middle of the Capture the Flag scenario, Igor answered his cellphone, and it was his fiancée, Anya. She was nonplussed that he was spending the day playing paintball with us rather than hanging out with her. The conversation was a short one. He recounted it to me after:

"I just wanted to tell you that I'm not pissed at you," she said.

"Baby," he said, "I'm busy right now. You know this."

"Fuck you," she said, and hung up.

Word began to circulate that I was not only a hamster but a foreign hamster. A foreign hamster on the paintball field. Suddenly everyone on the yellow team was gunning for me.

A whole commando unit, led every time, it seemed, by Vadim, hunted me down early in each scenario.

Misha announced a modification of the scenario rules, which Igor translated as "unlimited respawn." In unlimited respawn, returning to camp after you're shot brings you back to life. But upon my resurrection, I was instantly killed again and again. Sometimes it was funny for a yellow-team sniper to shoot me—in the back or in the ass—at the very moment of my respawn.

Big Al stomped back to camp for a drink of water. "I like paintball," he said. "But I don't like how fast I die." He cut back onto the field again, and Igor whispered, "Al is huge. Good target."

We paused for lunch, potato and barley soup. Igor and I shared the rest of his Thermos of hot raspberry tea. One wouldn't imagine Igor to be the type to bring a Thermos of hot raspberry tea to paintball, but there it is.

After lunch, we played everyone's favourite scenario: Narco-Traffic. One team member with a blue beach ball is the narco-dealer, and he has several points across the field to which he must deliver drugs. Our job was to cover him. There was no respawn on this one. I got shot in the side of the head, and I returned to base camp to inspect my welts and swab the paint out of my ear.

The final scenario was called Massacre. Every man against every man. Teams be damned. Igor and I decided to sit out the Massacre. We peeled off our fatigues by the trash receptacles made from real RGD-2 grenade crates. I had perfectly circular red welts all over me. I noticed that Igor had two of the nicotine patches I'd brought him from Canada duct-taped to his shoulder.

A black German shepherd puppy, Misha's paintball mascot, decided to sniff us out. It was named Russia—not *Rossiya* (a light, noble word, almost a whistle), which means Russia in Russian, but the English word *Russia* (which trundles out of a Russian mouth with a long rumbling *R* culminating in *sh*, like the dramatic *sh* of *shazam*, before exhaling into the final *ah*). At that moment, Vadim passed by and fired his paintball marker into the dirt. Russia scrambled under the van into the soft sand and whimpered. Vadim smiled, showing his grey teeth. (The next time we saw this dog, at another paintball game a year later, it was full-grown and fearless when it came to guns. To that dog, a paintball gun was just a ball delivery system, and he enjoyed nothing more than to be fired upon at point-blank range. He would be both the most fearless and the shortest-lived warrior on any real-life battlefield.)

A retro tourist boat—a replica of a Romanov-era ship—appeared, floating into the inlet from the Gulf. The tourists on the boat peered at us. You could sense from their body language that they were concerned by what must have appeared a sizable army of men with machine guns. "Cannon meat!" someone shouted. Everyone who had already been massacred snatched up their markers and rushed to the shoreline. The tourists on the boat hit the deck. A downpour of paintball pellets rained into the water just short of the boat's hull.

After playing fake war, I went to Moscow to talk real war with Denis Butov, who grew up in Krasnoyarsk in the centre of Siberia and was drafted into the army at the age of twenty. His assignment was rather benign: an internal troops brigade assigned mostly to field exercises near Krasnoyarsk.

The year before his draft, Butov had read an essay entitled "I Was in This War" by Vyacheslav Mironov, who is now a well-known war writer, also from Siberia. The essay had been reprinted in a Krasnoyarsk newspaper. It was about an assault on Grozny in January 1995 in which Chechens tortured and killed Russian soldiers. The story had a strong effect on Butov.

"I wanted revenge," he recalled of his thoughts at the time.

He went to the recruitment office and requested reassignment to Chechnya. They surely thought he was crazy. And they surely thought he was just the kind of soldier they needed in Chechnya.

I had discovered Butov's writings in an edition of the literary journal *Glas*, which publishes contemporary Russian work in translation. I thought his stories were powerful and wrote to him. He wrote me back, and I was surprised that a grizzled veteran of such a cruel war used smiley-face emoticons so frequently in his email correspondence.

We met at a café in downtown Moscow near the Tverskaya metro, where, on August 8, 2000, a Chechen terrorist bomb killed eight people. Nearly a decade later, the memorial at the underground crossing there was still flush with fresh flowers. Butov brought along his friend and fellow veteran Ilya Plekhanov.

Plekhanov was about six feet tall and in his early forties. He basically looked like somebody's dad, and because he'd spent much of his childhood in Australia, he spoke perfect English with an Australian twang. There was something darker in Butov. He was short and stocky, wearing a white T-shirt and jeans. His eyes were slightly crossed, and when we shook hands, I noticed that he was missing his ring finger above the first knuckle. He had a friendly and mischievous smile.

Plekhanov ordered a milkshake and Butov a glass of iced tea stuffed with herbs.

I asked Butov what he thought about his decision to go to war now, ten years after the fact, given everything that had happened to him.

"First of all, I was young and silly," Butov said. "I was kind of romantic, and I thought I must do it actually. Because I thought it was the right thing to do. I think it was the right thing at this moment. I wanted to go to war. I just didn't know what war was at that time. I'm not sure I'd ask to be sent to Chechnya if I knew what I know today. But what happened happened."

Butov's experience in Chechnya eerily echoed the Mironov story that had inspired him to go there in the first place. Butov's unit of thirty-two soldiers was involved in a notorious assault in Grozny in August 1996. "They liquidated all but four of us," he said. "It was kind of hell." Butov documented his experience in the autobiographical short story "Five Days of War," which he wrote one evening after he returned to Krasnoyarsk from Chechnya shell-shocked, poor, lonely, and totally misplaced outside a war zone. He found the website Artofwar.ru, where other veterans posted stories and reminiscences, mostly very bad writings with lots of gore and nationalism and melodrama. Butov's stories were different.

"Five Days of War" recounts how his unit was pinned in a bunker by an unknown number of Chechen rebel machine gunners trying to reclaim Grozny from Russian forces. After an hour of attack, there were ten of them left and only eight who could still fight. They held out for three days with more vodka than water and without the proper training to use their sniper rifles after their snipers were killed off. On day two, the seriously injured among them began killing themselves.

Butov and the remaining soldiers kept the machine gunners at bay and drank their vodka ("Some cause for cheer in this shitty life," Butov wrote) and had conversations about whose side God might be on in this conflict. "I don't think God is on anyone's side now," a soldier named Kuzya said. "It's just a couple of minor devils on dope playing for money . . . They cheat like crazy, and no one wins."

On day three, another unit rescued the four of them that were left.

Afterward, Butov returned to his parents' apartment in Siberia, where he became a shut-in and often contemplated suicide.

"Just leaving the army, leaving the war, I thought there was no place for me," he said. "I had physically returned, but my soul was still there."

Once, he took a girl on a date and tried to describe his alienation to her. She told him that only fools went to Chechnya. Anyone with any sense, she said, could have gotten out of it. She said that if he hadn't gone into the service, he'd have made some money instead of fighting and he'd be successful, but because he was drafted and especially because he asked to be sent to the Caucasus, he was a fool and a loser and no one would love him, and so on. Another time, walking through the park with a different girl, he mistook an electrical box with wires sticking out of it for a booby trap. Later, in the presence of a group of old friends, he explained why it was better to strangle a guard than to cut his throat. His old friends stopped returning his calls after that.

"I knew that I'm not a hero," Butov told me, "but I thought that I had fought for my country. I thought my country will meet me at least neutrally and not hostile. But it was very hostile. I needed rehabilitation. I needed some kind of therapy. I needed work, money.

"There was a problem, and there is a problem," Butov said, "in that service is not a noble thing here in Russia, unfortunately. If we're talking about during the Soviet Union, there would come a point when every man would have to serve some time. Now the common point of view is a real man has to buy his way out of the service.

"When I returned, I divided people into two parts: who served and who didn't. Friends who didn't were neutral at best. Or maybe enemies . . . It was not a single case. It is the common point of view of society on this problem. They hated us. We hated them. Now, I think different. I used to think that only people who had been to war could understand me. Then I came to realize that there were people who didn't serve who can understand me and even more people who served and they are morons actually."

I was hesitant to bring any of this up with Igor. Personally, I always felt guilty around guys my age who had gone to Iraq while I prowled bars and wrote my stories. And unlike Igor, I hadn't swindled my way out of the fate. Could what Igor had done even be considered a swindle in light of the immorality of it all? Wouldn't any reasonable ethicist say that he and the tens of thousands of others who'd done the same thing were in the right? Put in the same situation, I'd have done everything in my power—I'd have paid much more than Igor paid for an X-ray showing a non-existent crack in my spine. In any case, when

I described my meeting with Butov and Plekhanov to Igor, he listened thoughtfully.

I told him that I understood his decision perfectly and that I'd have done the same thing. "But," I said, "I also think, hearing stories like those people told me, I would feel guilty for having done it."

"Well, man," he said. "Better to be alive with guilt than dead without guilt. I was thinking at the time, 'Who the fuck needs it?' I didn't want to be *pushechnoye myaso*." He didn't want to be cannon meat. "This is the question of survival. It means I wasn't guilty. You can't be guilty for your life. How you can be guilty for your survival?"

"And if a soldier who fought came up right now and called you a coward?" I asked.

Igor paused. "It's a good question. I will say, 'It's your fate.' Basically, it is, I think. It was your choice. My choice was not to go on this war."

CHAPTER 7
SUMMER 2009

We wrestle the Red Dog into a cab at the Novorossiysk train station and drift in and out of sleep as the cab careens along the twisty mountain roads, passing in the oncoming-traffic lane around hairpin turns. Barges on the Black Sea dot the horizon under fluffy cotton-ball clouds, the kind that don't look real.

At last, we approach a set of massive cement-block letters reading *Welcome to the City of Your Dreams*. Gelendzhik is a rather small resort town that reminds me of beach towns in Florida, with houses painted in pastel colours and palm trees in the yards. It isn't long before the cab stops in front of a steel fence with Igor's uncle's address. Right across the street is a beer bar, which Igor calls Borya's Place. "We will spend a lot of time at Borya's Place," Igor says, paying the cabbie and fumbling the Red Dog out of the trunk.

Igor visited his uncle for the first time a few years ago. Like him, I'd grown up not knowing my biological father. I eventually met him in my late twenties. It wasn't exactly a Hollywood-style feel-good reunion where we instantly became best buds, but it wasn't awkward either. Somehow, it seems infinitely more strange to meet the identical twin of the biological father you've never known, as Igor did when he met Uncle Vova, than to meet the man himself. But Igor and his uncle had hit it off, and Vova took him in as family.

Behind the metal gate, in the driveway of Igor's uncle's three-storey house, is a light blue Zhiguli parked underneath a trellis of rusty metal fence. Grapes and flowers and the family's laundry hang from the metal rebar criss-crossing over the driveway. The driveway is lined with a flower garden of rubber trees, roses, elephant ears, and lilies.

Their house is about five minutes from the beach and you can smell the sea in the air. The view is spectacular. The mountain range to the north is covered in lush green trees. At the top of the nearest mountain is a sign, in the tradition of the famous Hollywood sign, that reads *GELENDZHIK* in big white letters. On the next mountain summit over is a neon advertisement, dwarfing and outshining the *GELENDZHIK* sign, for the Russian cellphone company Megafon. Because of this advertisement, we'll learn, the mountain has now been rechristened Megafon Mountain.

Uncle Vova sits at the outdoor kitchen table with no shirt or shoes, just a pair of shorts and a knee-high plaster cast on one leg. He has long hair and a wide, gold-toothy smile. He looks like Animal from the Muppets. A decrepit French bulldog woofs beside him.

Uncle Vova stands and limps forward, opens his arms to Igor, calls him *muzhik*. They embrace. Aunt Irina rushes out, shouting at her husband to sit down. Then she joins in the embrace, hugs Igor and hugs me.

We put our stuff away. Uncle's place is three storeys, most of which he rents out. He built it himself, and you feel the craftsmanship in the placement of every floor or ceiling tile and in the sturdy steps leading to the second-floor guest rooms and the third-floor guest apartment, all empty except for us. Then we return to the outdoor kitchen.

There's a thermometer mounted on the wall. Igor looks at it and then looks at me. "Like I promise you," he says. "Thirty degrees in the shade." It's nine a.m.

Immediately, Uncle Vova starts in on the crisis in Gelendzhik. It's still early in the season, but he has zero tenants lined up. He's unsure how it will develop as the season goes on. People may decide to save money on vacations to Tunisia and Egypt and instead come here. Or people may decide not to vacation at all.

We tell him about the empty train from St. Petersburg to Novorossiysk. Uncle seems despondent. He smokes. He ridicules me when I stir a half teaspoon of sugar into my tea. "Watch how I do it," he says. He dumps four heaping teaspoons of sugar into a small cup of coffee. "This is not sugar," he says. "This is vitamins." He slurps loudly and pounds the cup onto the table. I can't tell how old Uncle Vova is. Could be an excellent, spry sixty-five or a worn fifty. The resemblance between Igor and Uncle Vova is elusive, but I see it in the eyes and the nose and the exuberance.

Aunt Irina cooks a massive breakfast for us: bread caked with butter and layers of fresh salted red fish, sausages, scrambled eggs, and coffee.

Uncle Vova tells us that if his leg wasn't broken, he'd be out on the highway with a sign recruiting tenants. The competition is fierce. Almost every house in this area, within five to ten minutes of the beach, has a *Room for rent* sign in front of it. If he doesn't get tenants this year, he tells us, he may have to sell the house. His younger son Sergey should be hustling up tenants on the boardwalk, but instead he doesn't know what the fuck his younger son Sergey is doing. Certainly, it seems, not trying to help the family save the house.

"House," he says. "Reminds me of a little joke. Man catches a golden fish and the fish offers him three wishes. The man says, 'Okay, I'll have a new house, three million dollars, and that was just one wish.'" He and Igor laugh, and I laugh because their laughing individually is infectious but their laughing together is epidemic.

Igor's uncle hunches over the table and tells another joke. Igor fires back with one of his own. His uncle takes this as a challenge, spins out several stories and anecdotes, pounding the table with his fist, his long, thin hair flying around his head. Much of this performance is either beyond my Russian or untranslatable.

The joke/anecdote call and response between Igor and his uncle gets me thinking about Russian humour in general. For instance, here is a Russian joke:

A guy comes to a brothel and he picks out a girl. They go into a room and close the door. Five minutes later, she rushes out and screams, *"Uzhas-uzhas!"* The word *uzhas*, often whispered under one's breath, literally means "horror." So she rushes out screaming, "The horrors, the horrors!"

The madam sends in another girl. The door closes, and five minutes later she rushes out, screaming, *"Uzhas-uzhas!"*

So the madam says, "Okay, looks like I have to take matters into my own hands." She goes in herself. The door closes behind her. She's there for five minutes, ten minutes, fifteen minutes. Then she returns, visibly ruffled but composed. She says, "Well, yes, it was *uzhas*. But not *uzhas-uzhas*."

Another joke: A guy walking down the street sees a man fishing in a city park. The first guy thinks, *Okay, I'll come up to him and I'll ask him, "Anything biting today?" The fisherman will either say, "Yep, they're biting," to which I'll respond, "They're always biting for assholes like you," or he will say, "Nothing today," to which I'll respond, "They're never biting for assholes like you."*

So the guy asks his question. The fisherman turns around and says, "Fuck off." The first guy, with surprise and admiration, thinks to himself, *Eto tozhe variant* ("That's another possibility").

Igor and I walk to the beach with the good-for-nothing Sergey, Igor's cousin. The Russian word for cousin translates as "brother or sister once removed." (There is no word for *siblings* in Russian, or *grandparents* for that matter.) Igor, who is technically an only child, refers to Sergey as his brother. They've only seen each other once before in their lives.

"It's cool to have brothers here," he tells me as the three of us walk along the embankment, a perfect eight-kilometre semicircle.

Looking around, I realize that it's the only place I've been in Russia that reminds me of somewhere in the West. It really is like a Russian version of Florida. There are water parks and human slingshots, long-leaf pines and sunshine. The water is aqua and the sand white before turning to grey pebbles at the shoreline.

The beach is packed—thick as the Moscow metro at rush hour. Blankets and sheets overlap. Feet rest millimetres from heads and heads millimetres from asses. "Usually it's twice as crowded as this," Sergey says, and twice as crowded as this is difficult to envision.

Sergey is spindly and boyish, but there's something kind of Frankenstein's monster–like about him—the square head, deep-set eyes, slow and deliberate movements.

Sergey strips down to his tighty whities. We swim into the bay. I ask him if there are sharks and he says there aren't. I find this news—that there are no sharks in the Black Sea—incredibly liberating. I splash and swim with abandon, unafraid. In Florida, it's always either alligators or sharks or snakes. Here: a whole ocean and nothing capable of eating me!

Why, I wonder, are there no sharks? He doesn't have the answer.

He asks me whether there are sharks in Florida, and I tell him there are. He asks how many, and I tell him I don't know.

"A lot, I think," I say.

He seems concerned. He asks if there are shark watchers on duty. I tell him sometimes there are shark watchers on duty.

We swim back to shore.

"Stones here are perfect for skitting," Igor says.

"Skipping," I correct him.

"Yes, skitting stones perfect here."

He is right. The stones are perfect. And actually, *skitting* sounds like the better verb. So we skit stones for a while across the surface of the Black Sea.

"Once," Igor says, "in the sea, two sharks meet. The younger shark looks up and sees a swimmer. 'Oh, let's go eat it,' he says. And the old one says, 'Oh no no no stop stop stop. You know what you need to do. You need to go underneath while he's swimming and touch his ankle with your fin. Then go down again and wait.' The young one says, 'What the fuck? Let's just go eat him.' Old one says, 'No no no. Without shit it's going to be much more tasty.'"

Uncle smirks and shakes his head. He signals his turn by knocking on his cast. "Jeff, I have a political anecdote for you," he says. "Medvedev goes to visit Obama in New York City. They meet and have a very cordial meeting. They discuss and sit down to a grand meal. Obama's team serves him a first course, a second course, a third course, a fourth . . . and finally Obama asks, 'What else would you want?' Medvedev says, 'I'd like to eat the brain of a young negro child.' Obama doesn't flinch. He sends his people away immediately, and shortly they bring it, and Medvedev eats. A few months later, Obama comes to Moscow, and the same meeting of heads of state takes place. After the final course, Medvedev asks, 'What else might you want?' Obama says, 'I'd like to eat the brain of the deputy of your Duma.' Medvedev says, 'Okay,' and sends his assistants away. But one hour passes. They wait. Another hour passes, then three. Finally, Medvedev's assistants return, and he asks them what's going on. 'Where are the brains?' 'Well,' his assistant says, 'we've shot half the Duma already and we haven't found any brains, but if you like tongue, they have tongues like this.'" Uncle sticks out his tongue and holds his hand way out in front of his mouth and looks at me wild-eyed.

I ask where he heard this anecdote.

He says that it's an old one from the Brezhnev era. "I just updated it," he says.

I'd anticipated another racist Russian joke. There are many racist Russian jokes. But instead, it did something interesting. In this one, the joke turns on the Russian racist, ostensibly, in this case, Medvedev, and it becomes, from the Russian point of view, self-deprecating: no brains in the Duma.

Igor tries to tell another joke, but his uncle interrupts halfway through with the punchline. Igor looks slightly defeated. He is still an amateur in the presence of a pro.

After dinner—a huge pot of Uzbek pilaf charred in a cast iron dish—Igor asks where Uncle's other son, Dima, is, and an uncomfortable silence settles around the table. It seems like a good cue for me to give them some alone time, and I go to the bedroom for a while to catch up on some sleep. But soon Igor appears in our room with the news about Dima.

Turns out Dima left his wife and son, who moved in with Igor's uncle and aunt. Then he had an argument with Uncle that ended with a drunken Dima attacking his own father with a kitchen knife. He was subsequently banished from the family.

"It was a shock to me," Igor says. "Dima tried to stab Uncle. He has serious drinking and drugs problem. We won't be seeing him."

When we head out that night, Dima's wife, home from work in a trinket shop, is sitting on Aunt Irina's lap. She works several jobs every day of the week while Aunt Irina takes care of their son, Artyom. She gets home every day around nine and spends a couple of hours with Artyom before doing it all over again. She wears a silken Japanese-style blouse. Her mother–in-law fawns over her, petting her bright red dyed hair.

Sergey joins us as we walk down to the embankment and find an outdoor beer garden. Waitresses in Uzbek-style clothes bring us vodka and a beer for Sergey.

Sergey doesn't drink, he tells us, because of what happened to his brother. I guess he's afraid that he too might try to stab their father. After telling us this, he proceeds to consume a beer faster than I've ever seen anyone not in a drinking contest consume a beer.

Of course, like Igor, he doesn't consider beer alcohol. And so, by the end of that night, around four in the morning, the non-drinker Sergey is passed out face down on the table at the outdoor beer garden near the sea.

The mornings start with us walking downstairs to the outdoor kitchen, where Uncle Vova is waiting in ambush with jokes and anecdotes. Most of his teeth are gold and he has an aged dancing flamingo tattooed on his forearm. He is clearly going out of his mind with this broken leg. The guy is bursting with energy, which he directs toward entertaining Igor and me and berating Sergey for being a lazy piece of shit.

We head across the street to Borya's Place, where Igor orders a litre of beer. "Why I'm ordering a beer? I don't want beer," Igor says.

"I also don't want beer," I say, "but I'm the only one here not drinking it."

"Da," Igor says, "some sort of it."

We order borscht, but they bring us cabbage soup. "What the fuck the cabbage soup is doing here?" Igor says. But there is no arguing with the wait staff at Borya's Place. They are all

Borya's relatives. You eat what they serve you. Your order is at best a rough outline of your general preference. And borscht is essentially cabbage soup with beets, so in effect we have a kind of borscht minus the beets.

I finish the cabbage soup and order another. This time they bring cabbage soup with beets.

Igor gives me a look suggesting my Western weakness, needing so much food. "Look at me," he says. "I am not eating. I am not sleeping. I am spry."

At night, we return to Borya's Place for another litre of beer and then cross the street to Uncle's place to boil *pelmeni*, meat-filled dumplings, in the outdoor kitchen. There is a full-size fridge in the outdoor kitchen that doesn't stay shut. We have to tie orange twine around the door. The cupboards are plastered with eighties gumball stickers: Van Damme, Bryan Adams, Terminator, RoboCop, Transformers, Chuck Norris . . . Irina cooks dinner for Vova and her daughter-in-law and grandson in the indoor kitchen. We boil our *pelmeni* on the outdoor stove. And we all eat together outside.

Marusya, the thirteen-year-old French bulldog, begs by hacking at me while I eat and staring with bulging, sad eyes. The left side of her body is swollen from a tumour and her tale is mangy. If you pet her, she rolls onto her side to present her dirty belly to you. She spends the day coughing and skulking around the driveway in search of shade. They feed her once a day by throwing a raw chicken head—beak, comb, eyes and all—into the flower bed. She sleeps at night on the shoes piled outside the door, snoring loud enough to compete with Igor. She seems particularly fond of sleeping on my shoes.

She's out of breath summoning the energy just to beg for *pelmeni* at my feet. Igor looks at her with pity. He says, "Last time I saw her, she was spry."

Anya calls Igor every couple of hours. When he hangs up, he says, "She is worrying that I will have affair. She is saying, 'Tell me how you miss me. Tell me you love me.' Everyone is coming to Gelendzhik to have affair."

But we have come to Gelendzhik to get our positive on, and in so doing we will ride four-wheelers. We walk to the embankment to browse the wares of the multitude of four-wheeler rental operations there, and at the very first four-wheeler rental operation we find ourselves face to face with Dima. He is sitting on a blue four-wheeler in a Gelendzhik hat and faux Oakley sunglasses. Dima's whole vibe is very different from Sergey's. Sergey looks innocent and wide-eyed. Dima is lizardy. Sharp lines radiate from the sides of his mouth.

He recognizes Igor, and they shake hands. Igor introduces me. Igor tells him that we'd like to go four-wheeling. Russians call four-wheelers quadrocycles. Dima arranges for us to be picked up by one of the guides at Uncle's house in a couple of hours.

"Let me ask you something," Dima says. "Father is pissed off?"

"Yes, he told me about it," Igor says.

Dima looks at the ground. Then he looks at Igor again. *"C'est la vie,"* Dima says.

They chat awkwardly. It's heavy material, and this is only the second time they've seen each other in their lives.

Igor asks him what happened. "How could you try and stab your father?" he asks. "How could you leave your kid?"

"He said something wrong. I said something wrong," Dima says. "The wife was fucking my brain. So I left. That's it. The only thing I miss is the kid."

While they talk, Irina appears with Artyom. Dima picks him up and hoists him onto the smallest four-wheeler. Artyom pretends to drive. Dima gives him an eight-by-ten photograph of a sailboat on the water. Artyom takes it, still astride the four-wheeler, not quite sure what to do.

Irina, normally overflowing with warmth, chats with Dima through clenched lips. Then she picks up Artyom and he waves goodbye to his father and his father waves back.

We ride the quadrocycles for two hours up Megafon Mountain. We have three guides, eighteen-year-old kids. In a normal season, they do multiple trips per day with fleets of tourists. The two of us constitute their first trip of the week. One guide drives in front of us, the other two in back. They make us wear what amounts to full suits of hockey gear. They make us sign insurance waivers. ("Ten people flipped last year," one of the guides tells us.) They ride sidesaddle in bare feet and smoke as we navigate a technical course between trees, up the mountain. Igor keeps getting stuck between trees and pissed off. We stop on a ridge and the guide points out strange streaks in the rock that he says were made by a meteor.

I ask for one of our bottles of water out of his backpack. I drink it and take in the view. But for the four-wheeler trails and meteor tracks, it seems untouched. When I finish my water, I hand the empty bottle back to the guide to put in his backpack.

"Just throw it," he says.

I look around. It shouldn't surprise. In Russia, some products, such as Lambi toilet paper, are marketed specifically as having been produced with absolutely no recycled paper whatsoever. The Sierra Club in St. Petersburg has packed its offices with spent batteries in hopes that one day the city will introduce a program for safely disposing of them. These are the moments when I discover how deeply childhood recycling propaganda has affected me. "I'd prefer to take it down. I'll carry it," I say.

"Fuck it," he says. He snatches it from my hand and pitches it into a thick, bright bush.

We ride to the top of the summit, where we can see both the *GELENDZHIK* and *MEGAFON* signs. A perfect view of the circular bay. The bay too, says the guide, was made by a meteor, a different meteor than the one that striated the rock. We hang out for a while, gazing at the bay and, on the other side, the village of Divnomorskoye. The only sounds are the squeals of the grasshoppers. The dandelions up here are the size of softballs. On the way back down the mountain, the whine of the four-wheeler brakes is the exact same pitch as the grasshoppers at the top.

CHAPTER 8

gor, Anya, and I watched the 2008 Eurocup semifinals, Russia against Spain, at the Office Bar in St. Petersburg. The Office is a faux British pub, and we had a table reserved in the sunken basement right in front of the big screens.

The Russian national team's improbable showing in the Eurocup, matching up against one of the best teams in the world, with the chance to play in the Eurocup finals, had the unlikely alliance of skinhead hooligans and businessmen in the Office Bar losing their collective shit.

Everyone sang along with the new-old national anthem. But from the start, the team looked unsteady, playing under a downpour. Igor predicted, confidently, "It's going to be draw—0-0, 1-1, or 2-2." The crowd chanted, *"Rossiya! Rossiya! Champ-ee-on! Champ-ee-on!"*

A few years before this, at a party I threw in an apartment I rented in the centre of St. Petersburg, Igor got down on his knees in the hallway outside the apartment door and repeatedly bashed an empty bottle of Baltika into his forehead. The occasion at the time was the ousting of the Russian team from an early World Cup qualifying round. Back then, they hadn't stood a chance. Igor was practically crying that night, wailing, *"Rossiya proigrala! Rossiya proigrala!"* ("Russia lost, Russia lost") and hitting himself with the bottle. Neither his head nor the bottle broke, but the scene made a memorable entrance to the party for other guests.

By 2008, Igor's soccer enthusiasm was less fanatical. He was older and more low-key in general. Gone were the days of swimming the Griboyedov canal and smashing bottles on his head. After Russia went down 1–0, Igor altered his earlier prediction: "Will be draw at half. Then Russia will lose."

With their current star player Andrey Arshavin—the local hero from the Zenit team—playing an awful game, Pavlyuchenko picked up the slack. But when Spain took the lead and Pavlyuchenko missed a goal, the crowd—everyone—quickly turned on him.

The game is supposed to be a war and the Russian players formidable soldiers. The announcer called Pavlyuchenko a *pederas*, which means exactly what it sounds like it means.

A few plays later, Igor altered his prediction again: "I wasn't thinking that our defence was going to be so weak. Our defence is shit, man. Draw at half will be bliss."

The announcer derided the team more aggressively as Spain went up 2–0. Igor used the translator on his cellphone to explain to me the proper translation of the slang phrase the announcer was now using to describe the Russian squad, and it returned *mob of bendy-legged cripples*.

Anya sat quietly smoking Vogue Lilas the whole time, occasionally texting.

Seventeen minutes left. The crowd chanted, *"Davai, davai!"* ("Let's go, let's go!"). Then, from the middle of the field, a pass to no one and the ball went out of bounds. The crowd clapped sarcastically.

"Man," Igor said. "They are running in circles." On the ensuing play, Spain scored and went up 3–0. "The seven-year-old boys playing near my flat—they are better!"

"You think it's the rain?" I asked.

"No, in another case I will say yes. This, no."

Suddenly Pavlyuchenko headed one in. Everyone screamed. A meaningless consolation prize, but they were on the board.

"He was *pederas* earlier," Igor said, "but not anymore."

Any hope was short-lived. The temporary exhilaration of one spectacular goal faded. The outcome was clear. One very skinny girl periodically shrieked hysterically.

When it ended, the businessmen and hooligans collectively mumbled about the *suki* (bitches).

"Where was our defence?" Igor said, dropping his head in his hands. "I didn't see it."

We sat at the bar and listened to the news reports and post-game coverage. The announcer said that a St. Petersburg man threw a TV out of a fifth-storey window during the match, killing another man walking by down below.

"Bendy-legged cripples," Igor said.

He and Anya left because she had to prepare for her exams. I sat and drank and commiserated with the barman. He cried over Russia's loss. The front of his T-shirt read *Happiness is a mushroom cloud*; the back, *War is the answer*.

I had assumed I'd never hear from Igor again after our early morning billiards session at Panda in 1999, but he called me after a few days and invited me to the Russian banya, which he said was even more Russian than Russian billiards, and if I hoped ever to understand the simplest thing about Russia, then I needed to experience it. I didn't know if this was a good idea. After all, he was a dude whom I'd met in the middle of the night on the street who'd taken me to some criminal pool hall after exhibiting highly suspect judgment in swimming the Griboyedov.

But I decided to check it out. We met at the St. Petersburg landmark known as Five Corners, where five different streets converge, for the first of what would turn out to be countless trips to the banya. We walked to Dostoevsky street. He stopped under a black awning in front of a steel door that looked more like the door to a bank vault than a public sauna, and he said, "Citizen of the USA, prepare to suffer!"

We entered a cement and cinder-block foyer that smelled of chlorine. An old woman sat at a schoolchild's desk. The desk was covered with bunches of *veniki*, branches held together with twine, some oak and some birch. Igor picked up a couple of birch, shook them, smelled them, decided, based on some mysterious criteria, which two he wanted, and gave her a handful of rubles. I followed him up the stairs into a smaller hall with wooden dividers separating booths.

Igor ordered two hours of banya time from a shirtless guy in sweatpants. The guy was covered in faded prison tattoos (banya attendant seems to be one of the most popular jobs for ex-cons). Igor rented sheets and slippers for each of us and we paid what amounted to about twenty dollars.

We went to our stall and sat on leather-upholstered benches. Between the benches was a small table, about knee height, with an ashtray on it. I waited for Igor to undress first so as to understand the protocol. I went to one of those middle schools where you didn't dress or undress in front of anyone—ever. So going to the banya with Igor was my initiation into the getting-naked-in-a-manly-way-with-other-men thing. We hung our clothes on small metal hooks in the walls. Once we were swaddled into our sheets, Igor emptied the contents of his backpack: a bar of pine-scented soap, deodorant, mittens, a felt hat with earflaps and a Red Army star on the front, four bottles of Baltika beer, a vial of eucalyptus oil, three packages of squid jerky, and a whole dried fish wrapped in plastic. Then he snatched the branches and went to soak them in a bucket of hot water and eucalyptus oil.

At the time, it was all deeply confusing. I really had no idea what was meant by *banya* beyond the fact that it involved some kind of steam room.

Igor returned and ordered me to follow him. We left the booth and walked past a couple of guys kicked back on an orange couch. They were soaking wet with sheets tied around their waists like us. The TV was tuned to a soccer match. Two cigarettes smouldered in ashtrays in front of them, but they seemed to be asleep or passed out. We walked down a hall and into the tiled shower area. There were buckets sitting on concrete platforms and four shower stalls. An impossibly skinny dude with long hair lathered an old man's whole body with an oak *venik*. The look on the old man's face as the skinny dude washed him was piercing and severe. In the very back was a ladder leading to a small rectangular pool, about ten feet by six feet. The water had a green tint. Igor opened a wooden door to the *parilka*—the steam room.

"Ah!" he said. "It's a good steam. Now we begin. Find a place and lay down right away. Soon, I will come." He shut the door behind me.

There were three other guys in the steam room. I walked up the wooden steps and sat on the bench across from them. One of them had a huge ladle called a *kovshik*. He used the handle to open the black iron doors of a brick oven, then he dipped water from a bucket and splashed it on the rocks. One of the other guys shouted, *"Dobavim,"* meaning to throw more water on the rocks.

The water sizzled and a wall of two-hundred-degree wet steam pushed across the small room. It melted through my sinuses, and I ducked to get under it. The guys across from me squinted. The other guy shouted, *"Dobavim, dobavim!"*

I spread my sheet across the bench and lay down supine. The sheet was scalding. Hovering my arms and feet slightly, I tried to minimize the parts of my body that burnt when they touched the bench.

Igor reappeared armed with the two birch branches, one in each hand, both of them dripping water and sweet-smelling eucalyptus oil. His sheet was bunched around his waist, and he wore the mittens and the felt Red Army star hat with flaps over his ears.

He ascended the steps.

"Cover your dick," he said.

I covered my dick.

Igor whipped the branches in the air so the heat collected in the leaves. Then he lightly—surprisingly gently—smacked every inch of me, stopping only to push the leaves into my face and to poke my heels with the stick end of the branches. This was the second time I had met him in my life. It took about ten minutes, until the leaves—by then dry and crisp—singed the skin and Igor declared enough.

We hurried out of the *parilka* red and puffy. I gasped for

breath. Sweat stuck leaves and twigs to me. We hung our sheets on metal coat racks and jumped into the freezing cold pool. After about five minutes, we climbed out and returned to our booth.

"You feel the rebirth?" he asked.

"I feel it," I said. And I did.

I sipped from a bottle of beer. Every American sweatbox cautions against drinking and sauna, but you're unlikely to find a bathhouse anywhere in Russia in which sweaty, naked men (and for all I know, women too) are not consuming some alcohol or other. I got immediately buzzed and light-headed. I chewed a few strings of the squid jerky, which is like salted rubber bands.

Igor tore the dried fish (*vobla*) in half and plucked out a shrivelled thing the size and colour of a golden raisin that he insisted was its pancreas. "Eat," he said, holding it out to me in his palm. I shook my head.

He popped it into his mouth and then broke off pieces of the *vobla* and munched happily.

Then we did what you do in the chill-out hall of the banya: we talked. We talked about a lot of things. We talked about billiards: "Practise, practise, practise," Igor said. We talked about women: "The girls here don't understand that I am alive. I am not a slot machine. They only understand how to take."

We repeated the process—*parilka*–pool–booth–squid jerky–beer—three times, until we had the desired effect: skin spider-webbed with red blotches and mental relaxation to a degree requiring total concentration just to maintain consciousness.

"Do you understand why people are coming in banya now?" Igor asked. He didn't wait for an answer. "Probably they even doesn't think about it. But somebody, for entertainment like with their friends, to drink some beer, to talk and stuff without the girls . . . They still didn't realize that their lives are beginning again. Probably it's true."

Nine years later, on the day after the Spain–Russia World Cup debacle, Igor had one of his "day offs," as he calls them. We headed to the famous Bateninskaya banya on Karbysheva street, also known as the Round Banya, also known as Shaiba, "hockey puck." A white building with a hollowed-out space in the middle for an outdoor pool.

In those nine years, we had banya-ed countless times. We had hit most of the banyas in the city. And Bateninskaya was our favourite. It's unique, with its circular structure and outdoor pool, and the steam is often perfect. The possibility of running into naked girls at the shared outdoor pool was also an advantage.

As we entered Shaiba, we were surprised to see the same group of cops who had caused a ruckus here once before. That day, we were sitting in the chill-out room. We had soggy, cold sheets wrapped around our waists. We sipped beer, and I struggled not to pass out from too-frequent intervals in the steam room. A group of drunken cops settled up their bills and retrieved their valuables from the safe. As the banya attendant, a kindly middle-aged woman whose unfortunate job it is to sit in a room of naked, drunk, and sweating men, handed a service revolver back to one of the policemen, he fumbled and it discharged right over her head. Everyone in the chill-out room, including Igor and me, hit the deck.

Now the drunk cops were drunk again and leaving the banya. *"S lyogkim parom!"* the one who nearly shot the cashier in the head said to Igor. I've never heard a great translation of this phrase. Literally, it's "With a light steam." You say it to people as post-banya congratulations. It takes the same grammatical form as "Happy Birthday" or "Happy New Year," neither of which include the word *happy* in Russian. Instead, it's "With birthday" or "With the New Year."

The phrase is the alternate title of the most popular Russian holiday film, the Russian *Miracle on 34th Street*: *The Irony of Fate* or *With a Light Steam*. The plot is simple. A group of four friends go to the banya on New Year's Eve as per their long-standing holiday tradition. They get totally plastered there and two of them pass out. One of the men passed out is supposed to go to the airport for a trip to Leningrad, but the two plastered friends can't remember which one. They make their best guess and send the wrong friend to Leningrad. When he arrives, not realizing he is in Leningrad, he takes a cab to his address, 3rd Builders Street, Building 25, Apartment 12. The street exists and the building is the same as his, his key works in the lock, and even the decor is similar. A beautiful woman lives there, and romantic comedy ensues . . .

The drunken cop slurred and swayed as the banya attendant returned the officers' things from the so-called safe, a drawer behind the counter. They were trying to pay but seemed unable to find their money.

She produced a handgun snapped into a leather holster. With her free hand, she pointed to a hole, about the diameter of a number two pencil, in the wall behind her. "Last time you came in here and got as stupid drunk as you are now, I handed you back your gun and it went off. You gave me your gun with the safety off. You could have killed me, and you probably don't even remember."

"The safety is on, grandma," one of them said. "We're not going to kill you."

"You told me the safety was on last time, bitch. And now you come in here again, and give me your gun, and again you leave completely shit-faced."

She took their money and handed the man his gun. He laughed and dropped it into his sports bag and they left.

Then she turned to us. "See that hole? Do you see that hole?" She put her finger again to the bullet hole in the wallpaper. She shook her head and cleared her throat. "Now you," she said to us. "Who are you? What do you want? I will never take these assholes' gun again. Never."

Igor ordered two hours of banya time, two sheets, and two birch *veniki*. She assigned us to the booth the drunken cops had just left, number three. Each stall has small swinging doors, like in a western saloon, a picnic table, and two benches. The police had left a cheap Casio watch and rubles all over the floor in stall number three.

We sat down and changed into our sheets.

Igor and I ordered two mugs of kvass, a malted black bread beverage that comes in tall frothy mugs. A waitress, also middle-aged, busted through the doors of our stall and placed the heady mugs of kvass on our table.

"She doesn't seem at all bothered by us naked men, does she?" I said.

"She's seen so many dicks," Igor said, "she doesn't fucking caring."

The loud, jolly voices of thirty or so Russian men in the midst of their weekend steam competed with the famous voice of Russian soprano Anna Netrebko coming from the TVs mounted on the walls. Lots of bodies make for the best banya conditions.

One older guy sitting next to us asked if we were from Israel. Igor laughed and told him I was a foreigner and he was Russian.

A cricket chirped somewhere under the benches below us. Igor and the man didn't seem to notice it. Igor tried to explain the quality of a proper steam like this one: "You feel it with the lungs. It's what it means to sweat and not feel heat." And I got it. It's hot. Scalding hot, but not cutting. A light steam.

A little boy shielded his face with his hand and sat next to his father on the bench.

"Papa, it's too hot," the boy said.

"Okay," the father said, "we'll leave in thirty seconds."

The boy counted out loud—"Thirty, twenty-nine, twenty-eight, twenty-seven . . ."—and crept toward the exit.

I listened for the cricket. If it were a machine, some kind of recording, it'd have a rhythm. But this seemed a random, occasional chirp.

"I think it's a real cricket," I said.

"Man," Igor said, "no being could live in banya. Even cricket. It's bullshit."

We were on our warm-up steam. During your first go, you're absolutely dry, and the way you want to play it on your first go, according to Igor Rules, is to sit there only until you hit the sweat point, the moment your dry skin bursts into tears.

I told Igor to take his place on the bench so that I could beat him.

"You are not ready," he told me.

"I've studied long enough," I said. "I can't just be your birch branch bitch."

This was persuasive logic for him. He handed over the Red Army star hat, the gloves, and the *venik*.

The Russian banya habit is documented as far back as 1113 in the *Primary Chronicle* of Kievan Rus', a loose coalition of Slavic tribes:

> *They warm [the banya] to extreme heat, then undress, and after anointing themselves with tallow, take young reeds and lash their bodies. They actually lash themselves so violently that they barely escape alive. Then they drench themselves with cold water, and thus are revived. They think nothing of doing this every day and actually inflict such voluntary torture upon themselves. They make of the act not a mere washing but a veritable torment.*

There were Russian jokes during World War II suggesting that if they could only get Hitler into a banya, they could end the war.

But the ceremony of the banya is not wholly a torment. Only to the casual observer or the unstudied amateur is the lashing violent. There are massage schools in Russia that teach *venik* massage, but it's also a kind of folk knowledge, like reducing high blood pressure with leeches or curing a cold with onion tea. Igor learned from his uncle, his mother's brother, with whom they lived for a while after she and his stepdad split.

You start by shaking the branches lightly over the whole body. With one *venik* you hit the person, while you stir the air with the other. The leaves immediately dry out, so you have to periodically stop and rub them across the body to collect sweat. It may look as if the beater is wailing on the beatee, but the truth of the banya is that the beater is the one who really suffers.

After a minute or so, I was done; my hands burned, my heart pounded, and I felt as though I might pass out.

"You get B-minus," Igor said, and this was surely grade inflation.

The thing that makes Shaiba special is the outdoor pool, shared by men and women, that constitutes the centre of the puck. We swam a few laps then returned to our booth for beer and squid jerky. Igor peeled apart *vobla*. He opened them up lengthwise with his thumbnail and rolled out the pancreas. He offered it to me. As usual, I declined and he ate it.

"You know why you got B-minus?" he said. "You were too much collecting sweat. The next step after getting A in beating me, to fulfill the spirit of banya, is to eat this fucking fish with beer. The more stinky, the more tasty."

In this case, I am afraid that I may never fulfill the spirit of the banya.

CHAPTER 9

On the night of August 7, 2008, war broke out between Russia and Georgia in Tskhinvali, a city in South Ossetia. South Ossetia and North Ossetia are largely homogeneous ethnically, but they ended up across the border from each other in 1991 after the collapse of the Soviet Union— North Ossetia in Russia and South Ossetia in Georgia. The South had long sought reunification.

The conflict lasted all of five days, several thousand died, many more were displaced, and the world went into an uproar. It immediately became a campaign issue in the American elections, and French president Nicolas Sarkozy stepped in to broker a peace deal while Russian tanks rolled toward the Georgian capital of Tbilisi.

I had planned to spend my last few weeks in Russia that summer watching the Beijing Olympics on TV. Igor had to work every day and spend his day offs with Anya. I hoped to see the American-born J.R. Holden run the point for the Russian national team (he had been naturalized Russian by decree of Putin for the express purpose of running the point for the national team) against the United States. That match-up was not to be (Russia sucked in group play), and the whole Olympics paled against the war coverage.

I had the same armchair post as the rest of Russia, but for me it would be the first time I'd watch a major world event through the lens of a censored media.

August 8, the day of the Summer Olympics opening ceremony in Beijing, I turned on Channel One, the Russian state-controlled television station, to find out that Georgia had launched an attack against South Ossetia.

The footage of Georgian missiles falling on Tskhinvali played on repeat. The emphasis was on the fact that the missiles were launched in civilian areas. *Georgia blocks Internet,* the ticker read. One of the first interviews I saw was with a North Ossetian Cossack, a guy straight out of an Isaac Babel short story in silken red shirt and fur hat, who, speaking on behalf of patriotic Cossacks everywhere, proclaimed, "If Russia is involved in a conflict, we will all go there to protect her!"

In short, according to the Russian media: Georgia provoked aggression; Georgia's actions constituted genocide, the murder of around two thousand South Ossetians creating a humanitarian catastrophe; Georgians had been trained, provided with arms, and given the go-ahead to move in by the West, specifically the United States.

Later, at an Internet café, I looked up CNN. The talking heads were already questioning the Russian assertion that Georgia launched missiles first. Presidential candidate John McCain condemned "Russian aggression."

Soon, the Russian media announced that Russia had liberated the South Ossetian capital of Tskhinvali while Georgia declared a state of war. The Western media reported that Russian forces were sixty-five kilometres outside Tbilisi, sowing rack and ruin in their path. Grigory Karasin, Russian deputy minister of foreign affairs, described the Georgian offensive as "uncivilized," "criminal," "wicked." Medvedev declared that Russia was going to protect Russian citizens in South Ossetia and that many people had already died because of the "barbarous" actions of Georgia.

The Russian line about Georgian aggression seemed strange. Would Georgian president Mikheil Saakashvili really be so bold as to think the West would engage Russia in direct military conflict over Georgia?

The Western line, that Russia had prepared for and planned the attack on its end, made more sense.

There had been an ongoing Russian initiative to give South Ossetian citizens Russian passports, in effect instantly populating the conflict zones with its citizens. Russian troops who had been amassing in South Ossetia during recent months were characterized as "peacekeepers." It might have been a master chess move by Putin to set everything in place then wait for Saakashvili to get nervous.

In Medvedev's first appearance on the world stage, presenting Russia's position on the conflict, he sputtered out of the gate, reading from a prepared speech, looking worried and unsure. Meanwhile, French president Sarkozy, who had swooped in to broker a peace deal, played it like a master, practically dancing, all charisma and gesticulation alongside the wooden and bleary-eyed Russian president.

On Russian TV, the war was only ever referred to as "the humanitarian catastrophe in South Ossetia." Flipping through the channels, I saw that a little peace sign with a blip of text reading "No war" had been added in the corner of all Russian MTV broadcasts. Russian stations showed images of South Ossetian pensioners with bandages around their heads describing missiles arriving without warning. Western stations showed images of Russian troops hooting wildly and shooting up already dead Georgians on the side of the road.

Russian troops nearly made it to Tbilisi—it was unclear what would happen if Russia took the Georgian capital—but then they stopped short. And a nervous pause settled over the whole affair.

Much later, Human Rights Watch and European Union reports on the Russia–Georgia conflict appeared. Their conclusions: Georgia ignited the conflict *and* Russia was guilty of violating numerous aspects of international law in its provocations, including the amassing of "peacekeepers" in South Ossetia. The funny thing is that, in these reports, the majority of the blame is laid at the feet of the Western darling Saakashvili, who comes off as trigger-happy and wilfully reckless.

In the black-and-white story of the conflict, the real truth turned out, as it often does, to lie in the grey area. But from where I was sitting, the censored Russian media had the better claim to the more correct version.

I had a few days in Moscow before my flight back to Toronto. I looked up the Chechen vets Denis Butov and Ilya Plekhanov, and we arranged to meet at a beer hall near Mayakovsky Square.

In the courtyard of the apartment I was staying at, a group of young boys armed with butter knives viciously stabbed the ground. They seemed to be playing a game. The game seemed to be: viciously stab the ground. And they were quite good at this game.

I met Butov and Plekhanov and their friend Arkady Babchenko at the beer hall. Butov and Plekhanov were editing the Art of War site and print magazine. Babchenko had covered the war for both *Novaya Gazeta* and Artofwar.ru.

The waiter brought us massive one-litre mugs of Pilsner Urquell.

Hanging out with these guys made me feel as though I was among a different species of human being than myself, and while I wanted to steer the conversation to the Georgian conflict, they made it clear they were there because I had offered to buy them beer and that they, especially Babchenko, would talk about what they wanted to talk about.

Denis criticized the stories of another contemporary writer. "His soldiers are running around fearing for their lives everywhere," he said. "Yes, I feared for my life when they tried to kill me. But this feeling of fear goes away after a little while."

"For me," Arkady said, "the most important thing is, if we are talking about war, when you read the text, do you smell the smell or you don't smell the smell? Do you feel that heat or you don't feel that heat?

"The matter is in people, and people in all wars behave the same," he said. "In all wars, personal features and the behaviour on display during the war are absolutely similar. Consider any war movie with Chuck Norris. He has all the right equipment, all the right moves, but the behaviour at war and his personal characteristics are not specified. Then it's not real war."

"Leave Chuck Norris alone," Denis said.

Babchenko served his initial tour of duty in Chechnya in 1997 at eighteen years of age. He returned, got a university degree, and then re-enlisted for another six-month tour in 2000. In a photo of his family seeing him off for his first tour, he's skinny as a rail. He looks like a bird, like a joke. He looks like someone who wouldn't make it back from the Russian army once, let alone twice.

I asked him what made him enlist the second time, and what drove him back effectively a third time in August as a correspondent, as one of only a handful of journalists travelling directly into the line of fire.

"Nothing drives me to war, you understand," he said.

"For money, bastard," Denis said. "He's just bored at home."

"When the Russian soul is struggling and cannot find how to live anymore," Ilya said, "the Russian soul always goes to war."

Arkady ignored them both. "For me, the fact that I went to both wars is absolutely normal. Why no one else went? Why no one else went? That's the question. When in your country there is a war, why nobody goes to that war? Let's talk about South Ossetia. All Russian troops there were screaming, 'We are great Russia! We are going to conquer everyone!' How come nobody went anywhere, and how come nobody conquered anyone?"

"I don't know exactly what you mean," I said.

"That's the question," he said. "What do I mean? We're trying to answer it."

The night the Russia–Georgia conflict started, Arkady boarded a plane to the Caucasus. He attached himself to a Russian unit and sent a chronological photo record of their journey and his first war as a non-combatant. The images began in Vladikavkaz, where he met and interviewed those modern-day Cossacks lining up to go into war against Georgia to protect the Motherland. Then to the destruction of Tskhinvali. He travelled through South Ossetia and into Georgia. Charred bodies in puddles on the sides of the road as tanks go past. Fleeing Georgian troops.

The cover of the print issue of *Art of War* magazine featuring Arkady's South Ossetia reporting showed a young, tough Russian solider. His fatigues were open, revealing a gaping wound the size of a pear above his heart. The headline read, *Indestructible Union*.

The issue included a long piece about Babchenko's trip with the Russian unit. His journalistic style focuses on the gruesome details, the visual and situational details that are the reality of war, and the effect of bearing witness to it all. At one point he wrote: "I always dreamed of writing stories for children, but for nine years already I've written about bloated corpses in the heat on the streets of ruined cities. You want a great Russia? Here she is. Take a whiff."

When the bill came, Arkady wrote, *Why do you water down the beer?* and *From Russia With Love* at the bottom.

We walked down Tverskaya street and Ilya joked that the three of them were like the three heroes from Erich Maria Remarque's *All Quiet on the Western Front*. Butov bought cans of beer from a kiosk for all of us and we stood by the Mayakovsky statue in the cold.

Arkady bummed two cigarettes from an Italian tourist. After he smoked those, he approached another guy in a business suit, who gave him an entire pack of menthol Vogues. Denis refused to smoke them. Arkady sucked one down.

"Every time I'm around you guys, you talk to me about stories," I said. I had wanted to discuss the particularities of the conflict with them, and they had wanted to discuss the authenticity of war stories.

Arkady told me that if not for the stories of Remarque, he probably would not have gone to war to begin with. This reminded me of Butov's statement that the stories of Mironov led to his request for assignment to Chechnya.

Arkady despises writing that dramatizes and romanticizes war. He's afraid it will influence young readers in the way he and Butov were influenced. "You should write only about how war is awful," he said.

Though he has now become the famous writer of their group, Babchenko was initially attracted to the Art of War (kind of like an Internet community, a Veterans of Foreign Wars post, and a psychiatric support group for veterans all rolled into one) by Butov's stories of Chechnya. Veterans and combatants from every war in recent history have posted their stories there. It's how the three of these guys met.

Arkady said that he was perusing the site and read Denis's work. It moved him to write to Denis and to return to his own memoirs, which he had abandoned out of depression, memoirs that would eventually become the book *One Soldier's War*, a harrowing and graphic account of his time in Chechnya.

"Arkady wrote me a big email letter," Denis said. "I thought he was the typical dickhead."

"He just learned this word today," Ilya told me. "Now he will say it all the time."

Ilya had a similar experience, drawn into the site in large part by Butov's Chechnya stories.

Denis seemed embarrassed by his friends' praise. He recalled meeting Ilya for the first time on the train to Odessa for an Art of War conference there.

"He was drunk and very aggressive," Denis said. "Then we drank some, and I came up to his level."

"We are beating around the bush, Jeff," Arkady suddenly said to me. "Do we have a generation of Chechen war writers in Russia right now or not?"

He posed the question that I did not ask. Then he answered it.

"Dostoevsky was right: there are those who dare and those who are afraid. Will we talk about the war or will we be still silent? If we were to meet three years ago, I would say we don't have writers about these wars. Now I can say that there are."

I asked him about the common viewpoint that the Russian army damages young men.

"I want to tell you that if five years ago I felt like a leper, nowadays I don't feel like a leper," he said. "I feel like one of the normal people in society. I think that we are normal. We are normal. And it's not that this world is normal. It's us who are normal in an abnormal world. And that's what I am happy about. I am really happy that I found people who think the same way. And I am happy that we have our own brotherhood."

When we finished our beers, Arkady and Ilya ran to catch the metro home to their wives and children before it closed at one a.m. Denis, who lived with his brother and worked in IT, walked a little way with me. He told me that Ilya's and Arkady's wives hated him because every time they got together with him, they ended up drunk.

"I am the enemy of the state," he said.

I emailed Igor when I got back to Canada and told him about meeting again with the Chechen vets and Babchenko's perspective on the war. He responded by sending me a video clip from a Russian site that showed a series of nuclear explosions wiping out the major cities of the world. He wrote, *all world in dust man, everybody are prepared.*

Doom was already on his mind. I had arrived in Russia at the beginning of the summer of 2008. I had arrived in a resurgent country. When I left at the end of that summer, new blood had been shed and the world was tipping toward crisis.

CHAPTER 10
SUMMER 2009

gor reports to Uncle Vova that we saw Dima, the knife-wielding would-be prodigal son.

"Was he drunk?" Uncle Vova says, his face souring.

"No," Igor says. "He was working."

We sit at the outdoor kitchen in silence.

"I'd like to see you back together again, and to help make the first step," Igor says.

Vova instantly turns bright red. He enumerates how much money he's spent on keeping Dima out of jail and raising his children, only to be attacked with a knife.

"It is the end," Vova says.

Silence again. Igor clenches his lips. I can see him considering whether to push this thing further or let it drop.

We all look at Artyom. The boy refuses to release even for a second the photo of the sailboat that his father gave him. He clutches it in one hand as he rides his tricycle in circles on the driveway. The photo is already creased and torn and covered in greasy fingerprints.

I receive a text message on my mobile that reads *I am in the hospital, please, as soon as possible help me by adding money to this phone number?*

It's a scam I heard about in Moscow. I pass the phone around, and it cuts the tension of the moment. Irina tells us about the SMSs she's been receiving: she wins the lottery, she wins a new car. At first she thought they might be real and got excited. "Then I called and they told me all I had to do was to pay a small fee that was not so small," she says. She brandishes her flip-top cellphone while she tells the story, proudly showing off the photo of an Orthodox icon on the home screen. When she closes it, there is another photo, this one of an elaborate Orthodox cross, on the exterior mini-screen.

After everyone goes to bed, Igor and I sit drinking beer from coffee mugs in the outdoor kitchen. The unfortunate part of living so close to the water is the soundtrack from the terrible clubs along the embankment. The ubiquitous Russian pop music echoing through the quiet night is enough to ruin the effect of the plush scenery and the fresh sea air. The same playlist plays every night on repeat.

First up would be Dima Bilan, the man whom I believed to be personally responsible for the resurgence in popularity of the mullet haircut among Russian men. The English version of Bilan's "Believe" won the 2008 Eurovision Song Contest. Russian president Medvedev, who was reportedly watching the contest live, immediately called Dima to congratulate him.

The recent hit "Digi Digi" follows, a riff that goes on for

approximately three minutes, repeating the refrain: "They saying digi digi digi digi / Ya they say, oh / They saying digi digi digi digi / Ya they say, oh / They saying digi digi digi digi / Ya they say, oh / They say, oooh, they say, ooh / They say, oooh, they say, ooh . . ." The flicker of the neon *MEGAFON* sign on Megafon Mountain sometimes syncs to the incessant beat of this one.

Then, in my humble translation, the existential nonsense poetry of the Russian song "Bad Girl": "Wild beast, my lord / my cradle is your abode / And you already decided that the bad girl / will do everything for sure."

"Stop, Where Am I Going" is sung from the perspective of a woman unsure where she is going: "The wind is carefully rocking a branch / and I am strongly drawn away from it to you / Why is my heart melting? Stop, where am I going? / How did this happen?—I don't know / I have become completely tamed by you / Why is my heart melting? / Stop, where am I going?"

The next day is Russia Day, and I wake up convinced that I have swine flu.

We find Irina, Uncle, and Sergey in the outdoor kitchen. Sergey is once again "waiting for his ride" to get to work. He has been waiting for his ride to work every morning since we've been here. And the ride never shows. Today it's again getting late. Uncle is wondering where this mystery ride is. When we hear the sound of a car pulling up outside the gate, Sergey says goodbye. He wears a camo backpack packed with his tools. The gate clanks behind him and there's a brief flicker of satisfaction in Uncle Vova's eyes.

After a few minutes, Sergey returns. He says that wasn't them. He calls someone and after a brief conversation tells us, unsuccessfully masking his giddiness, that they've apparently decided to take the day off.

Uncle curses under his breath.

Sergey walks with us to the end of the block.

"Why you are not helping father?" Igor asks. The diplomat has turned suddenly into the scolding older brother.

"I don't want," he says.

"You want to eat?"

"Yes, I want." He steps on his cigarette and turns around, leaving us.

We walk around Gelendzhik. Neither of us says much. I sniffle a lot. It's the first gloomy day we've had here. The resort town has become kind of boring. After so many days getting our positive on, we go a little bit negative.

"It's some sort of raining. Feel it?" Igor says, holding out his hand, confused.

It rains for a while and we huddle under a bus stop shelter with other tourists in bathing suits. Igor ridicules me for applying sunscreen when it's overcast, just as he ridiculed me for applying sunscreen when the sun was out.

"You're going to die from the swine flu anyway," he says.

His back is spotted and red and peeling. He looks like a giant crab. Even he is impressed at the severity of his sunburn.

When the rain lets up, we sit on a bench on the boardwalk. The weather has scared people off the beach.

Igor says, "I had a dream last night that I was married. I remember clearly the ring on the finger."

"To who?" I ask.

"Don't know," he says, "just married."

After the rain stops, snails the size of Ping-Pong balls appear everywhere. They crunch under our feet on the sidewalk. My head is in some kind of feverish fugue. Igor suggests that we try to find a beach with some cover in case it starts raining again. We walk along the embankment. We see a cement overhang on the beach below and turn down the steps past a female police officer.

"Stop," she says. "You must have a pass for this beach."

"We don't have it," Igor says. "Where can we get it?"

"You must be born with it," she says.

She explains that this is the FSB beach, only for officers and their families. We crane our heads around the railing to see what a beach full of FSB officers looks like. We don't see Seryozha or Masha from the train—just a bunch of doughy beachgoers. Where are the buff Putins and Ivan Bondoviches? Apparently they do not attend the Gelendzhik FSB resort.

We stroll further along the embankment than we've yet strolled. At one point a small island of grass appears in the centre of the embankment. A well-manicured oak tree sprouts from one end of the grass median. A golden chain with links that would fit around my waist encircles the base of the tree. At the other end of the median stands a statue of a bronze cat dressed in university regalia reading from a book.

Igor instantly announces, "It's Pushkin, man," and he begins to recite in Russian the prologue to Pushkin's *Ruslan and Ludmilla*:

> *On seashore far a green oak towers,*
> *And to it with a gold chain bound,*
> *A learned cat whiles away the hours*

By walking slowly round and round.
To right he walks, and sings a ditty;
To left he walks, and tells a tale . . .

What marvels there! A mermaid sitting
High in a tree, a sprite, a trail
Where unknown beasts move never seen by
Man's eyes, a hut on chicken feet,
Without doors, without windows,
An evil witch's lone retreat;
The woods and valleys there are teeming . . .

"I don't remember any more," he says.

"How do you remember it by heart?" I ask.

"From school. This is Soviet school."

"You haven't been in school in fifteen years."

"Of course."

We stop at Krasnaya Talka, a closed beach connected to a sanatorium. You are supposed to pay to get onto this beach, but Igor negotiates with the ticket-taker at the entrance.

"Come on, man," Igor says. "What do I need a ticket for?" (Literally, what he says translates as "Fuck tickets" or, even more literally, "Tickets to the dick.") "We come here every day," Igor lies.

The boy considers this argument—we don't need a ticket because we come here every day—for a few seconds. Then he concedes, nodding, and we pass by.

"See, man," Igor says. "I said five words to him. You must negotiate, man. There is always a rule. The rule is, Fuck the rule. In Russia, everything happening."

Even though he has the equivalent of a ninth-grade education, Igor can recite Pushkin from memory. Then he can turn around and, expertly using the Russian slang dialect *mat*, talk his way past a gangly security guard onto a private beach. I do not know any poetry by heart, and I am an English professor. I wonder whether Igor is better off in any way for knowing Pushkin by heart. This quality does not make him unique among Russians of his generation and older. Soviet schools forced kids to memorize the great Russian poets, especially Pushkin. But I have often wondered what good it's done them. You cannot expect many farmers in Mississippi to quote Whitman, while you can expect every farmer in Krasnodar Krai, the region surrounding Gelendzhik, to recite you a verse of Pushkin or to pick their favourite from among Chekhov, Dostoevsky, and Tolstoy. Surely there must be some appreciation for language and for beauty, and there must be something worthwhile in the fact that there are all these texts that the whole nation shares—poems, fairy tales, great social novels, absurdist short stories . . . all these shared prisms to see the world through. And yet, in comparison with the stability of the West, with our lack of shared literary reference points, everything in Russia is governed by degrees of chaos. Is there something about wide-scale appreciation for art that leads to chaos?

I begin to realize that my thoughts have gone loopy. The fever has depleted me, and I lie there like a puddle in a white plastic beach chair.

The beach at Krasnaya Talka is a stunning cross-section of Russia. Topless girls lie with small flat stones over their nipples. A pack of virile young lifeguards try to trick one of these girls into sitting up by squirting her with a squirt gun. She smiles but doesn't flinch. Old men eat sunflower seeds, spitting the husks into the water.

And because it is a sanatorium, there are people in wheel-chairs and not a few with pink scars criss-crossing their bodies. The occasional one-armed or one-legged person emerges from the water.

The lifeguards not hitting on the topless girls paddle around the reef (concrete pylons stacked in a line about thirty metres out), fishing the seaweed out and packing little kayaks with it. Dogfish, which Igor calls "dogs," slither in and out of the sea-weed along the iron steps to the concrete platform.

On the other side of the bay, an aquatic passenger plane takes off from the water.

Igor swims and I sit on the cement ledge where a pack of kids repeatedly jump into the water. There is one boy who looks exactly like a young version of Igor. He even behaves like him. He takes great pleasaure in telling all the other kids where the warm spots in the water are. Whether he created the warm spots in the water before directing the other kids to them I cannot be sure. He performs acrobatics, shows off. But basically, I can tell he's lonely. How silly that when Igor and I were this kid's age, we were supposed to be enemies.

The Russia Day celebration at Vova and Irina's is one of those special occasions when Irina allows Vova to drink.

Sergey kicks off the celebration by standing and giving a surprisingly eloquent speech about the environment. He's concerned about the ecological destruction of the Gelendzhik beaches by tourists. I hadn't expected this from him. Igor's extended family is full of contradictions and surprises, I think, like Igor himself.

Vova, Igor, and I finish the first bottle of vodka, and we start talking about the war in Georgia and who's to blame.

Sergey, who drinks a pink soda, interjects. He says that he thinks war in general is fought over financial considerations. He adds, "Furthermore, in any quarrel, it's never only one person's fault."

Igor derides Sergey's position, calling it maximalism.

"South Ossetians are such good people," Uncle Vova says. "Once, I sat at a table of South Ossetians, and you can't leave until forty cups of corn vodka have been consumed. Children serve the table, and everyone says toasts. The toasts go on so long because everybody needs time to sober up. 'What the fuck?' I kept saying when they toasted. 'Did you eat the radio?'"

Igor watches his uncle, and his uncle watches Igor. A son who's never known his father looking into the eyes of his father's identical twin; a father with problematic sons looking at a version (perhaps preferred) of a better son, at least one who might go to work and refrain from stabbing him.

Igor keeps encouraging me to drink. The Russian belief is that vodka cures everything. Even swine flu. But after a brief reprieve, it is making me feel worse.

The deaf bulldog, which we already fed ten *pelmeni* and three whole cucumber peels, coughs at me because it wants sandwiches.

Suddenly, Danzig's "Mother" plays, Igor's ring tone for his mom. He picks up the phone and goes inside the house to talk.

Vova gazes thoughtfully at his wife, and he asks me where my wife is. I tell him the deal. My wife is in her home city in

Siberia. We are separated. I tell him that it looks as if it's over.

"A man without his wife, Jeff, is like a tree without a caterpillar," he says.

Soon Igor emerges from the house with tears streaming down his cheeks. He sits down at the table and puts his face in his hands. He lights a cigarette. "My grandfather died," he says. "He was like my real father. He was a real Georgian."

Irina sits down on the bench with Igor and strokes the back of his head.

After his cigarette, Igor calls and speaks to his grandma. She says the main problem, because of the recent conflict and border disputes, is that Valiko's son in Georgia can't get a Russian visa to come to the funeral.

We sit for a while and eventually Igor stops crying. I also lived with my grandparents when I was very young, and spent long stretches of my childhood with them. I tell Igor about when my grandfather died a few years ago. It was both really sad and strangely emboldening. I felt like everywhere I went after that, he was with me, watching me, and I wanted to behave honourably because of that.

Vova tries to lighten the mood. "A Chukchi is being asked what he thought about Peter the Great. 'Liked him,' the Chukchi says. Alexander I? 'Liked him.' And Ekaterina II? 'No, didn't like her.' Why? 'Why the hell she didn't sell us along with Alaska?'"

Igor's tears begin to dry up. The vodka keeps going down.

A couple of days later, cured of my swine flu, I awake before Igor and go downstairs to read in the outdoor kitchen. Vova limps out. He asks what are the pills I'm taking. He looks surprised when I tell him they're vitamin supplements. "What," he says, "you have wrinkles on your penis already?"

But Uncle Vova doesn't even smile at his own joke this morning. His new cast is bothering him. It's stiff and his foot is sore.

Uncle yells at Sergey to go to work.

"I wanted to work," Sergey says. "It's not my fault. I got the job. They didn't come to pick me up." Sergey really tries to play it off, calls the driver *mudak* (asshole). Uncle tells him he's a lazy bullshitter. Sergey storms up the stairs.

When Igor comes down to smoke, he asks if Sergey is at work. "What do you think?" Vova says. "He doesn't have a single kopeck. We are not giving him money. And he doesn't want to work."

"He is not a damn Burov," Igor mutters. Igor has reached the obvious conclusion that this business about Sergey's having a job is bullshit. Igor thinks he's lazy. Igor has emerged fully in alliance with Vova. The general consensus seems to be that Sergey is inventive and well-meaning but a total slacker.

"I will take him and teach him what it means to be a Burov," Igor says.

Uncle Vova looks at Igor approvingly, fondly. It's hard to imagine him looking at either of his own sons like this. The look says it might be possible for Igor to move into this life, take the place of the ingrates Sergey and Dima, who have the luxury of a father.

"Does being a Burov mean drinking every day?" I say.

"Only when not working," Igor says. He smiles. I refrain from bringing up the fact that Igor is himself unemployed.

We walk around to the various restaurants and construction sites to teach Sergey how to be a Burov. "Let's see how you operate," Igor says. He sends him to a barman at a circular outdoor bar, saying, "Go, go ask him for work."

Sergey approaches the barman and says, meekly, "Are you looking to hire anybody by any chance?" The barman shakes his head, and Sergey returns holding his hands in the air.

Igor takes him by the back of the neck. "Fuckhead," he says. "Look, you are doing it all wrong. The proper way: You are coming, and saying, 'You have some work for me? I am ready to work.' This is Burov style. I know how these things work, especially from the perspective of human resources. I know people, man."

We stop by a few construction sites, but while there seems to be work in progress, there are no workers or foremen around. Most of the job sites seem abandoned. Igor's strategies may in fact bolster Sergey's character, but if the crisis has decimated all the jobs, I'm not sure how much help it will be.

When we finally find a hotel with some workers out front, Sergey uses Igor's approach. Maybe it's bullshit, but the foreman tells Sergey to call him on Monday, that it's possible they may just need someone. Sergey returns to us in a state of shock. Igor's chest puffs out. Here is his triumphant big brother moment.

"Next order of business," Igor says to Sergey, "is to get rid of this moustache. If you're going to shave this forgery, it will then grow into real one."

Our departure day is cause for yet another celebration. This time Igor and I buy the food. We stop by the beach on our way to the store for a final dip.

Igor tells me to look for a stone with a hole in it. "It's called chicken heart," he says.

"Your favourite food," I say.

"Different kind chicken heart," he says. "If you find one, it means in your life you'll come back to this place."

The stones are grey and black when dry, but when they're wet, the moisture brings out a million shades of brown. They are worn smooth by the water.

"I found one," he says. He shows it to me: a grey stone ringed by a white stripe, with a toothpick-sized hole on the thinnest edge.

I scrounge around for a while, upturning stones by the handful, and eventually I find one too.

On the way back, we get some roast chickens and vegetables and *gorilka*—Ukrainian pepper vodka—and we buy two extra roast chickens and boiled eggs and cheese as well as beer and water for our trip.

Igor asks Uncle about the story we heard from one of our guides, that a meteor created the perfectly circular Gelendzhik bay. Uncle says: "You know, every year I am turning on the imagination and spinning some story about this. Don't pay any attention to it. It's legend. If you're telling a story and not lying, it's nonsense."

Vova tells us Gelendzhik is derived from the Turkish word meaning "little bride." It started as a slave market, and that's how it got its name. I ask if that's a yarn like the meteor stories. He says, very seriously, "No. This is true. But, by the way, you know how I know Russia is better than America? You only have one-headed eagle, we have two-headed one. Now, give me a theme," he says, "and I'll tell you an anecdote on this theme."

"About rabbits," I say.

"Oh, rabbits! How many do you want to hear about rabbits?"

A bottle of *gorilka* later and we're in a Hyundai Accent driven by one of Vova's friends, a former FSB officer, who is taking us to the train station in Novorossiysk. The antiseptic spotlessness of the car's interior is disrupted only by a small plastic snake on the dashboard, a throw pillow matching exactly the multicoloured zigzag of the upholstery, and a military cap, which he keeps under the rear window and which keeps falling into the seat beside me.

The FSB officer drops us off, and Igor wrestles the Red Dog onto the sidewalk. One of the suitcase's wheels has cracked and the other seized up, making it impossible to roll and difficult, because of its bulkiness, to carry. We realize that we've left all the food and supplies we purchased for the trip back in Gelendzhik. I am inclined to go buy another bottle of *gorilka* for the trip, but some police have taken notice of us, so I do my best to walk straight. Igor, with the Red Dog on his back, swerves from side to side down the sidewalk. He drops the suitcase and stumbles a little bit. Oblivious.

Then they are on us. Here it's the opposite of St. Pete, where I, the foreigner, would be the target. I take off my shades and look the two cops in the eye when I hand them my passport, but Igor's passport is in the Red Dog. He throws it open and all our clothes go flying, making a ridiculous spectacle. He finally finds it and they tell him, "Igor Yurievitch, you're being arrested for public drunkenness."

"Our train," Igor says, "leaves in ten minutes."

I glance at my watch. Less than ten minutes.

"Your friend can take the train, but you will go with us," the cop says. "We're calling the medical attendant to have your blood tested."

Several other officers emerge from the station and converse with the two cops arresting Igor.

"Give me three hundred rubles," Igor whispers to me. I fumble in my pockets, trying to nonchalantly slip three hundred rubles his way. The cops aren't looking at us, as though they're giving us space to figure out how much we're willing to pay to get out of this. I give him three hundred rubles, about ten dollars. He identifies the sergeant by uniform and asks if the two of them can have a little chat. The sergeant agrees, and they walk away together.

This is the moment that gets me. The offer. I have this fear that the one cop I try to bribe will turn out to be the one honest cop, that scene from countless American movies. I have not yet met that cop in Russia, but one of the most popular stories in the many soap operas and dramas on Russian TV, according to a friend who is a tele-serial writer, is that of the honest, non-corrupt cop, the one that few believe exists.

I hear Igor say to the sergeant: "We are leaving right now. What you want from us, and we will leave in ten minutes? We are just coming from the resort. We don't have any money. All I have is three hundred. This will be the fine."

"Fine for public drunkenness is seven hundred to one thousand," the sergeant says.

"Three hundred rubles is all we have left," Igor lies.

The sergeant keeps saying no. Igor keeps saying, "This is all we have." This is the process: the sergeant must say no a few times and Igor must repeat his offer.

"I will give you fine and I will leave in five minutes," Igor says. He says this as if he's using a Jedi mind trick. The sergeant confers with the other officers, for whom our offer constitutes less than a hundred rubles each. That's three or four bucks apiece. Or maybe three mid-range bottles of vodka? A nice box of chocolates for one of their families? Who knows?

The train whistle sounds. Two minutes to go.

"Three hundred rubles we lost, and I am upset," Igor says as we pull away from the station. "It is good price. Negotiating, negotiating, negotiating, and fuck it! Excellent rate. But still, little upset."

Our train attendant on this trip is older than our previous Lena. And considerably more severe. She calls Igor Citizen Burov and so we call her Citizen Alexandrova.

We had pre-agreed that we wouldn't drink much on this leg of the trip. But the first thing Citizen Alexandrova does is present us with two cans of cold White Bear beer without asking if we want them. Surely we are being overcharged for them, but they are cold and good, and we are supporting Citizen Alexandrova's side business.

We have been assigned a single coupe with only two beds. But one of our tickets doesn't have the seat marked on it. Citizen Alexandrova returns to have a discussion about the situation.

"For a little extra, you can stay here, and I won't have to move you," she tells Igor.

He steps around Citizen Alexandrova into the corridor and looks down the aisle. The entire train car, once again, is practically empty. She says it will fill up at subsequent stops. And while ordinarily this might be true, we have had experience of the trains in crisis-era Russia and suspect she's bluffing.

"I'm not paying, and I'm not leaving this place," he says. "I like this place. I already paid. This is my position."

She looks at him. He's emboldened by his successful negotiation with the cops. She understands that she won't be able to budge him. She stares blankly for a moment.

"In that case, Citizen Burov, why don't you two buy me a bottle of champagne for my hospitality?"

II.

LOVE

CHAPTER 11

Even before the global economic crisis, Russia was embroiled in what some described as a crisis of the family. This crisis of the family enveloping the nation had many dimensions and direct connections to other social ills: alcoholism, domestic abuse, divorce, low birth rates, etc. The population of Russia had been in decline for more than a decade and was expected to drop by 667,000 in 2008. Add to that high divorce rates (65 percent of marriages end in divorce—the second-highest divorce rate in the world, after Belarus) and a lower life expectancy for men (a 2009 study would show that 50 percent of all deaths of men in Russia since perestroika were alcohol related) and the absence on the books of a single domestic violence law . . .

The Medvedev government addressed the problem head-on by instituting the president's wife's plan: the creation of a new holiday. July's Day of Family, Love, and Faithfulness was conceived as something of a Valentine's Day for the entire family unit. (Along the same lines, one region of Russia anointed

September's Family Contact Day, which urged married couples to stay home together and engage in contact so as to patriotically produce children nine months later—if perfectly timed, on June's Russia Day.)

Further, the year 2008 had a theme. It had been christened by Putin himself as the Year of the Family.

Igor and Anya had been together for four years. They worked together at the Atrium café, and although she lived with her parents and he lived with his mom, they spent most of their time, physical and virtual, together. Last year, Igor had chipped in to help her buy a car, a maroon Honda Civic. When Anya didn't sleep over at Igor's place, they spent the night chatting through V Kontakte, the Russian Facebook, and playing electronic games against each other.

Of course, like all couples, they had their issues. It was no secret that Anya had long wanted to get married. When discussing it, Igor, skeptical about the meaning behind civil institutions, would say, "What for I need another stamp in my passport? What for I need a ring on my finger?"

One can hear in this, if one wishes, only assholitude. Or one could say that Anya's desire for the trappings of family are in conflict with Igor's disdain for the corrupt structures of power, the same corrupt structures of power that, in the form of the Putin–Medvedev administration, he sort of supported. Further, according to Igor, there were two finite difficulties in Anya's character: (a) she was constantly "fucking his brain"; and (b) she exhibited a tendency toward what Igor had dubbed the Duality.

The Duality could be seen in several different phenomena: her doing something herself and becoming angry when he did the same thing (changing her V Kontakte status to single after an argument and becoming enraged when he reciprocated); her telling him one thing one day and the opposite another (acquiescing to his pursuit of a job in Sochi and expressing outrage when he got it); her telling him that she would do one thing and then doing another (declaring that she would not visit work during her day offs and showing up anyway).

In Bruce Hopper's 1931 book *Pan-Sovietism*, he essentially (and without a tinge of political correctness) accused the Russian people in general of the Duality: "For all his capacity to suffer, the Russian is a contradictory animal."

Like many Russians, Igor himself both loves and loathes the West. He loves and loathes Russia. Russians are known simultaneously for their great capacity for hospitality to strangers and for hard-core xenophobia. There is a set of rules governing just about everything, and then there is the way things actually work, a duality implicit in driving, the legal system, you name it. He is a contradictory beast in a contradictory habitat.

Igor's uncle had lorded over me the extra head on the double-headed eagle from the coat of arms of the Russian Federation versus the single eagle from the Great Seal of the United States. He was joking, but come to think of it, symbol or not, when was it ever a good thing that a creature had two heads?

Decorum precludes me from interviewing my friend's girlfriend about their relationship. But it is easy to sympathize with Anya. Igor is not undifficult. During many of their arguments, the main point in his defence is "Man is first!" Given all this, a little duality is certainly forgivable. Yet the 2008 Year of the Family version of Igor was the most domesticated I'd ever seen him.

My friend the *samizdat* writer and émigré from Leningrad, Mikhail Iossel, who founded the writers' festival in St. Petersburg, describes his city as artifice incarnate. If not for the perverse imagination of Peter the Great, a seven-foot-tall madman, three hundred years ago, this unlikely city, built in a swamp on the bodies of more than a hundred thousand serfs, would not be. The architects of the city were steeped in the Italian Baroque style, so when you walk along the streets it looks European, but that visual aesthetic does not compute with the indescribable Russianness. This strangeness is compounded by the otherworldly summer light and the punishing winter dark. With the proper application of enough alcohol (and even sometimes without), walking in St. Petersburg is the equivalent of walking in a dream.

The inside of the Atrium café in downtown St. Petersburg, a spacious courtyard enclosure under skylights, was designed to be a sanitized inversion of the exterior. The pale and faded pastels of the outdoor facades were bright and vivid inside. An impossible indoor version of itself, a Bizarro St. Petersburg streetscape with an upscale Stokmann's department store and a spitting lion's head fountain.

You entered the Atrium through hallways converted into jewellery stores, the walls aglow with golden and silver necklaces and watches. Older Swedish and German and Finnish couples mobbed the place. It smelled of lavender soap from the L'Occitane kiosk.

This is where Igor and Anya spent most of their time before he quit and we went to Gelendzhik and he broke up with her, before it eventually closed down in the financial crisis. He doubled and tripled as the manager and barman and barista;

she waitressed. There was a narrow bar about twenty feet across with coolers at both ends. On one end were the cakes (Marzipan, Royal Truffle, Mango Sour Cream Shake Cake, Boney M) and at the other end were the ice creams (coconut sorbet, grape, bilberry). Little coat hooks were attached to the brass bar railing with decorative leather ties. The food elevator had two compartments hidden behind polished steel sliding doors. Food came up the food elevator from the kitchen in the basement; dirty dishes went down. Igor's domain included the espresso machine, the beer taps, and the full bar. One of his industrial juicers had a motorized knob into which he pressed halved oranges and grapefruits. The acid in the citrus had eaten away at the skin and the cuticles on both his hands. The other juicer was for carrots and apples and beets.

Two months before the conflict with Georgia in summer 2008, and before the economic crisis, I was in St. Petersburg working at the writers' festival. The Year of the Family was to be the festival's last year.

For ten years (I'd been involved for nine of those) the festival had been bringing the most interesting writers from around the world and inflicting powerful hangovers upon them. It had been feasible when the ruble was weaker, but every year the ruble crept up and up, costing the festival thousands of dollars that it didn't have. On top of that, the bribes—after all, we were rich Americans, and what difference is there between Coca-Cola and a non-profit literary organization, anyway? How were they to know? But the combination of the strengthening ruble and the higher bribes made it untenable, and that last year was bittersweet.

I had chaperoned countless of the finest representatives of contemporary North American literature to Bar Dacha, one of the sleaziest, most glorious holes in the wall imaginable, while they danced till dawn. I had taken an Ivy League professor to a party hosted by Igor at a nearby restaurant, and the impression it made on him could in part be measured by the fact that he was forty minutes late for the workshop he taught the next morning. I had taken my friend Adam, one of my favourite young American novelists, out for a night on the town only to run us right into two drunk cops who took all our money. It was hard to believe it was all coming to an end.

I walked down Kazanskaya, past the crumbling, magisterial Kazansky Cathedral and Nevsky Prospekt, and sat at the bar of the Atrium with Igor. He was in the middle of a rush. He poured me a glass of carbonated water from the four-nozzle, German-manufactured fountain, which read, from the customer side *Trink Coca-Cola*. I drank it and read at the bar.

Anya took an order. She banged the keys on the computer. She propped one foot on the counter and fussed with a cigarette. "What do they need, baby?" Igor asked. She turned away from him. She threw aside one of the food elevator doors and ran a ten-dollar plate of three sunny-side-up eggs drowned in bacon grease to some Germans. The check, after a short delay, printed. Igor snatched it and whipped up a cappuccino. He set it on the counter for her.

"Everything okay?" I said.

"Like usual, she is fucking my brain," he said.

When things slowed down, Anya greeted me and lamented her upcoming exams. She told me that when she wasn't at work, she was spending all her free time studying, but that soon she'd graduate. Despite the fact that Anya majored in English, she only spoke to me in Russian. She was timid, the opposite of Igor.

The sun shone through the glass ceiling and Igor cranked out the yellow awning over the café. He wore a black apron, a black polo, thin black slacks, and a pair of plastic purple sports sandals. For some reason, Russians in service jobs often wear the cheapest possible purple sports sandals with socks.

He peeled a small onion and popped it whole into his mouth.

"For some reason," he said, "every day I am wearing these nicotine patches, I am eating a raw onion."

"But you're not smoking?"

"I'm smoking and eating raw onions."

Igor handed me the book he was reading, a thick hardcover. It was called *The Ship of Sludge*. I flipped open the first page, where there was an ornate signature. "He signed it for you?"

"No, it's mine signature. I do this in all my books."

"Why do you sign your own books?" I had other friends who did this but hadn't expected it of Igor.

He thought for a moment. "I don't know . . . It is about navy. It is funny as fuck what these naval officers are doing. It's about life on the submarines. Lots about Kursk. Lots about Americans."

"It's fiction or non-fiction?"

"Well, basically, it's non, but from the tenth teller it will be different."

The accountant came in. She was a statuesque blonde with cat eyes. She appeared once per day, ostensibly to tally the books, but basically she flirted with Igor and smoked and drank coffee. She took a stool at the end of the counter near the juicers. Igor brought her an espresso and the daily receipts. Anya was also beautiful, but short and sometimes, it seemed, full of self-doubt. When the accountant came in, Anya softened toward Igor a little bit. She spoke the next order to him directly, but clipped: two mimosas with grapefruit juice, fresh squeezed, instead of orange. And a brandy.

He juiced two grapefruits on the juicer with the motorized knob. After he conferred with the accountant, he returned to the barstool across from me.

When Anya went by again, I asked about her sister, who was studying Chinese in Beijing right now, and she told me she was doing very well there, planning to attend the Olympics at the end of the summer and return to Petersburg afterward. It was an interesting choice. Her sister didn't have any particular interest in China, and just a few years ago any upwardly mobile young girl would certainly have studied English.

"This reminds me of little joke," Igor said. "Do you know the word *optimist*?"

"Yes," I said.

"How about *pessimist*? *Realist*?"

I nod.

"Okay, so there's three guys—one is optimist, one is pessimist, one is realist. Optimist chooses to study English. Pessimist studies Chinese. Realist studies AK-47."

CHAPTER 12
SUMMER 2009

The initial thrill of bribing the police subsides and the cumulative effect of two weeks of hangovers sets in. We are both exhausted and sleep for almost twenty-four hours straight. I even sleep through Igor's snoring.

We wake up simultaneously in the middle of the night somewhere in Russia. The train is stopped and silent. Outside, a shirtless man squats by a small campfire. We make tea and talk for a little bit.

"What will you do when we get back?" I ask Igor.

"Find a job," he says. "Any job. I am pissed off to sit at home since January." We have not checked, but we hope that the situation in the country is improving. (It's not.)

"You'll get one," I say. Then I ask something else I've been wanting to ask: "Have you ever wondered why we became friends?"

"You can't just say like this," he says. "No answer question. Let it be. You can answer this question?"

I think for a minute. I recall an Aristotle quote: "A friend is another Himself," which I'd always read as "A friend is a version of the self." I wondered at the Igor part of me. And the me-part of him . . .

"I can't explain to you," Igor says. "Better you explain me why you are breathing. Why you're not forgetting how to breathe?"

The train jerks, startling us, and moves again.

Our coupe reminds me of a coffin. A lot of human transport devices in Russia remind me of coffins. Or maybe not a lot, but at least two: this coupe and most elevators. I start down this line of thinking and out of nowhere remember a conversation with an old friend about his greatest fear.

"I have this friend from Ohio," I say. "His greatest fear is that the car he's driving will break down in the middle of an intersection."

"It means to go straight to the psychologist," Igor says.

"Probably. But I don't think it's uncommon for Americans. You know, in the US, if your car breaks down in the middle of the intersection, first of all, it means your car sucks. It means you're poor. And probably that means you're a loser. Also, you inconvenience people and they look at you and think that you're poor and in their way. So there's this shame that goes with it."

"In Russia, if your car breaks down, it means your car is shit. Everyone's car is shit. Someone will help you. Others will drive around."

What he says is true. Russians, as far as I can tell, do not invest themselves in their cars the way it seems Americans do. And probably any given Russian does not necessarily regard his or her personal poverty as something to be ashamed of, like many Americans I've known.

"Just out of curiosity," I say, "what's your greatest fear?"

He thinks for a moment. "Loneliness," he says.

As we travel north, the rain falls harder, the temperature drops, the blue sky rusts and then goes grey.

Igor grows flustered searching for a missing black sock.

"I have only one sock," he says. He holds up the lone black sock. Printed on the toe in white lettering is *No nonsense.* "I'm thinking someone stole the other. It's disturbing, man, if someone stole one sock."

By the time we arrive in St. Petersburg, it's like we never left, like the journey never happened. We got our positive on, but the positive is all gone. Back to overcast crisis. We've been through some kind of shared hallucination of a tropical place in Russia which could not, in the same nation that we've just arrived in, possibly exist.

Igor fumbles the Red Dog out from under the train seat. Surely it's seen its last journey.

On the way out of the station, he throws his stray sock into a garbage can.

Back in Gelendzhik, in the evening on Russia Day, the day I'd been convinced I had the swine flu and the day Igor got the news that his grandfather had died, Igor had decided to end it with Anya. While all the couples who had patriotically screwed on the previous Family Contact Day were giving birth to children, Igor ended it with his girlfriend of many years.

Not that this was a huge shock. Before we'd left for the south, he had put her on relationship probation. They'd been arguing non-stop. Every time they'd argue, she would change her status on V Kontakte from engaged to single. After a big spat, she posted the status update *Men are like blenders, you think that you need one, but you're not sure what for.* He had been thinking about ending it for some time, and something about that day in Gelendzhik and the news of his grandfather's passing made his decision.

We were at a café on the Gelendzhik bay. It's hard to remember which one, all their names blend together—Mr. Pizza or Café Pizza or Pizzeria Fast Food or Santa Fe or Malibu or Dolce Vita or Tropikana or Chili Pepper or Tijuana. We were celebrating the Russian Constitution and drinking vodka, which Igor insisted would cure the swine flu, at one of the cafés—they were all pretty much the same. We were both walled inside our heads, me from sickness and Igor from grief.

"There is some psychological square," he said.

He drew a strange equation with pluses and minuses and, if I'm not mistaken, the symbol for the chemical element neon on a napkin.

"This is psycholinguistic programming, just advice to make you think. Say I am trying to decide what I will do, if I will break up with Anya or not. In top left, I think, 'What won't happen if I break up with Anya?' In top right, I think, 'What will happen if I break up with Anya?' Below left, negative negative, 'What won't happen if I don't break up with Anya?' Below right, 'What will happen if I don't break up with Anya?' I am using this process a lot with all decisions."

"What will happen?"

"Lots of things. What won't happen if I break up with Anya? She won't be fucking my brain. This is most important thing."

"So you made your decision?"

"I told her today that we are splitting when I am home. You know what she replied? 'So I can start a new relationship, then?' This is not the thing to say. And she knows it." He'd hung up and she called back to apologize. She said, "I was just angry. That's why I said it."

"I can't tolerate this kind of character, man. This duality. Fucking duality," he said to me. "I told her the terms of probation: if you are saying one thing, this is your position. I suggested going to Sochi like Al"—there was good employment in the service industry in the resort town of Sochi, which was then hot in preparation for the 2014 Winter Olympics—"and she told me, 'Okay, you should go.' I asked Al, and he found me some work. Then I told her Al found me some work in Sochi and she said, 'No fucking way you are going.'

"She doesn't want to live with me, doesn't want a baby, doesn't want to cook, doesn't want to clean. The main thing she wants is to check how I am doing two times per day. I am fed up with it." He threw back another fifty grams and refilled our shot glasses from the carafe. "Fuck Anya. Fuck everything. I am alone. It is easier alone." He raised his glass.

There were a lot of things I could have said at that point—but I was too sick. Despite the fact that she was the most balanced girlfriend he'd been with since I'd known him, and despite the fact that she seemed to do him great good, his mind was made up. We clinked glasses and drank.

"I don't think I should be drinking. What if I really have the swine flu?"

"This is not drinking. This is medicine. This is cure," he said. He had told me this once before, and it hadn't ended well.

I felt despondent. I didn't open up about my relationship

the way Igor did. That was one of the things I admired about him: he knew exactly what the problems were and put them all out there. I bottled mine up more. Maybe these characteristics were American of me and Russian of him. Or maybe it was just me and that was just him.

I tried to apply Igor's psycholinguistic square to my own situation. What won't happen if Yulia and I get divorced? What will happen if we do? What won't happen if we don't? What will happen if we don't? I didn't have any of the answers. What I knew was that Yulia and I had become siblings, roommates. There was no affection. We didn't talk. But I felt the end of the marriage was like a death. And I didn't know if I could bear it.

We had met in grad school in upstate New York in the late nineties. She was totally new to the United States and a lot of things were confusing to her. I consoled her after her landlord chastised her for hanging her laundry to dry on the front porch. We were different in pretty much every way—she liked to shop and I liked to skateboard; she liked pop music and I liked punk rock; she liked to stay home and I liked to go out—but somehow that didn't matter.

If I tried to pinpoint one specific reason, if I tried to say in some definitive language what went wrong, I couldn't. There were all kinds of reasons; all kinds of things went wrong. We had treated each other shabbily. She was stubborn. I was stubborn. We were too different. We had grown apart emotionally over years of living apart physically—she in Ohio and me in Arizona for a year, and then me in Michigan and she in Atlanta for two years and Toronto for a third. And then there were the summers—every summer I went to Russia to work for the writers' festival and she taught Russian at a language school in Vermont.

Ironically, she stayed in my country while I went to hers. If you added up all the time I'd spent in Russia since 1999—more than two and a half years in total—only about a month or two overlapped with her. In 2007, I'd gotten a job in Toronto as well and joined her there. Things had finally come together as they were supposed to, but instead of working out, it was all combusting.

Next thing I knew, Igor and I were completely sauced at a club called Cool, and Igor was dancing with two Moskvichkas to that godawful playlist that I knew by heart. He and I might as well have been on different planets. Between my frequent trips to the bathroom—toilets in the Black Sea resort area, porcelain holes in the floor costing ten rubles a go, were among the worst I'd ever encountered, the last place one wants to be sick—I sat at a table and hoped I didn't have swine flu. All I wanted was to sleep, to recover. He was celebrating Russia Day, celebrating the demise of his relationship, and coping with the death of his beloved grandfather, which he'd taken pretty hard. I didn't have the heart to caution him off his high. And even if I had, he wasn't to be daunted.

I tried to hang with him, but it was obvious my presence there wasn't doing him any good. I decided to go. I approached him on the dance floor, unsure what to make of this Igor I'd never seen before, Dancing Machine Igor, wearing a T-shirt that read *Never dance alone*. He introduced me to the Moskvichkas. One was tall and brunette, the other short and blond like Anya. He spun the short blonde around and then swung her back into his arms. She hit his body with a thud.

"You are so huge," she said to him, "like a wall." She batted her eyelashes.

I told him that I needed to nurse my swine flu, and I walked home.

In our dorm-style room back at his uncle's place, we had single beds separated by a nightstand. I couldn't sleep when Igor was awake because he always wanted to talk. I couldn't sleep—even with headphones—when he was asleep because of his snoring. I passed out hoping he wouldn't come home and force me to drink beer with him. I slept the best I'd slept since the journey began, and when I woke up, I felt better; the swine flu, or whatever it was, had ebbed.

At ten in the morning, Igor's bed still empty, I sat in the outdoor kitchen with Sergey. Soon Igor slammed the steel fence gate and stumbled in. He looked surprisingly spry. I'd seen him in far worse condition. He told us that he and the girls had hung out on the beach all night, drinking a little champagne and swimming at sun-up. When I came to the room later to check on him, he was snoring like a herd of buffalo.

In St. Petersburg, each of us goes his own way for a while. We need it. He has to deal with Anya, and we both need some rest and sobriety. I retreat to my small rented apartment near the end of the metro line, at metro Prospekt Bolshevikov. I chose to stay out here to get a different take on the city. I'd always lived like a tourist somewhere in the centre. It'd be inconvenient as hell, but I wanted to distance myself from things and get a taste of real life in Russia.

I sleep soundly without Igor's snoring, as soundly as I slept the one night I ditched him at the club. I do pretty much nothing but sleep and embrace sobriety for a few days. Then I explore the area around metro Bolshevikov.

It's not the worst part of the city, but it's not one of the best either. Solidarnosti street, the main street in front of my apartment, is always dotted with skanky prostitutes in short skirts and stockings. Dangerous-looking drunk men haggle with them on the sidewalks. Sometimes these drunk johns and the prostitutes sit drinking malt liquor on the bench outside my apartment building door.

But like Anya, the region around metro Bolshevikov has its own duality. There's a moment, somewhere between five and seven every day, when families claim the streets. The skinheads, hookers, and drunks make themselves scarce for a little while, and the sidewalks fill with young couples walking dogs and kids.

Not far away from the apartment, there is a Papa John's, which is an upscale sit-down place in Russia, and a Pizza Hut. Beds of red-hot salvias and marigolds decorate the courtyards.

A few steps away from the apartment is something called a Vertical Turbo Solarium in a bright orange building. English graffiti over the orange paint reads *Go Vegan* and *Emo sux*.

The most striking feature of the landscape is the monstrous hospital Alexandrovskaya Bolnitsa, with broken windows and crumbling exterior brickwork. When Igor first showed me the apartment, I asked how long the hospital across the street had been shut down. "Dude," he said, "it's working."

Inside, my apartment building has the traditional pee-scented entryway. The dark stairwells seem specifically designed to produce as many shadowy corners as possible. The elevator, perfectly coffin-sized, also serves as a common urinal, and sometimes worse. The apartment is on the ninth floor and has an excellent balcony. At sunrise, crows dive-bomb the balcony's tin roof. They land there and fight, making a sound like thunder. I bang on the balcony ceiling with a broom and they swoop away.

Alone in Russia, one easily gets into a Raskolnikov/ Underground Man state of mind. Gunshots occasionally ring out. Or maybe they're cars backfiring. Sometimes I hear a woman screaming in one of the apartments around me, but it's impossible to tell if she's having sex or being murdered.

The hot water is cut off with some regularity; centralized water heating systems are repaired in the summer months. To take a bath, I boil water in pots on the stove and in the electric kettle. It takes about two rounds of each plus some cold water from the tap to get the temperature right.

There are no proper chairs in the apartment, only a couple of paint-splattered footstools and an ottoman. I need a chair with a back to write, and so I *marshrutka* over to Igor's and borrow a flimsy dining chair.

I take the chair home on the metro. In the subway car, I put it down next to the bench and sit in it. This act catches no one's attention at all, a foreigner sitting in a wooden chair on the subway.

CHAPTER 13
SUMMER 2009

Igor bangs on my apartment door at nine in the morning with three bottles of Baltika Light. "I only wanted to buy one, but they didn't have change," he says.

Last night, he tells me, he got together with some old friends from school. They drank a lot of beer. He is surly and gloomy.

We have returned to his reality, and his reality is crisis. He's put out some feelers, but he knows the prospect of finding a job is slim right now. At the end of April 2009, the Russian Statistics Service reported that 7.7 million people (10.2 percent of the workforce) were unemployed. Since April 2008, there'd been a 71 percent growth in unemployment.

Igor's mother has asked him to renovate the apartment while he is out of work and she's on vacation in Abkhazia. He asks if I might be interested in helping, and I agree. We take the number 284 *marshrutka* to his place, through the industrial parts of town, where prostitutes stand in dirt driveways off the main road, leaning on dump trucks.

I've only been over to his apartment a few times before. Normally we meet somewhere in the centre. His building is across from the Piskaryovskoye Memorial Cemetery on the Avenue of the Unvanquished in the area of St. Petersburg known as Piskaryovka, which is lush and green. Development is restricted near the national cemetery.

The siege is the defining historic event of St. Petersburg. There is a museum dedicated to the siege that is one of the most horrifying museums I've ever seen. With food supply lines cut off for nearly three years, the city starved. They ate belt and shoe leather soup, their pets, each other. The stories of those who survived are some of the most harrowing survival stories ever told. One photo sequence at the siege museum shows a young girl's photo taken just before the siege and then at roughly one-year intervals during. The effect of seeing someone age thirty years in two years is stunning. Living in Piskaryovka, lush and beautiful as it is, Igor is confronted with that history every day, and while he's not likely to admit it, it must make him think about death and the past a lot. How could it not?

It certainly stayed on the minds of other denizens of St. Petersburg. Over the years, I'd been invited to a number of apartments for dinner—that famous Russian hospitality—and one question kept popping up, especially among those whose parents' generation fought in World War II, in which Russia and St. Petersburg sacrificed so much and which is referred to as the Great Patriotic War. After a little food and a little drink, someone would invariably ask, not accusingly but with inquisitive, disbelieving eyes, eyes that really wanted to know: Is it true that Americans think they won World War II?

In the elevator of his building, Igor's neighbour has installed a mirror so that when he comes home drunk, he can check himself out before seeing his wife.

Igor's apartment is a stuffy two-bedroom flat he shares with his mother and his two cats, Russian blues. The apartment breathes about as well as a banya, and I imagine that I can still smell the ancient grease from the days of the potato chip makers. The small kitchen has a balcony looking out on a cheap hotel frequented by tourists from the Stans.

The apartment has been under renovation ever since I've known him. There are always wires poking out or half-constructed shelves. Now he has scraped the old wallpaper off the walls to replace it. We will also replace the old wardrobe and install decorative Styrofoam tiles on the ceiling. It's a job that should, given a generous ratio of slacking off to work, take us about one week.

The cockpit of Igor's room is his cluttered computer desk. The old PC there is constantly downloading movies, games, and TV shows, and it is perpetually logged into V Kontakte. Scattered among the ashes and beer spills on his desk, there's a DVD for quitting smoking, two Arabic language learning discs, video poker, *Professional Coffee: The Barista's Bible*, and the musty hardcover English-to-Russian and Russian-to-English dictionaries whose pages have separated from the glue in the spine. There is also a model ship that I suspect, at one time or another, was encased in a bottle.

There's a hookah in the corner of the room. A painting with tribal text reading *LIFE*, his own artwork, hangs on the wall suspended from two chains, and amulets dangle from the corners of it. Above his bed are framed collections of beer coasters from his old job at the restaurant Chaika. A few photos of Anya are propped here and there, their edges curling. Several *No smoking* signs are taped to the walls.

In his mother's room, he proudly shows me the photo taken the time Putin and Gerhard Schröder came to Chaika. The photo shows Putin in close-up with the smiling face of Igor at the bar in the background. There's another photo of him striking a Schwarzenegger pose during his weightlifting days.

He smokes and plays me some of his favourite YouTube clips. One shows two teams of Japanese guys playing soccer with binoculars taped to their eyes. Another one shows Medvedev and Putin with several former prime ministers of Ukraine standing stoically at some formal event. Yanukovych (who, at the time of writing, has just been deposed as leader of Ukraine), offers a sunflower seed to Medvedev, who accepts. Then he offers one to Putin, who shakes his head politely but firmly.

Igor smokes seven cigarettes. We drink a couple of cans of Nevskoye. Then we take a walk to Sberbank to pay his bills.

"Anya is calling to me," Igor says, "saying, 'I am missing you. Can we meet?' 'What for?' I say."

He tells me that if he doesn't find a job soon, he will follow through with his earlier plan to join his friends Katya and Big Al, who are working as cooks at a resort near Sochi. They had already gotten him one gig, which he turned down because of Anya's duality. Her duality is not his problem anymore.

"If you go there, how long will you stay?" I ask.

"Don't know," he says. Thanks to the 2014 Olympics, it's the only place in the country where jobs are actively being created. The pay is very good, an apartment is generally included, and he can easily visit his uncle and family in the winter.

"Won't you miss St. Petersburg?" I ask him.

He looks out the window. "Man, now I have hangover. I am getting it only in St. Petersburg. Not in the sea air. It's always too hot or too cold here. Today too hot."

His normally spry demeanour is tempered. He loves his city and here he is demeaning it. The crisis, the unemployment—it is all starting to get to him.

CHAPTER 14

Professional matchmaker Anatoly Ivanovich's office is near the former Romanov Winter Palace, the Hermitage, on the embankment of the Neva River. A prime piece of real estate. I meet with Anatoly Ivanovich, self-declared expert on love in modern Russia.

One of the curious cases he presents to me is that of one of his clients, a wealthy Russian construction tycoon who lives in Canada. The tycoon is rich, young, and good-looking, and the attributes he's seeking in a partner are fairly easy to satisfy among the general population of Russian women: roughly twenty-four years old and hot. But every time Anatoly Ivanovich arranges a suitable girl for him, she balks upon finding out that he lives abroad.

"They don't want to leave their country," he says. "In this regard, the situation changed dramatically after Putin became president."

For a time in the post-Soviet era, matchmaking services in Russia focused on hooking up Russian women with foreign men, and vice versa. Love was tied inexorably to escape, and a whole industry of foreign and Russian companies sprang up to facilitate it.

One of the most fascinating texts of this period is the *English-Russian Dictionary-Phrasebook of Love*. Arranged in alphabetical order by keyword, the entries provide phrases in English and Russian that an anglo suitor might find useful in wooing a potential Russian mate. For instance, if one needs to say something like, "When my lips and tongue revel on your beautiful, luscious body, they will hear your moans of pleasure in South Africa," this is the ideal book. Alternately: "I watch your mouth forming sounds, moving and undulating so supplely, so softly, so enticingly and I am seized with a raging impulse to fuse my own mouth together with it and once and for all revel in its sweet softness."

The book is also packed with practical usages. Under *period*, there are the following: "Are you having your period:" "When will your period be finished?" "My period will be finished in two days" "I'm overdue with my period" And "There's a required waiting period after the divorce."

Still others: "Our bodies will fuse together in exquisite pleasure until we are flung into a wild sea of passion" and "You have opened the floodgates of my womanhood."

Clearly, a useful codex in countless situations. But according to matchmaker Anatoly Ivanovich, such a text has far less applicability today than it may have had in the days when the Russian economy was in a shambles and many women were eager to shack up with any Joe from the American suburbs.

To be fair, the Russian bride business is still relatively healthy. For a few thousand dollars, if a foreign man is inclined to combine adventure and courtship, he can still easily arrange whitewater rafting in the south of Russia with a boatful of women seeking thrills and mates. But there was a time in the nineties when it seemed most girls, and for that matter many boys, would jump at any chance to escape. Demographic statisticians track this as quiet or soft emigration. Independent research reports suggest that between 2003 and 2008, more than 400,000 people left Russia through soft emigration. The Russian Ministry of Statistics (RossStat) reports that over a six-month period in that same time frame, six people renounced their citizenship. Such confusing statistics leave the situation sufficiently fuzzy that one might as well rely on the observations of Anatoly Ivanovich.

Anatoly Ivanovich laughs exactly like the Russian villain in any Western movie you've ever seen with a laughing Russian villain. He also has the same voice as the beloved Russian actor Yevgeny Leonov, best known for voicing the Russian version of Winnie the Pooh.

He is quick to mention that he loves his profession. "After the army, I studied business," he says. "Then I decided to do what I liked, social psychology and interpersonal relationships. But do you know what I really am? A parachutist infiltrator. I studied with Hugo Chávez. Hugo Chávez was learning from me. No, I don't mean he was learning from me, but we were studying in the same academy in Ryazan."

Anatoly Ivanovich styles himself as a provider of many different things for many different clients. For the women, he is a father or big brother, checking up on their prospective suitors and keeping them safe. For the men, he screens out the gold diggers—he's a friend, a big brother, a guiding force . . . Checking up on prospective suitors ranges from the obvious sorts of things, such as checking their passports for previous marriage stamps, to using his contacts in the police force and medical fields to investigate their criminal histories, tendencies toward alcoholism, and medical screens for diseases.

He has a database of hundreds of carefully screened clients of both sexes. The youngest is nineteen; the oldest is eighty-four.

In terms of potential available partners, the demographic situation in Russia clearly favours men. There are, according to census figures, around eleven million more women in Russia than men. This is in large part due to the history of wars—from World War II to Afghanistan to Chechnya—and the brutality of the military, but also to alcohol, which is largely responsible for the lopsided average life expectancy of men (sixty-two) versus women (seventy-six).

"One or two men from my database die each year," Anatoly Ivanovich says. "Last year, this man died." He clicks over to a fresh-faced 57-year-old. "But not a single woman has died in all these years. Another man died this year. He was only fifty years old and he made twenty thousand dollars a month. Bad health. Men die a lot here."

This is an interesting and depressing observation: men die without finding love, leaving their entries like ghosts in Anatoly Ivanovich's database.

But death notwithstanding, in Anatoly Ivanovich's universe, Russia is flooded with good, successful men and women, and awash in riches and possibility. Love is on everybody's mind, but it's an elusive thing to find on your own.

He clicks through the database, showing me more examples. Another man, a top executive at Singer. "He writes music very good," Anatoly Ivanovich says. "We can't find anyone for him.

We did find a 32-year-old woman with a child, and he decided to take her, but then it turned out that she swore too much, so he broke things off."

He clicks to another. "This client is right now looking for a girl thirty-two to thirty-eight years old. He's ready to give her a Lexus and 100,000 to 200,000 rubles per month for her personal expenses. I already sent three women his way, but the selection process works this way: First his assistants screen the women. And only if they approve does he meet them. And out of these three, he met only one. But she was also rich and she was driving her own Mercedes."

Second half is roughly the Russian equivalent of the English *soulmate*. And Anatoly Ivanovich says that he spends most of his time trying to find his clients' second half.

"If a man is looking for his second half, he doesn't have to take all of St. Petersburg to restaurants," he says. "I had one client who wanted to meet 110 women, and I told him, 'No, this is too many. Try and select fewer.' So he chose 97 and said, 'I really like these ones.'"

His assistant, a woman in her late thirties who tells me that she met her husband with Anatoly Ivanovich's help, chimes in: "The problem is, our men are all looking for the same market segment—age, qualities, and look of the women. They all look for good-looking, maybe not extremely beautiful but attractive, family-oriented, interesting to communicate with and pleasant in communication, educated women, and, well, they have problems finding these women of this age and this look and especially of this character."

In short, the men have unrealistic expectations roughly in line with Igor's "man is first" mantra. Journalist Anna Nemtsova has a slightly different take. In an article entitled "Russia's Single Ladies Fed Up with Country's Useless Bachelors," she wrote: "The litany of complaints that Russian ladies have against their male counterparts is long: They smoke too much and drink too much. They cheat shamelessly and curse freely. They expect their girlfriends and wives to clean for them, cook for them, and to look like models." This seems for the most part to be a fair characterization. And on top of it all, the men have the demographic upper hand. No wonder Anatoly Ivanovich has such trouble finding some men a second half.

Based on her photo, one of his female clients is a tall, sporty, blond supermodel. She is in the process of finishing two dissertations—in what exactly, Anatoly Ivanovich is not sure. But two dissertations. The problem, he says, is that she doesn't know how to communicate with a man. Anatoly Ivanovich tries to set up situations in which two people will be able to communicate, and he tries to teach them how to communicate more effectively: how to talk to a person of the opposite sex and how to understand that person.

"When women come to me for the first time, I tell them, 'Let me teach you how to communicate with a man.' They say that they don't want to learn that from me, that they don't need my advice, but then, when a woman meets someone she really likes, she calls me back and says, 'Anatoly Ivanovich, how much do I need to pay you to make this man mine?'"

While we're talking, the phone rings. Anatoly Ivanovich answers and his side of the conversation goes as follows: "Yes . . . Okay . . . So how much younger do you expect the woman to be? Nine years. And how old are you? Forty-five? Okay, for this service it will cost you three thousand rubles. For women who request the same thing we charge them five thousand, but we give a discount to men . . . You will definitely find someone in a short period of time. We have a wide selection." He hangs up.

I asked him how, pray tell, he teaches women to communicate. "Simple," he says. He starts with Dale Carnegie's *How to Win Friends and Influence People*, a wildly popular text in Russia. "First of all, I give them Carnegie to read, and after that we have a discussion about what they read. Then they do two tests. The first test is how to win over a man or how to win over a woman, depending on the gender. Actually, women do both tests and they keep retaking this test as long as they are my clients, so they think more about it and slowly start to understand what they actually need to do.

"I teach them everything. For example, I teach them how a woman should react if a man has a problem performing in bed. Not only young women. When I offer them my help, they say, 'What can you teach us when we are sixty years old?' But then, when I ask them simple questions, they don't know how to answer."

Anatoly Ivanovich got his start in the matchmaking biz quite by accident. A friend asked him to write some materials for her profile on a Russian version of a dating site Previously she had hits only from creeps, but after Anatoly Ivanovich got involved, she began to attract some more interesting prospects.

He basically took over her profile. He coached her on her photograph. "The facial expression and the imprint of thought in the face is very important. Open face, not clenched jaws, mouth relaxed, eyes want a man . . . She must have a sexy expression in the eyes so the man would want her and choose her out of a thousand."

When men started responding to his friend, he continued managing her correspondence. The meeting requests, the dates, the follow-ups all rolled in. She told her friends about her success via Anatoly Ivanovich, and they asked him to help them as well.

So he found himself managing the romantic affairs of a group of women, spending most of his time tending to their correspondence.

"Women tend to write some garbage like, *I like the murmur of falling leaves*. I tell them not to write that. Here's what you need to write: *I'm looking for my one and only and I will give you children. I'll take care of you, etc.*"

His assistant adds: "It's not about the woman's interests. It should be addressed to the man."

Only one problem: "After I wrote those letters to men, they met the women. They were very disappointed. Because when I wrote to those men, I understood them. And when they met the woman, she didn't understand them.

"I played on the man's sense of self-importance. And all the men were mine."

I had initially wanted to meet with some of Anatoly Ivanovich's male clients, but he tried to arrange several meetings and they all fell through. During another visit, he showed me the profile for Natalya, someone he'd been working with for several years and hadn't yet found a match for. I was intrigued why someone would stay with the same matchmaker for several years if the matches he brought in kept not working. So I asked if I could meet with Natalya.

Anatoly Ivanovich seemed suspicious that I wanted to meet Natalya. And with good reason. She was gorgeous and, according to her profile, she seemed smart—a biology teacher. But he arranged it anyway.

As I walk to the small café near the Pushkin statue in downtown St. Petersburg where we are supposed to meet, I imagine a grand Anatoly Ivanovich chess move: suspecting me of trying to get around the agency's aversion to foreigners with this elaborate writing-about-love-in-Russia thing, he acceded to my request to meet Natalya because he had a hunch that she and I might just be a good match. And maybe this fantasy of mine is right. Maybe on some level I am hoping to meet Natalya and to fall in love with her.

Natalya has a perfect French manicure, a fresh bob, a stylish black and white skirt. She looks nothing like anyone I might imagine needing Anatoly Ivanovich's help in finding a partner.

So, perhaps a little too enthusiastically, the first question I ask is why she utilizes him.

"Anatoly Ivanovich is the kind of man who is really interested in his work," she says. "He really wants people to find each other, and is ready to teach them what's necessary. Usually a person has a problem, that's why they can't find a partner. Anatoly Ivanovich helps to solve that problem. For me, my goal was not to necessarily find a husband but someone who will be a good match for me, with whom I can feel comfortable and confident. That didn't happen. Other people find their second half. He marks them with hearts."

"If he is such a good matchmaker, isn't it surprising that you've been with him for several years and haven't met someone?" I ask.

"I met different people and sometimes maybe from the first time you meet, that's not someone you're looking for because something in the person's behaviour may be crude. One time is enough for me to understand that I don't want to see this person again. If you find someone normal who you can hang out with, then maybe they have their own reasons or fears not to like me. Maybe I'm not who they're looking for. Sometimes there are people who I met six months or a year ago through Anatoly Ivanovich and from time to time they get in touch and give me a call. They are good people, but I didn't have any feeling in my heart.

"And this is only one of the ways of going through this process with him. I'm still in control, and I make the decisions whether I like this or that person or not. You can meet people in a club or in a restaurant, but Anatoly Ivanovich is just a way of meeting people to broaden your circle of communication."

Natalya is nearly thirty. She comes from a small town in Ukraine and moved to Petersburg three years ago to stay with her sister and take advantage of opportunities in the big city. She is a biology teacher by training, but since her divorce and her move she has had a hard time securing a new teaching position. She's recently been working at a kiosk in the market.

"You seem very independent, and comfortable with your independence," I say. I am not sure if I'm flirting with her or simply proposing stupid and insulting topics for discussion.

"Yes, these ideas are a sign of our times and, personally, I would rather have a man who would take care of me, but because this type of man is extinct, I have to take care of myself and not rely on anyone. Moreover, women are more responsible. A real man is a man who you can rely on, but now it seems that men can manage to take care of themselves and organize their own little worlds somehow, but they have a lot of fears, and they're not responsible enough to be able to also take care of a woman. I mean, he can make sure he has clean socks and a few cans of beer, but taking care of children and summer vacations for the whole family is already beyond him. They run away from responsibility."

"What in your opinion makes a real man?"

"He must be responsible and he has to be mentally and spiritually healthy, not a pervert. He has to be attentive and caring and, if possible, honest. Cultured."

"This is difficult to find," I suggest in my most attentive, caring, honest, and cultured voice.

"Yes. But I'm a diamond also."

"Do you think the idea of love in Russia right now is different than it was before—say, during the Soviet times?"

"I wouldn't make any distinction between love before and love now," she says. "Love is always the same. There are a lot of definitions of love. One of them is when two people are looking in the same direction."

She explains that primarily she is looking for someone to communicate with, and only then for love.

Communication keeps coming up in her answers, and I start feeling kind of sad. Yulia and I had never been able to communicate. On our first date, I had asked would she mind if I kissed her, and she said yes, which I read as yes, she would mind. So I got up and left, figuring she wasn't interested.

And my attempts at improving communication down the road were misunderstood. At one point, I bought her a book called *Wedded Strangers: The Challenges of Russian-American*

Marriages. I had intended it as a way to open things up between us. She became offended when I gave it to her, and it had sat on her shelf unread ever since.

Natalya tells me about her divorce. "When I was marrying him, he was great, very attentive. He put me up on a pedestal, was very loving, but then he became a member of a religious sect, and they explained to him that family is not important and family is an obstacle on the path to his spiritual development. So his personality and his values changed completely."

"I'm glad that you got out of that situation," I say.

I don't bring up my situation. I am still wearing my wedding ring, but this isn't always clear in Russia, because Russians wear their rings on the opposite hand. Every time I hear about someone else's relationship problems, they are always much more dramatic than mine—involving a scandal or a religious sect. Part of the problem is that, while I know that things are over, I feel guilty for knowing that things are over and for not doing more to make it work. On the other hand, staying in it seems to just be prolonging the misery for both of us.

"Sometimes a person finds herself in a situation that feels like a swamp and there is no hope and then the person either perishes in that swamp or gets up and tries to do something," she says.

"I know exactly what you mean," I say. "I hope that Anatoly Ivanovich finds you someone great."

"Me too," she says.

It occurrs to me as we part that I could try to set her up with Igor. But he isn't exactly the cultured diamond in the rough that she's looking for. He can clean his socks and acquire bottles of beer, but his "man is first" mantra would not go over well with her.

And also, it doesn't seem like a good idea to interfere with the matchmaking of a parachute infiltrator who studied with Hugo Chávez.

CHAPTER 15

Igor's idea of a university graduation party—vodka aplenty, food aplenty, reserved tables at some restaurant, dancing, proclaiming, eventually passing out on reserved tables—did not gel with Anya's idea. It went to a central split between them: he was social and outgoing and reckless and hard-partying; she was shy and liked to spend time with her family.

Her graduation coincided with the one-year anniversary of her grandparents' burial. Her grandfather was so in love with her grandmother after a lifetime together that he had died just a few days after her. They were buried at a cemetery not far from the family dacha, their graves marked with temporary wooden crosses with their names and dates carved into them.

This was what Anya wanted for her graduation: After the customary year, her family and Igor would erect proper gravestones over her grandparents' graves. This and an iPhone. Igor came through on both counts.

Anya's family's dacha was far outside of town, near the edge of the Leningrad region. And across the street from the graveyard was a cement factory. The cement factory kept the air powdery, and everything was always covered in dust.

They pulled up to the graveyard in Anya's father's car, with the gravestones in the trunk. A cement dust–covered pigeon lit on the hood of the car. Anya tried to stir it away, but her uncle said that the pigeons were spirits from the graveyard.

Igor and Anya's father lugged the permanent, polished-granite gravestones from the trunk to the graves. They cleared away the temporary wooden markers and levelled the earth. The gravestones weighed about one hundred kilos each. Igor called the gravestones "monuments," as in, "Monuments are fucking heavy, dude."

By the time they moved the gravestones into place, Igor was covered, like the pigeons and the trees and the ground and everything else there, in a layer of fine cement dust. When he breathed, it scratched his lungs. He coughed.

"In the US, people bury our dead for us," I told him later. "I'm pretty sure it's illegal to do it yourself."

"This is disrespect. You need to do it by your own forces," he said.

After installing Anya's grandparents' gravestones, Igor spent the next day with her brother, moving sand. There was a fenceline and a pile of sand, and the pile had been deposited on the wrong side of the fenceline. The rationale for moving the pile of sand was that, if it remained on the side of the fenceline where it was, it might be stolen.

While they were shovelling the sand, Igor noticed that Anya's brother was wearing combat boots. This surprised him. It was summer, and it was hot. He asked him about them.

Anya's brother told Igor that he kept being robbed at the

subway station. Thugs had stolen three of his cellphones in three separate muggings. After the third one, he decided he would wear combat boots everywhere from then on, so as to kick any would-be assailants.

Moving the pile of sand took an entire day.

Anya spent the weekend trying to figure out her iPhone, Igor's graduation present. She loved it. Simply typing out an SMS got her incredibly giddy.

Anya's family dacha was nine hundred square metres. It wasn't modern, not what they call *Yevropeyskiy remont* (European renovation), but they were updating it bit by bit. Igor helped Anya's father repair a door frame and install some bathroom tiles.

The whole affair was a kind of test run, and Anya and Igor both knew it. He was auditioning for a part in the family life she imagined for them.

Igor went to the banya with Anya's father and her uncle one day during their memorial trip. Igor had brought along the new paintball gun that I'd imported for him. Her father and uncle, both military guys, scoffed when Igor told them about paintball. It's a rub Igor gets sometimes.

"You weren't in the army," they said. "That's why you like paintball."

They cool-guyed him. Then he switched to automatic and began painting the roof of Anya's uncle's banya. The older men were suddenly impressed. "Give it to me, give it to me," Anya's uncle said. From a distance of about fifty metres, he hit the banya's exhaust pipe.

A little boy walking by on the road shouted, "Mama, Mama,

what is this sound?" His mother saw the three shirtless men firing what looked like a machine gun at their banya, snatched the boy's hand, and ran away.

"Oh," Igor said, recounting the story later as we sat having beers. "Anya's uncle has Staffordshire terrier."

"What?"

"Staffordshire terrier. What's in English the common attack command for dogs?"

"Sic 'em."

"Sic 'em? In Russian, this is *fass*. But Uncle trained this dog not *fass*, not . . . how it?"

"Sic 'em."

"Not sic 'em, but *Nemtsi*."

"Germans?" I asked.

"Germans. And the dog like this, *Nemtsi, Nemtsi*." Igor made a series of woofing sounds.

"Was her uncle in World War II?" I asked.

"No, just thinking all Germans are assholes."

"That's a good one."

"Hey, you told me a lot of times that Russian are xenophobes."

"It's true," I said.

"It's really funny, man. I need to make a picture or a video clip."

"Does the dog ever really attack someone?"

"It will attack," Igor said. "It will for sure, but it's well trained. The dog is patrolling the area for Germans or somebody else or whatever to destroy it. The dog is the kindest being I ever seen. Except when someone says, 'Germans.'"

While Igor was off bonding with Anya's family, anti-German

dog included, I hung out with some American writers who had just arrived for the literary festival. I had taken them for dinner and drinks. We'd been together an hour or so when one of the women with us said to me, "Your English is fantastic. You hardly have any accent."

This was the first time I became aware that I had begun speaking English with a Russian accent. I'd always had this subconscious thing that I was embarrassed about where I'd pick up someone else's speech patterns. The year I lived in Arizona and hung out with a guy from Wisconsin, I latched on to some of his Northernisms. As soon as I arrived in Canada, I'd claimed the "eh" particle as my own. I'd even started shortening the *a* sounds in double-*a* words the way Canadians do: *dra*ma, *Maz*da, *ban*ya . . . But the Russian accent was more insidious because, while the modifications were still subconscious, I was saying words as Igor said them, and using Russian grammatical forms when speaking with Russians in English because it facilitated understanding. Then I'd get used to saying it that way and the form fixed in my regular speech.

I might have cured myself of this by simply speaking Russian and Russian only with Igor, but he still insisted that my Russian hurt his ears. And I was damned if I did and damned if I didn't, because all my formal Russian language teachers had been women. Women speak Russian in an almost singsongy way. They modulate their intonation, playing the language like a xylophone. But men tend to speak in a gruff monotone. They garble all their words. They also use a lot more *mat*. Through no fault of their own, female language teachers teach foreigners to mimic their intonations, giving their speech an inherently effeminate inflection.

I explained this to Igor at the Atrium. He seemed impressed by the information.

"Say something in Russian," he said.

"*Ty ochen krasivy,*" I said.

"Hm," he said. "Yeah. You do sound like gay."

"Is that why it hurts your ears?"

"No. Sounding gay is okay. Will help in picking up chicks. Hurts ears because of mistakes. Keep study, grasshopper. Practise practise. One day."

CHAPTER 16

gor and I went to the banya again, and he violated his cardinal rule. We had been talking, as we sometimes talked in the banya, about women. One thing he had said about Anya stuck in my head: "I am trying to figure out whether she is the shadow or I am."

Then, while we sat in the chill-out area in between steams, he ordered fifty grams of vodka.

I called him out. He had once commanded me that, whatever I did, I must never drink vodka in the banya. A good friend of his died after drinking vodka and passing out inside the *parilka*.

"This is not alcohol," he said. "This is medicine. This is cure."

I refrained from accusing him of the Duality.

He shot the vodka and clanked the glass on the table. "We are now entering Heathrow Airport by Jeep!" he said.

Later that night, I invited Igor and Anya on the traditional closing boat ride for the writers' festival. Every year we rented a big boat stocked with alcohol and, around midnight, cruised the canals for an hour. Then the captain steered the ship out onto the Neva for the raising of the bridges. The river was mobbed with boats small and large.

The first time I'd heard of this spectacle, I didn't quite understand it. "We are going to look at drawbridges go up?" I asked. But it's difficult to describe the collective feeling of joy that the sight inspires.

And in the summer, city life in St. Petersburg revolves, to some degree, around the bridges. Each bridge goes up on schedule, and if you don't leave the centre by the scheduled time, you have to wait until the morning when they come down again. Every night, cars scream toward the bridges in hopes of making it just in the nick of time. Some of them invariably don't. Long lines of traffic are always blocked in for the night. Taxis hurrying to get their final fares across the bridge are stuck. They turn off their engines in the middle of the road and sleep for a couple of hours until the bridges go down again.

The bridges are brightly lit on the sides, and they rise slowly. From the water, the view is stunning—the Winter Palace on one side and the Peter and Paul Fortress on the other. Thousands of people line the banks. The boats sputter and bob in the choppy water, dangerously close to one another. They jockey for position under this bridge or that one as it rises. On one boat they're having a dance party, on another a wedding celebration, everyone shouting and partying. Sometimes there's fireworks over the Hermitage. And after the bridges are up, the massive barges and cruise ships wind their way up the river.

Our boat that night carried a group of about a hundred North American and Russian writers, and Igor and Anya. It was the closing night of the final year of the festival. And I was thinking about those nine years roaming the nooks and crannies of that ethereal city, drunkenly chaperoning drunken writers—some of my heroes—home from those nooks and crannies, wandering fictional paths taken by great fictional characters—Dostoevsky's murderer Raskolnikov and, of course, Gogol's person-sized nose. All that time, I hadn't only been drinking and sweating at the banya with Igor. I'd sat in on seminars on Russian punk rock and Russian translation. I'd heard Mikhail Iossel's stories about being a part of the artistic underground there in the eighties, with the KGB constantly hassling writers. I'd met an entire new generation of young Russian poets, one of whom had told me the first time we met that he was trying to write works that actively resisted commodification, which blew my mind because back then I'd just come out of a writing program in which lots of people were actively trying to write whatever Random House could sell. That last boat ride was a big night.

Igor sat at a table with Anya for as long as he could stand the boredom and lack of social engagement. Then he started walking around the boat talking to everyone.

I sat with Anya for a little while. Once Igor was gone, she grew even more quiet and a little sulky. Meanwhile, Igor was on the outside deck, infiltrating group after group, sharing shots of vodka. At one point he threatened to throw a Russian poet whom he disliked overboard. There was uncomfortable laughter. Everyone, especially the Russian poet, hoped that this was a joke.

When the ride was over, we docked on the Fontanka canal and no one wanted the night to end. We careened down the street toward Dumskaya street and its legions of sleazy bars. Igor wanted to join us, but Anya took him by the arm and led him away.

Around eleven the next morning, on the Day of the Family, Igor called. "Wazzup muzzafugga!" he said. He sounded wasted. Sober, he typically didn't use this particular refrain, very popular on one of the local radio stations. "I will be in Suliko in five to ten minutes," he said.

"I thought you were working," I said.

"I don't feel like working today. So you'll meet me there in five to ten minutes?"

"Okay," I said.

"Okay, see you, man."

I'd slept for only a few hours. It took me a little while to get myself together and head down to Suliko, the cheap but tasty Georgian restaurant behind the Kazansky Cathedral. When I walked in, he was slumped in a booth in the corner. There was an almost empty carafe of vodka in front of him, and he had finished a business lunch, the typical midday restaurant deal including, at Suliko, fish soup, beet salad, meat and rice, and a cup of *mors* (boiled fruit soaked in water). He seemed practically asleep, wearing his work uniform. The black apron was tied around his waist.

"Wazzup muzzafugga?" I said.

"Hey man," he said. "I am not spry. Nothing is interesting. It's autumn depression. I need to see the first snow."

"It's summer," I said.

"In Russia, summer is autumn depression."

He forced me to drink vodka with him. I noticed that his right knuckles were like hamburger. He told me that, on the way home from the boat ride, he had made Anya stop the car. He got out and started a fight with a brick wall. Surprisingly, the brick wall won.

"I told you, man," he said. "Never drink vodka in banya."

He fumbled his cigarette, mumbling and slurring. I ordered more bread to keep him eating.

"How did you get out of work?" I asked.

"Just left. Said I wanted to leave. Director said no. I drank some whiskey. Then director said, 'You are drunk, get the fuck out of here.'"

"Are you going to be fired?"

"No, just day off. That's all."

The real deal started to come out. He and Anya had reached an impasse. She refused to move in with him without being married; at the suggestion of marriage, Igor's refrain kicked in. "Why do I need another stamp in my passport? Why do I need more ink on my hands? A ring on the finger? I hate rings."

Marriage in Russia is a rite of passage that sees the permanent modification of the passport with a marriage stamp, to go along with the other stamps designating your city registration and place of work. To Igor, it was just more bureaucratic officialese, just like any other engagement with the system in Russia: meaningless. He'd rather they just got a place together.

He said she'd stopped by work that morning, and they had a fight.

"It is like how I already told you. How House MD says, 'Everyone lies.'"

"Well, happy Day of the Family, man," I said.

It was unclear how many people noticed the new holiday. There was a municipal banner hung downtown that read *Day of the Family. Love, Dedication, Trust.*

Igor's friend Big Al suddenly arrived, and he immediately understood the situation.

"We need to get your drunk ass home, Igor," he said. Big Al pulled him into a standing position and Igor slung his arm over his neck.

"See you tomorrow," I said.

"Tomorrow never dies," Igor said. He smiled and his eyes closed. Big Al walked him out of Suliko.

After they left, some guy tapped me on the shoulder. "Excuse me," he said. "I can't help hear you talk English. May I ask you please, do you happen to have the email address of Al Gore?"

CHAPTER 17
SUMMER 2009

I n our efforts to complete the renovation before Igor's mother's return, we spend an entire day, until well into the evening, wallpapering the apartment. The next morning we wake up late to find the wallpaper, our single accomplishment so far, shredded by Dorofay the cat. There is a brief moment of defeat.

But we do not lose hope. We push on. We pull the old wardrobe away from the wall and find years' worth of trash back there.

There are ancient copies of the *St. Petersburg Times*, an old telegram from his grandmother in Abkhazia congratulating him on his birthday, and an actual chicken foot. Igor holds up the latter and laughs. "Cat was playing with it," he says. Dorofay again. He tosses it into one of the green garbage bags stuffed with old wallpaper.

I glance at the old newspapers. They're from 1999, the year we first met, from the era when Igor used to read this very paper from cover to cover to learn English.

The big news was coverage of the fighting in Chechnya. There's a surprising photo of a very young and trim Putin shaking hands with Bill Clinton. Another photo is of a dust-up between Shaquille O'Neal and Charles Barkley during an NBA game. There are mentions of some local bars and clubs we used to go to in the events section, and five different classified ads for foreign marriage agencies.

We disassemble the wardrobe, but it is slow work. We stack the heavy wood of the wardrobe in the hallway. We try to measure and apply some of the ceiling tiles, which are about two feet square and made of Styrofoam. The tiles don't quite fit in the spots we allot for them, and they are not flush. The seams are just untrue enough to be noticeable. It's a mess.

We begin to realize that we will never make the deadline of his mom's return.

We're discouraged by our own slacking and ineptitude, and so we slack some more, taking a break in the courtyard.

I hang out for a little while, but I get the sense that maybe it's been my influence that has kept us from getting the work done. Every day Igor emails applications for jobs, but he doesn't even get called in for interviews. I suspect that he is falling into a depression over his inability to find a job in a country in which there are no jobs. So I return to my apartment at metro Bolshevikov.

As I'm waiting for the *marshrutka* to take me to the subway, a guy in a pink snow-bunny coat stumbles out of the woods carrying a five-litre water bottle filled with beer. He staggers across the street, staring with fear at the traffic because, it seems, he has not the mental processes to get out of the way of anything, only some primordial directive to move forward.

After a few days, I take the *marshrutka* back to Piskaryovka to meet Igor and go to the banya. I step off the bus and he is standing at the stop dressed in grey from head to toe. The sky also is grey, from horizon to horizon. His clothes and mood match the sky perfectly. Even his eyes, I notice, are the exact same shade of grey, the colour of his cats. He syncs somehow with Petersburg, like a chameleon.

We wait a long time for another *marshrutka*, going in the direction of the banya. We don't talk much.

I ask him if everything's okay.

"I'm still have no job, man," he says.

He tells me about "the talks" with Anya. This is how he refers to them. "We have had many 'the talks' with her." He sums up their whole relationship: "We are going round and round. This is her character." He doesn't want to discuss it any further.

It's a weekday. Others are at work or at home saving their money. We are the only ones at Shaiba, which means it will be a crap steam. We walk in and I note once again the pencil-width bullet hole behind the check-in woman's desk.

"You're getting fat, man," I say to Igor.

"Of course," he says. "I'm drinking beer every day with you. I'm not supposed to do it."

I tell him what I had for breakfast: ramen noodles, two fried eggs, yogurt, bread, sliced tomato.

"I ate today one pickle, two sandwiches, and an apple. That's all."

I call the number for the café on the in-house phone and tell her that I want a mug of kvass. She tells me the price. Then, after I put the phone down, the door behind me opens and the woman I spoke to appears. "You just ordered?" she asks. I nod, and she goes to get our kvass.

"Chill," Igor says. "I am going to smoke."

In the *parilka*, Igor lets me have another go at the *venik* massage. This time there is no B-minus, or even a C-minus. I have no strength at all in my arms. The greyness and depression of St. Petersburg have depleted me. I too have absorbed the great weight that is a gloomy summer in a world in crisis.

"More amplitude!" Igor shouts. But I've got nothing.

He sits up and snatches the *veniki* from me. He beats himself, standing in the middle of the *parilka*. Flakes of his skin, the remains of the Gelendzhik sunburn, and leaves fly around him.

Back in the chill-out room, I announce that I can feel my heart beating in my legs.

"It means the arteries are like this," he says, making a huge circle with both arms. "You need fifty grams of cognac . . . or vodka. Wait. Which increases arteries and which decreases? I don't know. You need it. One hundred grams and you will be the happiest man in the world."

We leave the banya and stop by the Ryumochnaya. Igor asks the bartender whether cognac or vodka narrows arteries and she says, "How the fuck should I know?"

We have plastic cups of vodka with tomato juice and mini-pickles.

"I'm exhausted," Igor says, "but coming back to life a little bit."

I hadn't known what to anticipate this summer. It is the first summer in ten years that I'm not working for the literary festival. I had planned to hang out, write. I'd intended to travel, but I didn't know to where. Eventually, I planned to land in Krasnoyarsk, where Yulia is visiting her family, and see what is left of my marriage. Since Igor isn't finding work anyway, and since we can't manage a single, simple, productive thing such as finishing the renovations on his apartment, I wonder whether we might downshift—whether we might get our positive on—a little more.

"I know what you need," I say.

"What I need?" Igor asks.

"Another trip."

"Trip to where?"

"Come to Baikal with me. We've been south, let's go east. You can swim in the Russian soul."

Lake Baikal is the largest freshwater lake in the world, a legend of mythic proportions in Russian culture, a spiritual place, one of the crown jewels of the Motherland. We have both talked often about wanting to see it.

"All right," he says. "Better do that than sit here boring. I think people are just bored. This is the answer for everything. They are bored from life, bored from everything. Sometimes the boredom is pissing people off. It's the usual thing."

"Maybe you're right. Maybe you're right. I can't imagine we'll be bored at the biggest lake in the world."

"I have a sister and brother near Irkutsk, and my real father lives there."

This is news to me. I've never heard about them, and I had no idea that he knew where his father was, much less that he was still alive. I haven't even seriously given any thought to the idea of Igor coming with me, or what we might do. And now we are suddenly en route to seeing the family he never knew.

"Have you been in touch with them any?" I ask.

"A couple times, but we never met. I will see them and then I can tell Uncle how they are."

I had visited my biological father for the first time in California a decade earlier. I was glad I had done it. I tell Igor how strange it was to see an expression that you had always only seen in the mirror on the face of someone you'd never met.

"I don't need to see him for this. I already saw my face on Uncle's. Now, about this trip, just one thing."

"What's that?"

"Fuck the fucking train. We will fly."

The train is slow, so I figure we might as well fly. And like the Russian Federation's, Igor's currency reserves, his savings from the oil-rich Putin years, are still strong. We have a great feeling as we finish the meal. So what if the world is still in crisis? We are invested with purpose. We are men going on a trip. A couple of strangers on the road again.

CHAPTER 18

In one of our Skype conversations in the fall of 2008, Igor informed me that he had been playing paintball recently in the woods. "The best is when the snow is up to the knee, and you are jumping like a goat," he said.

"What's going on in your life there, man?" I asked him.

"I don't know," he said. "I want a baby. And Anya not."

"A baby?" I asked. This was the first I had heard about it.

"A baby," he said. Then he quickly changed the subject. He told me that Anya had gotten a new job working for a Finnish construction company on English translations. She would work at the Finnish company and at the Atrium.

"This is a very good opportunity for her," he said. "It's a good company. She will make a good career in it. And the main boss, he likes to drink and he's fond of paintball. Oh yeah, I will help her with translations." It is true that Igor's English, at least conversationally, is far beyond Anya's.

Then he dropped the bomb. "I made—how you say in English?—proposition—proposal to Anya. She said, 'Yes, I agree, I agree.'" He trails off.

"You proposed to her? I thought you didn't need another stamp in your passport. When?" First a baby and now this. I wondered if Putin's Year of the Family was getting to him.

"I don't remember," he says. "Maybe two weeks, three weeks ago. It doesn't matter. I don't remember the date. Fuck it. So I made the proposal: 'I am making official proposal. I am not going to visit your parents, I'm asking you, only you.' Then, later on . . . Then, on this day later on in the evening, I said to Anya, 'Tomorrow we need to go to state registration to make application forms.' She said, 'No.' I said, 'What the fuck you say, "no"?' In Russia, this industry, marriage industry, I don't know how to explain it. It takes, like, three months. This is the law. Anya said, 'If we are going to make application forms right now, I don't need it. I need sun and green grass and everyone is happy and it's warm on the streets.' The Duality. I said, 'Okay. We will wait until February.'"

I laughed, thinking he was joking.

"Funny?" he said. "All my life is funny to you? No, no, man, it needs to be done, because she was fucking my brains for two years. I am fed up with it. No, really. She can't understand this is another ink on the finger and another stamp in the passport. Okay. Let it be. Fuck it. But don't fuck my brain."

"It's a very beautiful and romantic story," I said.

"Yes, it is," he said.

It was hard to understand. Igor had finally proposed to her and now she was waffling. Was it because he was so crude about it, or had she changed her mind? The Duality. I certainly couldn't call myself an expert on marriage. Yulia worked upstairs in her office on the second floor of our house in the east end of Toronto. I worked in my office in our basement. We didn't communicate much. And we had our own duality. Instead of talking about how to fix things or how to communicate better, we wondered whether we should try to have kids or break up.

When Barack Obama was elected in November, Igor left a message on my cellphone. "Hey man," he said, "congratulations on the Obama!"

The *Yes we can* and hope and change, the enthusiasm for which even carried across the border into Canada and spread around the world, was soon overshadowed by the global economic crisis, the worst since the Great Depression. And while the effects were brutal in many countries, Russia was already in an economic tailspin after the Georgian conflict, and matters kept getting worse.

The price of Urals crude, the linchpin of the Russian economy, which had been US$140 in July, dipped into the low fifties. By the time it was all over, the Russian stock market would shed more than one trillion dollars. The ruble, which the past summer had been as strong as twenty-two to the dollar, slipped toward thirty. The Russian government aggressively deployed its massive but quickly depleting—to the tune of tens of billions of dollars per week—foreign currency reserves to prop it up.

Putin reassured his citizenry with a US$20-billion economic stimulus package. "We will do everything," he said, "everything in our power . . . so that the collapses of the past years should never be repeated in our country. We will do everything in our power to defend the deposits of our citizens in the bank."

By winter, the crisis (which is pronounced in Russian like *creases*) was in full swing. The National Bolshevik Party posted signs over ATMs all over Moscow that read *Citizens, Take your money—before it's too late*. More than a quarter of all consumer savings were withdrawn from deposit accounts. The licences of nine banks were revoked by the end of November. The Kremlin began bailing out, one by one, its oligarchs.

Within just a few short months, Angelina Jolie kisses on the lips of Russian heartthrobs were all but forgotten. Just before I returned to Russia in early December 2008, Standard & Poor's cut the country's rating to two levels above junk.

The price of a barrel of oil dipped further, below forty dollars.

St. Petersburg was snowy and dark when I arrived that December, the first time I'd ever seen the city in the winter.

Through some unlikely connections, Igor had arranged an apartment for me in a music school affiliated with the Mariinksy Theatre, one of the most famous in Russia, where many of the nineteenth-century greats played.

Carrying my luggage through ankle-deep snow, we followed the directions he'd been given down a little side street across from the Mariinsky to a children's music school. The director of the school, a woman with a round face and a stern brow, greeted us abruptly. "You must be our distinguished foreign conductor?" she said to me.

I looked at Igor. I hadn't heard anything about this.

"Yes," Igor said.

Her face was skeptical. I didn't know what a conductor looked like, but I definitely didn't look like a conductor, and Igor definitely did not look like the type to be escorting a conductor. Bodyguard, maybe. Still, she let us through.

The building smelled like a school. Children tussled in lockers, packing and unpacking instruments. The director retrieved some keys and introduced us to the security guard, a shifty-looking character with a thin moustache.

He shook my hand and told me that the curfew was eleven p.m. Igor and I once again exchanged looks. Curfew?

"They are playing concerts sometimes late at night," Igor said to him.

"There are no concerts after eleven," he said. "The door locks at this time. For the children."

Igor nodded. I knew what he was thinking: we will bring the guard a present and my curfew will be extended. We followed the round-faced woman with the stern brow into the courtyard. In the middle of the courtyard was a small stand-alone house. She unlocked the door for us and gave me the keys.

The apartment was magnificent—spacious and recently renovated. Something like this should cost a couple of hundred dollars per night, but on my special conductor arrangement I paid a mere six hundred rubles per night, twenty dollars.

When she left, Igor said, "Welcome to your quarters, guest conductor."

"Who exactly am I?" I asked.

"I think probably you are a German conductor. Be whoever you want. Just some conductor. No one's fucking caring who."

The apartment had a bedroom with two dorm-style beds and a living room with a giant flat-screen TV and a plush Western-style wraparound couch. I got the strange sense that it had all been assembled just for my arrival. The screws on the IKEA coffee table were only in halfway. Everything seemed brand new.

I suggested that we go get a beer.

"Fuck beer," Igor said. "I don't drink beer in winter. I have better idea."

We walked toward the Mariinsky. Several of the cafés we passed advertised anti-crisis menus. We stopped at a place that specialized in *pirogi*, pies, one of my favourite aspects of Russian cuisine: you take something wonderful like mashed potatoes or fried onions and bake it into bread.

Igor ordered rabbit pie. I ordered salmon pie.

He smacked loudly, enjoying the hell out of it. He made sure that I understood this was pie made from *krolik*, domesticated rabbit, and not hare. It was important to him that I was cognizant of this distinction since he knew that Americans tend to call anything that hops and has big ears a rabbit. Just another example, for him, of the American failure of precision, as with the colour blue, which Russians break down into two separate words for light and dark shades.

He brought me up to speed on the crisis situation at the Atrium. To say the least, business was not looking good. He sat behind the bar smoking and reading, serving the trickle of customers. He and the cook, Small Al, had spent an entire day filming a clip on their cellphones called "Fruit Salad," in which they exploded various of the Atrium's fruit inventory in the basement with M-80s.

Anya called from the Atrium while we were sitting there and fucked Igor's brain about a personal problem she was having with the other barman at work. Apparently, she had become offended that the other barman constantly talked to her about his sexual conquests and she asked him to stop. Subsequently, the offended party had offended the offending party. A scandal was brewing.

Igor and I both drank cappuccinos, and he chain-smoked. He stubbed out his cigarette in the remaining crust of rabbit pie. He had long since gone through the nicotine patches and gum I'd brought over the summer, with no discernible reduction in his smoking. The only outcome was that, since he'd run out of nicotine patches, he no longer ate an onion every day.

The general docility of Winter Igor surprised me. I wondered if it was possible that he was the hard-partying force I knew him as only in summer, that he hibernated, in a sense, come the long, dark Petersburg winter. Was this a result of him getting older, becoming engaged?

We bought two extra slabs of rabbit pie, one to take to Anya and a piece to use as a preliminary bribe for the security guard.

CHAPTER 19
SUMMER 2009

gor's mood registers a slight uptick after the decision is made to go to Siberia and Lake Baikal. It's July 1, and a new gambling ban has gone into effect. We walk around downtown and watch men loading all the city's slot machines into big blue trucks. Then we shoot back up to Akademicheskaya, a stop away from Igor's place.

There are wide asphalt sidewalks, parks, and student cafés for the foreign students of St. Petersburg State Polytechnic University nearby.

We pass a middle-aged couple on the street. The woman is drinking a can of beer while the man eats an ice cream.

We stop by Igor's favourite café and grab a seat across from an aquarium where catfish mate. The aquarium needs better filtration. The glass is clear, but the water is heavy with sediment. "Hotel California" plays over the restaurant sound system.

"This is my place," Igor says. He comes here sometimes by

himself, usually for breakfast. He always sits at this one table in the back facing the aquarium.

We watch the catfish do it. Igor orders some Caucasian dish made from eggs, chicken, and potatoes fried together with spicy tomato sauce and fifty grams of vodka.

"In Irkutsk, I will see my sister and brother," he says. "I decided I will not see Father. He is not like Uncle. I will just get the information what he is doing from sister and brother, to tell to Uncle. It's not right that twins should be so far apart, not even knowing where the other one is for two years." He orders another fifty grams and drinks a dark Kozel beer. It is clear that things are weighing on him, this business about his father. He's negotiated with the workers doing the renovations on his neighbour's apartment to bring down the old wardrobe we disassembled.

I stumble across an article on alcohol in the newspaper. A study suggests that there is more alcohol purchased in Russia today than in the chaotic and stressful nineties. And this statistic doesn't even cover illegal sales. Some grandma cooks up some hooch (which is called *samagon*) to supplement her meagre pension, selling it to neighbours, and it kills every old alcoholic in the neighbourhood.

Igor is discerning in his vodka choices. Some small bottles can be had for as little as seventy rubles. It is not as bad as the turpentine the *samizdat*-era writers used to drink, but close. He sticks with the moderately priced Green Mark and its Fresh Vodka slogan.

I tell him that Fresh Vodka is a very funny slogan for me.

He says, "And for me it's very funny to see the expiration date on my vodka."

"You think you're an alcoholic?" I ask.

"Probably I am drinking too much," he says. "Beer mostly. Vodka rarely. In the winter, as you saw, I am not even drinking beer."

There is a slight awkwardness in the air after I ask this question. Then it passes.

We decide to walk back to his apartment, along the Avenue of the Unvanquished. This area along the avenue, bordering the siege cemetery, accounts for some of the greenest parts of the city. It's wooded, and we walk down trails far away from the actual street. The trees—pine, blue spruce, birch—are lush and dark.

We pass flocks of massive grey and black crows, which, I tell Igor, are the most terrifying crows I've ever seen.

Igor says, "I will tell you the story with crows. You know they like shiny things. In Abkhazia, tourists are losing these shiny things. When I was a boy, I would go hunting in crows' nests, and sometimes was successful."

I tell him about a documentary I saw in which crows drop nuts from traffic signals for cars to break open.

"Actually, crows very smart beings," he says.

We are not far from the centre of St. Petersburg, yet we wander through a horse farm and a thicket of woods before emerging into a big wholesale market. We're across the Avenue of the Unvanquished from the cemetery.

"Bodies are not only there," Igor says, pointing to the cemetery. "They are here." Now he points to the ground we're walking on. "Besides the law, it's another reason no one will ever build here. Dig and you will find bones.

"Kostya's grandma lived here during the siege. She said they would bring bodies from all over the city. They were everywhere. We are again walking on them now."

I look down at the sandy path.

"Imagine," he says, "starving people were bringing the dead here in winter, with no strength to dig, especially in frozen ground. They were lying everywhere here."

We cross the street and enter the Piskaryovskoye Memorial Cemetery. There's a dried-up lake to the left of the cemetery. A mother and two children walk in their bare feet in the mud. A sign instructs the public not to fish.

"It's bullshit," Igor says. "I was fishing all the time here."

The monument in the cemetery is called Motherland. There are vast stretches of communal graves, elevated platforms with date markers designated by year only. The eternal fire is surrounded by wilted bright red plants. The fountains are dry like the lake.

"It used to be beautiful here in the nineties," Igor says, suddenly and unexpectedly angry, "especially during every May 9 artillery show. Now, no one is caring. Veterans are dying more year by year. I think in thirty years no one will remember."

Back at Igor's place, there's a toupée-sized jellyfish fermenting in a three-litre jar of brownish water on the counter with cheesecloth over the top.

"What is it?" I ask.

"Chainiy grib," he says. "Bacteria and yeast."

Literally, this means "tea mushroom." I know of only one type of mushroom associated with tea, and this is not that.

He tries to explain: "It is not a real mushroom, it is bacteria, man."

I ask where he got it.

"I asked my friend," he says. "It's Japanese stuff. I can get it easily, maybe from someone's grandmother. Just asking. He gets it from somebody and somebody is giving to someone else."

He begins enumerating all the diseases it cures. He says it's especially helpful for the liver. We look it up online and find out it's a kombucha colony.

Igor will leave it there for nine days.

"It's a little bit alcoholic."

"You believe in it?"

"I think so. People aren't drinking shit, man."

"But do you feel something when you drink it?"

"No," he says, "just tastes a little bit bitter."

We leave the *chainiy grib* to buy some beer at the store downstairs.

On the way, we run into a group of Igor's friends going to play PlayStation and smoke weed. We greet them and exchange a few jokes and then carry on our separate ways.

"Do you ever join them?" I ask.

"Rarely."

"Why not?"

"Because they will be smoking ganja and dancing like morons and smiling."

I have long known that Igor doesn't like weed, but the downer on dancing and smiling is something new.

We bump into those same friends again the next night. They are running across the parking lot to the car driven by a Hello Pizza! delivery guy. They buy the pizza off the delivery man by offering to outbid the person who ordered it. They bring it to Igor's apartment.

These are real Russian stoners.

They smoke from a one-hitter and smile and dance like morons, just like Igor said, in the kitchen. They drink cheap Chilean white wine and speak with long strings of *mat* such that it's difficult for me to get what they're talking about.

Ilya works at the Grand Hotel Europa. Anton is a carpenter. Alex works in merchandising. They laugh and trade quotes from *The Simpsons*. Ilya mimics a conversation between Hugo Chávez and Obama. The joke is that Chávez exposes Obama as a transparent smooth talker with no substance. But the three of them don't even know that Obama was recently in Moscow. It hasn't been a high priority on Russian news.

They ask me the requisite questions, such as how much does a house cost in the West? And when they leave, they suggest that we join them later in the courtyard.

Igor has a special connection with these friends from the neighbourhood, most of whom he grew up with, went to school with, has known forever. With these kinds of friends, life is like an American sitcom—to the degree that life in Russia can be like an American sitcom. They pop by anytime, and Igor can just pop by their places anytime. They congregate daily in the courtyard. It's extended family.

"This is my place, man. I can go to anyone's apartment around here anytime and sit and drink or just have tea and talk," he says.

We inspect the wallpaper again. Dorofay has continued to shred it, burying her claws deep in the soft, thick material. Not an inch of wallpaper below four feet has been spared.

He goes to the closet and digs out Dorofay's pedigree. He showed her a few times while he was at the shipbuilding university and won a few ribbons. Igor is full of surprises. I wouldn't assume that the young hooligan who posed for photos like Schwarzenegger and skipped all his classes (except badminton) would have been into cat shows.

He logs onto V Kontakte. Anya is posting love poems on his wall.

"I don't love her anymore," he says. "For girls, love is eternal. For men, it's not."

Right now, he's particularly into the V Kontakte game City Bandits, a role-playing game in which one slowly builds a crew of mafiosi in competition with other players. He mindlessly taps at the keyboard, robs a few banks. He's made something like seventy thousand euros today.

We head down to the courtyard, but none of his friends are there. So we sit in the sun on a bench.

"I think it's time I learned some Russian *mat*," I say.

"You think you are ready?"

"I am ready," I say.

"What was your last grade on *veniki* beating?"

"Doesn't matter."

"You failed. It means you are not ready for Russian *mat*."

Which is likely true, but he explains anyway. There are two main words, he says: *hui* and *pizda*.

"I can easily make twenty swear words from *hui* with different prefixes and suffixes," he says.

It is difficult enough for me to pick up the sense of Russian spoken in the monotone in which Russian men speak it. What I hear when Igor talks to his friends in real *mat*, especially when drunk, generally goes something like this: "Motherfucker, to the dick [something, something] fucking shit, pussy [something] dick this, fuck that [something something something] whore cunt ..."

He takes my notepad and makes two columns. One column is a positive variant and the other is a negative variant. For example, very bad adverbs: *huyovo* (I feel like fucking shit), *pizdets* (I'm totally fucked). Good adverbs: *ohuyenno* or *pizdato* (I'm fucking awesome or I feel fucking good).

"Then, you can use them together for more emotional thing. Can use good with good and bad with bad, but can't use bad with good. And if you're changing the endings, you can play with it."

The true inferiority of the English language with regard to swearing becomes clear in any discussion of Russian swearing. The sheer number of possibilities and the sophistication—the only word that covers it—make Russian swearing vastly superior. I can say, in English, "Motherfucker, shit cocksucker damn," and it's expressive but sounds absurd. Russia's great *mat* speakers are street poets, but to be a poet you can't simply have an intellectual understanding of the language; you have to feel it. And I can't feel it.

This doesn't stop me from trying. He teaches me to say *Ya segodnya ni huya ne sdelal* (Today I didn't do a motherfucking thing). And my attempts leave Igor in hysterical tears.

"Goodie one," he says. "Excellent."

CHAPTER 20

gor and I trekked around the wintry city looking for currency exchanges with euros. Before the ruble sank further, he wanted to convert his pay. We didn't discuss the fact that just six months earlier, in some nationalistic urge, he'd proposed converting his entire savings to rubles. All the exchanges we stopped at were out of foreign currency. We finally found one that could give him a maximum of one hundred euros, and he took it.

When we passed a Glinka statue, Igor asked, "You know Glinka?" We stopped and read the inscription, his dates of birth and death.

"Yeah," I said. "The father of Russian classical music, but I didn't know that he died at fifty-three."

"Fifty-three is enough," Igor said.

The traffic snarled around us, the historic streets feeling the crunch of millions of people opting to be warm in their cars.

We crossed over the frozen Fontanka via the Anichkov Bridge, with its four horseman statues. The scrotum of one of the horses, according to local legend, was etched with the likeness of the sculptor's cuckold. Groups of tourists sometimes stood on the bridge peering intently at the horses' genitals, trying to discern a face there. This was the same canal that Igor had his dock on the one summer he tried out free enterprise in Russia. It was the same canal where I once saw a boat cop chasing down three jet skiers.

As it neared four p.m., it was already almost dark.

At Shaiba, the round banya, a guy wrapped only in a sheet rolled around in the snow on the sidewalk out front. His bright red skin steamed. It was my first time at the banya in the winter.

"Listen, man," Igor said, "if anyone asks, you're Canadian, not American."

I laughed. "You never asked me to do this before."

"Before, there wasn't elections," he said. "If you say America, they will ask about Obama, about Bush. All this shit. No one knows who president of Canada is or when are elections."

Every time I came to the banya, I understood it a little bit better. I watched Igor prepare the steam room, splashing the rocks with water then wetting the *veniki* and beating all the walls to moisten them. In order to prepare the banya for the proper humidity, to achieve the right character of steam, you must first massage the banya itself.

Then we sat in the chill-out area and perused the meat appetizers: beef, pig, chicken, turkey, horse, deer, moose.

"I would like some moose," Igor said, "but it is crisis."

We sat in the prepared *parilka*'s good light steam until we couldn't take it anymore. Then we rushed outside to the pool deck, where it was minus-seven degrees Celsius. I stood knee-deep in snow, my feet pulsing, staring up at the white sky.

We dove in. My banya-heated body didn't register any temperature difference between the air and the water. The banya had cancelled out all feeling. There were only the textural sensations of air and water.

"Let's go jump through the ice into the Neva," I said.

"Fuck it," Igor said. "My days of swimming in those waters are over."

Steam rolled off the surface of the water. A group of naked girls clung to one side of the pool near the entrance to the women's banya. Protocol with naked woman in the banya pool seemed to be: do not acknowledge. They clung to their side of the pool and we didn't approach out of courtesy.

As we climbed out, my warm and wet hands stuck to the ice on the pool railings. The wind blew little bursts of snow off the roof.

I became cold once I was out of the pool. My sheet, which was hanging on a hat rack, was frozen like a massive strip of phyllo dough. My slippers had frozen also. I shuffled into the *parilka* again to defrost the sheet and slippers. It took all of maybe ten seconds before they were warm and pliable again.

In the chill-out area, we sat sweating, our heads spinning, our skin turning that blotchy leopard pattern.

"Man," Igor said finally. "Earlier today it was hard talk with Anya. "It was so stupid. You see, the problem is, she is fond of Atrium. After the job she's coming to the Atrium. She's coming with her mom. And not so rare. Two or three times per week. It means she is working there one or two days per week, and she is coming there three days a week. She is coming and I am saying, 'Go.'"

"Why does she go there?" I asked.

"I don't know. She is fond of it. And she knows I'm pissed when anyone from staff is coming to say, 'Hello! Hello! I'm not working not working! Hello!' I'm not coming on Nevsky Prospekt except when you are in St. Petersburg. I am already ten years working there. I've seen these faces. I know a lot of taxis and they are already saying, 'Hello, Igor. Hello.'

"For example, explain me one thing. She is coming with her mom. Today was this question: 'You want to see me?' I said, 'No.' The problem is, I know her character and before she asked me she had already decided to come to Atrium, and when I said no, she had already made up her mind. I knew it before, if she is asking this question, she already decided and she will be here without any doubts. Of course, she shows up.

"I say, 'You are the master of the questions with no answer.' She says, 'You always have the choice to say yes or no.' I said, 'I already said no, and you are still here. It makes no sense answering your answerless question,' and she was pissed off about it.

"Then she says, 'Okay, I've got your position.' And in the evening still it was two hours of talking. Why does the woman likes to talk about all this shit?"

I tried to offer some helpful advice. I suggested that it might all work out a bit better if he was nice to her and happy to see her and communicated this rather than asking her, upon her arrival, "What the fuck are you doing here?"

"Probably you are right," he said. "I am just trying to break her character. There is a poem about it. How is it in English? *Ukroshcheniye Stroptivoi*? *Tameness of Willful*? *Taming the Obstinate*?"

"*Taming of the Shrew*?" I said.

"Yes, Shakespeare. So for me this is this story."

His allusion to Shakespeare's classic misogynist play made me realize that Igor's interactions with everyone, including his romantic relationships, were all about breaking the other person and winning. He wasn't working on his communication. He was adept and practised at conflict, whether it was an outright fight or some kind of power struggle or negotiation, and that was the mode he operated in.

Outside again on the pool deck, the slippers froze to my feet and the sheet to my waist.

"Anya is happy when I am hanging out with you," he said. "I am not getting so drunk I am fighting."

We shaved and dressed. I never cool down enough to stop sweating before we leave. We overstayed our two hours a little, but the woman who was almost shot in the head by the cop's gun didn't charge us any extra.

Igor walked toward his home and I toward my conductor's palace.

As I crossed the bridge to the music school, I noticed that, even though the winter was now technically receding, the ice had spread further across the Moika canal. It was the winter solstice, when the days begin to count down, ever so slowly lengthening toward summer and white nights again.

CHAPTER 21

The name Krasnoyarsk means "red pit." The valley the city lies in is sunk below a lip of reddish clay earth.

I left St. Petersburg and the harmonic music school apartment to fly to Krasnoyarsk, in Siberia, in the dead of winter. There I met Yulia, and things were not harmonious.

She had grown up in Kras, as it's often shortened, and much of her family still lived there. The first thing Westerners think of when they hear "Siberia" is, of course, gulags, but Krasnoyarsk is a normal city of about a million, the third largest in Siberia. The magnificent Yenisei River cuts through the centre of town.

We stayed in her mother's apartment on Karl Marx street, a one-bedroom flat, with her mom, two insane Yorkshire terriers named Risska and Zhulka, and her sister, who was visiting from Moscow.

The first day I was there, we went for a walk around Krasnoyarsk's Red Square, a small park with a phallic monument, and looked at the swimming-pool green buildings. On his travels across Russia in the late nineteenth century, Anton Chekhov was particularly taken with Krasnoyarsk's beauty, and there is a statue of him there. As in all Russian cities, there is also a tremendous Lenin statue.

As you move east across the country, Russia gets more extreme in every respect. In St. Petersburg, it was cold. Here, my nostril hairs and eyelashes froze. This is how cold it was: After walking for a while, we wandered into a grocery store. I took off my glove and grabbed a bag of frozen peas. The frozen peas felt warm to the touch.

To anyone accustomed to the *Romper Room* safety of North American streets, where everything is padded and railed and of a certain height and of a certain specific design to avoid even the remotest possibility of human injury (and the subsequent lawsuit), the basic infrastructure of Russia can be a shock. In Russia, ordinary objects seem intentionally designed to pose safety risks. There are literally holes in the street. Also, poles and pipes and stakes and protrusions from buildings and vehicles and surfaces. When walking on the sidewalk, one keeps a sharp eye out for icicles dangling off rooftops. The street surface is a skating rink, and the ice forms severe transitions from the street up to the sidewalk. Traffic is even more treacherous than usual in such conditions. If you miss your footing crossing the street, you slip backward underneath the car that is too impatient to give you a berth.

"I think our marriage is over," Yulia said.

I said nothing.

In these kinds of crises, I guess, they say that you are supposed to talk. You are supposed to formulate some new policies to get you out of the debacle, spend down your foreign currency reserves to support the ruble, and so on. We did the opposite of what you are supposed to do. We ignored everything that was wrong. We didn't talk.

We passed by Krasnoyarsk's Havana Club. A banner hanging out front read *Pay Half, Hang Out 100%. Party in Crisis Style at Havana Club. Cheap!*

While I was there, we mostly sat inside and watched TV. Yulia's sister Sasha was on an all-day-every-day *Dom Dva* binge. Something like *Big Brother*, *Dom Dva* (*Second Home*) was one of Russia's most popular shows at the time. The premise was simple: a group of whiny twenty-somethings trapped together in a house fuck and fight and try to become stars.

During a commercial break, Sasha told me about her plans for the near future. She would stay in Krasnoyarsk to have her son. She would return to Moscow on her own in May to fetch spring clothes. She'd spend the summer in Kras and then go back to Moscow with the child.

"The most important thing," she said, "I want to find a man as soon as possible. I don't know how to raise a boy."

The father of her child hadn't wanted anything to do with her once she became pregnant. Even worse, once her employer found out, he fired her from her secretarial post. Appalling but not uncommon. The world of business is one that largely excludes women except as eye candy or maternalistic administrative assistant types. Only three percent of the country's senior executives are female.

I ask her what the dating scene in Moscow was like.

"Women don't meet men in nightclubs or cafés anymore,"

she said. "They meet them in cars. You can meet men in the metro. But it's a different classification of man."

"They meet in cars?"

"All my friends who have cars met their boyfriends that way. The man pulls up next to her. Lowers the window. And they exchange phone numbers."

"This is the new tradition of courtship in Russia?"

"Yes, and I don't have a car. It means I don't stand a chance."

When I would next see her in Moscow, her son had been born and she was eagerly enrolled in a driving course. So I think she really believed this. And who's to say? Maybe she was right.

In that short break before *Dom Dva* came back on, I asked her what, if any, was the effect of the ratio of men to women in Russia, in her opinion. The fact that there are eleven million more women than men must make what might ordinarily be a challenge into a competitive sport.

"Men already think of themselves as a present," she said. "They don't need to do anything but wait for you to come up to them."

When foreigners travel for more than a few days around Russia, they're required to register their visas at the post office. This is often a lengthy bureaucratic hurdle because of long lines, so I was psyched when I walked into the post office with Yulia's mother and there were only two people in line. Yulia's mother went up to the woman at the end and asked her the typical question: "Are you the last one?" An old man sitting on a bench on the other side of the room said, "I am the last one. And all these people are before me."

The room was filled with benches and the benches were filled with people. So while only two people were standing in line, a sum total of twelve people were actually in the line. The entire room was in the line. She told the man, "We are after you." Then she told me she was going to run some errands and I should hold our place.

I wasn't sure if I should sit down or stand. So I stood.

The next person who came into the post office asked me if I was last, and I said yes.

"I'm after you," the man said, and found a seat on a bench.

In one story in Tom Bissell's collection *God Lives in St. Petersburg*, which is mostly about Americans fucking up in big ways all around eastern Europe, a character named Donk divides the world into Chaos People and Order People. He says that Americans are Chaos People who think they're Order People, and that Russians are Chaos People who know they're Chaos People. Even though I don't think Donk gets Americans right—to me we seem very much Order People who think we are Order People—he hits the nail on the head with Russians. The system is pure chaos, and it is the system that Russians embrace.

American lines occasionally honour a request to "hold a place," but even then, it seems to me, it's done with some reservations. We want to enforce order, and a violation of order to us means you lose the right to your spot.

Russians, of course, have a long history with lines. The Soviet period required standing in a queue at length for anything, and often required standing in many separate queues to get everything you needed. Mothers would assign their whole families to various lines and agree to rendezvous later with all the goods. The Russian writer Vladimir Sorokin wrote a brilliant novel, perhaps the last great Soviet novel, called *The Queue,* in which a cast of characters spend their lives wandering in and out of a line, waiting for what they don't even know.

North Americans will generally sense the chaos approach in their first ride in a Russian car. Russian drivers pay little attention to the lines on the roadway. They will drift out to pass while going around sharp curves, and it's the responsibility of any oncoming traffic to get out of the way quickly.

The chaos is even built into various systems. There are pedestrian walkways in the subway tunnels of Moscow—a subway system that accommodates ten million people per day—in which two lanes of human foot traffic suddenly switch sides in the middle of a turn, resulting in a flustered and chaotic X of people running right into each other.

My line at the Krasnoyarsk post office became confused when a second window opened. Everyone got up to re-establish position. Everyone seemed to know whom they were after, and I stuck to the person I was after. That is why the initial question is key. Your place is dependent on someone else's place. Our "lines" were one amorphous mass of people who all knew whom they were behind.

Then an old woman came in.

"Who is last at window number four?" she said.

A girl at the back said, "I am standing in both windows."

"You can't stand in two windows. You can only stand in one window. You have to choose."

"I am standing in two windows," the girl said.

"Is this two lines or one?"

"It is two," one younger girl said.

"It is stupid to stand in two lines. Let's make it one."

The girls behind the counter pursed their lips in barely suppressed amusement. If, as in North America, they were to come out and settle the situation, organize the line, surely the crowd's fury would turn on them.

"It is one," another person said.

"Where is it written there should not be two lines? Who is last in the line this girl is not in?" No one answered. "All right, I am going to stand right here and I am behind this woman and that's where I'm going to stand."

The woman in front of her said, "No, the girl who stood behind me was behind me. She's going to be in front of you, lady, and you should be after her."

I'd been standing in line for about an hour and a half and I was somewhere between three and seven people back.

The old woman looked to the bench where the girl who was behind the woman at the end of the line sat. She sighed. She was not pleased with this development, but she trusted that the chaos would get her there eventually. She went and sat next to the girl on the bench who was currently last in one of the lines or the other or both. "I'm behind you," she said.

Yulia introduced me to three of her friends from school. Their stories were remarkably similar. They had all gotten married right out of school and within a year they were pregnant and, within months of giving birth, their husbands, heavy drinkers, punched their faces, and then they all got divorced and moved back in with their parents. Compared with their relationships, I thought, what kind of problems did Yulia and I have?

We met one of them at a café. Tanya was the only one whose

lifestyle and successful business made it possible for her to meet us in a café—an extravagant luxury for the others. She had started her own kitchen design company, which was doing very well. She had long blond hair and big blue eyes. She was soft-spoken and smart and savvy and beautiful. She was really into these audiotapes that are all about positive thinking leading to positivity in life and negative thinking leading to negativity in life.

"The problem, Jeff," she told me, "is that there are no men in Russia."

Tanya liked to emphasize, when showing off her car or her rings or her apartment, that all of it was paid for with her own money. The money she earned from working. She didn't travel much, and when she did, it was on the cheap. Many Siberians don't travel much. The average salary here was around two hundred dollars per month. A reasonable rate for a plane ticket from Krasnoyarsk to Sochi, a popular Black Sea resort town, runs much more than that. The train is an option if one is willing to give up four days to a week on either end, depending how far you're going. So, Tanya explained, you save for the ticket. Then, once you get there, you rent out a room in a house with some grandma, stock the fridge with food from the grocery store, and take the shuttle buses to the beach.

Yulia asked Tanya what she thought about a new decency law proposed in the Duma that would prevent girls from wearing revealing shirts in public.

"I am all for this law," Tanya said. "Let me tell you why. I don't have a nice belly. These girls, they have very nice bellies. Much better than mine. So if my man—I don't have one—sees her nice belly, he will go after her."

Cars idled in rush hour traffic. Yulia and I walked along Mira street faster than the cars moved. The idling buses were packed full of people exhaling so much collective hot breath that a layer of ice formed on the windows inside. Passengers' fingernails chipped away at the ice as we passed.

The entire city centre of Krasnoyarsk was lit up like a Christmas tree. Lights hung over the streets, fake trees with electric branches lined the sidewalks, animated creatures of all sorts adorned the street lights. Everything was lit up except the park at Lenin Square, where the complete absence of lights made for a shroud. You could only barely make out the silhouettes of the two massive objects there: the statue of Lenin pointing to Moscow and the cement exhaust pipe, part of an abandoned subway construction project, standing ominously together in the dark.

A higher-up whom Yulia's mom knew at the Pushkin Theatre had gotten us tickets to the dress rehearsal for the new production of *A Streetcar Named Desire*. The crowd included punk rockers in spiked belts with dyed pink hair and more proper theatregoers in evening gowns, as well as the casual masses in jeans and sweaters.

Yulia pointed out a guy who spent all day every day on the streets outside the theatre, begging for money until he had enough for a ticket. He took a seat in the third row.

Streetcar is my favourite play. And I liked the bizarre performance: Tennessee Williams filtered through a twenty-first-century Russian lens with a psychedelic seventies aesthetic bent. The men were manly and powerful and sexy—Mitch like Indiana Jones; Stanley, a New Russian Scarface—and Blanche was a fragile but electric Russian call girl–cum–lingerie model.

The production said a lot about gender roles in Russia. There was the macho, violent, crude, aggressively sexual Russian man—a type personified by none other than tiger-hunting, bear-tranquilizing, fighter jet–piloting judoist Vladimir Putin.

Because it was a dress rehearsal, the director—a man with curly shoulder-length hair, spectacles, a blue blazer, and a white dress shirt—spent the entire play pacing the aisle, chain-smoking, and barking directions at the actors.

There was a bed on wheels that rolled away under the propulsion of Stanley's thrusting when he and Stella went at it. There was a quasi-stripper scene with Blanche dancing in the kitchen in her underwear. And when she was led away to the crazy place, the stage lit up with palm trees and carnival lights. Something seemed to be missing from the final scene, in which Stella should find herself torn between her repulsion for Stanley for raping her sister and her animal desire for him (or whatever that desire has become by the end). They shared a vacant, resigned hug, and the stage went black.

A great moment for me was when Blanche called Stanley a polack, and he said, in perfect Russian, *"Ya stoprotsentny Amerikanets!"* I am 100 percent American!

Afterward, I saw the theatre-beggar at the coat check retrieving a mink coat.

One morning, I took a *marshrutka* out to the state-run Crisis Centre for the Assistance of Families and Children in the suburb of Shinnikov, in the Leninsky district. I wanted to understand what kind of support there was for girls like Tanya and others in Krasnoyarsk. The ride was a convenient hour and a half from the city centre. When I got off the bus, I saw a shop-keeper from one of the kiosks burning old fruit boxes beside the streetcar tracks. A couple of stray dogs came close enough to sniff the smoke and ran away.

The crisis centre used to be a pharmacy. Inside, the first thing you saw was exercise equipment: a treadmill, a pull-up bar, an exercise bike. No windows. Various offices housed different kinds of family specialists. A sign on the door of the woman who dealt with children's issues read *Session in Progress*. The Russian word for "session" is pronounced *seance*, and whenever I see it in this context, my immediate register is always: "Seance in progress."

The crisis centre had opened almost nine years earlier. At first, the plan was to offer counselling and shelter, but even though they had the sleeping space and multiple bathrooms, the authorities required a special room for disinfecting clothes, so the idea was quashed. Now the centre basically offered day services, legal assistance, counselling.

Galina Fyodorovna met the women and families who came here in a room stuffed with plaid and paisley armchairs. She had been working there as a psychologist for six years. I sat across from her in one of the paisley chairs. A stuffed white bear sat on a speaker next to me.

Galina Fyodorovna told me some basic facts about their situation. Almost every abuser they dealt with was under the influence of alcohol. The police perceived such domestic abuse as a personal matter that should be dealt with among the family, and they refused to intervene.

She told me that it was a frustrating predicament for her. "People have lots of ideas, ways to make the country better. We all have a lot of ideas, but no way to put them to work. If you start doing it, they'll stop you. There is a frame in which you can act, and if you go outside the frame, you'll be stopped. If, for example, the project is not directly beneficial for the government, it won't be approved. Whereas in other places, in other countries, projects are initiated and evaluated for their benefits later."

I spent two hours there on a Tuesday afternoon. No one in crisis came through the door, and I asked Galina Fyodorovna how many cases of domestic violence they'd had that past year. She told me there had been a total of five, which is a rather small number in a country where thirteen thousand women are murdered by their partners each year.

"They seldom come here," she said. "They are afraid their husbands may take revenge. But when they do, they come because their feelings and their inside world has changed, and during our discussion, during our talk, I understand that they are being beaten. Women here think it's usual and not a very serious crime. I mean, the women, when beaten, they know it's an offence or crime, but they don't pay attention to this."

So she and the psychologists on her staff were diplomats of sorts. Since they were limited in what they could do, they did what was possible. Once a complaint was lodged, they invited the man in for a talk.

"If the husband agrees to come in, they will achieve the point where they have good relations—by, for example, resolving conflicts between the husband and wife through argument rather than through a physical fight. We talk to the person who commits the violence. We talk to the man, and after that, usually, the man becomes better."

If the man refused to come in, they took different approaches. They invited the children in and taught them to protect the mother. They also taught the wife how to respond without provoking the man.

I asked her for some specifics on how women could respond without provoking. She didn't give me specifics. She called the techniques they taught techniques of "usual communication." I was reminded of Anatoly Ivanovich, the matchmaker, speaking in similar terms about instructing women on how to make themselves desirable to men.

Galina Fyodorovna approved of the Year of the Family and the new holiday about love, because she saw the Russian family as an institution in crisis.

"The responsibility of men continues to drop. The role of the father weakens. On the whole of civil society, it's noticeable that the value of the family as a unit is disappearing." She worked with kids in schools, and she told me that in one class, out of twenty-five kids, twenty were being brought up by single mothers. "We don't know exactly the cause of divorce in these situations. But we can say that violence is a primary cause of divorce in general."

One change she had noticed was that more middle-aged women and even pensioners in abusive relationships were seeking help, and she attributed this to some feeling of hope.

"They were hopeless because women thought that's the way life was supposed to be like, and now they can see the situation," she said. "Now older people see the way young people build lives and relationships and think they can rebuild their lives."

On the Western Christmas Day, Yulia's grandmother was travelling by train to have some special mineral mud treatment on her knee. While she didn't have to be at the station until ten in the morning, we left the house at seven to pick her up, load her things, and take two buses to the train station.

On the way, we stopped at a kiosk. In front of the kiosk, a man was lying on the ground. Probably he was drunk, but it was minus-twenty Celsius. People stepped over him to get to the kiosk, bought their produce and whatnot, and stepped over him again when they left.

Yulia's mother noticed some yellow stuff bubbling out of the man's mouth and nose. They asked the owner of the kiosk to call emergency services. By the time they arrived, he was already dead. We said farewell to her grandmother at the train station, and when we walked by the kiosk again, the police investigator was standing next to the man and writing a report. Someone had pulled his coat over his face.

CHAPTER 22
SUMMER 2009

The INGO crisis centre in St. Petersburg is situated on the Fontanka canal. It was founded by Natalya Khodyreva, an activist for women's rights and professor of gender studies. I imagined that a crisis centre led by such a person in Russia's second major city might have better experiences serving women in unfortunate circumstances than the crisis centre on the outskirts of Krasnoyarsk, in Siberia.

The centre is small and dingy. There is a room to the left full of bikes, a small office with a little kitchen nook, and a doorway leading to the hotline room, which is currently quiet.

Natalya is not there when I arrive. Instead, her 23-year-old daughter, Asya, greets me. She wears a plain brown dress and has big frizzy hair. Asya used to work officially in the centre, but right now they can't afford to pay her, so she is a volunteer. It's kind of a funny situation since, in a sense, she grew up here. Or, as she says, "I have always been working here."

Asya did her sociology thesis on the prostitutes of St.

Petersburg. She spent months talking to the girls, hanging around in the most dangerous parts of town, handing out HIV/AIDS information and condoms, asking them to take surveys, and spreading the word about the INGO hotline. She would go with them to detox because, she says, "It's important to have someone with you when you're trying to change your life."

But right now she is adrift. She's unemployed and living off her boyfriend, a fact that mortifies her mother. Asya shrugs it off. Her focus isn't on making it, on career, on how to better her life materially. I can tell instantly she is torn. She wants to be doing something important, but she also wants to be a 23-year-old girl. And she seems not to know quite in which direction to move.

We sit down for tea and Yelena, INGO's 27-year-old executive director, joins us. Yelena has long blond hair and wears stylish orange glasses, a tight half shirt, and a short skirt.

She starts by rattling off statistics. According to a 2004 sociological study in Moscow, a city in which there is not a single women's crisis centre, 18 percent of women are beaten regularly, and in more than 40 percent of families a husband has hit his wife at least once. Forty-eight percent of men admitted to having beaten a woman severely and 54 percent of women were subject to economic violence, such as being required to hand over their earnings or being prohibited from working altogether.

She tells me there are three major problems facing women in Russia with regard to violence and justice. The biggest of these is that there is no existing legislation against domestic or family violence. Any potential prosecution has to be run through a combination of criminal, civil, and family courts. Meanwhile, because of living conditions in Russia, very often the abuser lives with the abused during the proceedings.

One story highlights both of these problems. A man was regularly beating his wife and fourteen-year-old son. He strangled the boy viciously. The mother came to INGO and with their help launched a case against him. The case took two and a half years to wind its way through the courts. One of the issues prolonging it was the father's countersuit alleging that his wife was beating *him* regularly. During this time, the whole family lived together in two rooms in a communal apartment. In the end, his punishment was a small fine.

"The fine goes not to the woman but to the state," Yelena says. "He'll only be imprisoned when he murders her or throws her out of a window, or when she really suffers such physical assault that she, for example, cannot work any longer. Unfortunately, our laws are for those who commit violence rather than those who suffer from it. Right now they are still living together."

The third major problem is the general social attitude, which constitutes a roadblock at every turn, Yelena says.

"In one district in the city," she tells me, "the police wouldn't take the claim of one woman because, they said, 'We don't want to spoil our statistics.' The same thing happens when victims come to doctors. 'You were raped? Maybe you wore a too-short skirt?' Like this." Yelena stands and points to her skirt.

She tells me the story of another woman who was raped. At first the lead investigator wouldn't take her case. But the woman kept visiting him. She found out he had a daughter and asked him to imagine that his own daughter was raped. She brought him gifts, and after a month he took on the case.

"It worked?" I ask.

"In this specific case. There are so many cases in which nothing works."

At one time INGO had a shelter, a modest one, with four or five rooms. Asya used to work there when she was a teenager. But it was routinely audited by health services, and renovations required to bring it up to code were too costly, so they shut it down.

Asya tells me to imagine a woman who is beaten and kicked out into the street in her slippers in winter. "She really has nowhere to go," she says. The few shelters available can only house her for a month or two, maximum. She has to return to the same flat with the same partner.

There is a buzz at the door and Natalya Khodyreva, the founder, comes in. She and Asya have the same brown, frizzy hair. She sits down across from me and looks nervous. "We are trying to survive," she says. "We will serve our fellow women, but we don't know how to work without money."

I ask her how times have changed since the days when she founded the centre, in the early nineties. "Now the situation is much worse than during Yeltsin's time," she says. "Then we worked without any fear. Now there's high pressure from the conservative government. Very discriminating ideas about women."

As quickly as she came in, she leaves. She has another appointment. She welcomes me to talk further with Asya and Yelena. And so I do. They try to leaven all the terrible stories they have to tell me. They laugh when they talk about rape and abuse, and it's pretty clear this is how they deal with it. "Tragically funny" is their favourite phrase. The abuse, the authorities' reaction to the abuse, all of it—tragically funny. It cracks them up.

So far this year, the INGO crisis centre has taken more than 2,500 calls.

"Now," Yelena says, "the major idea of our state is to preserve the family, even if he's violent, even if he's an alcoholic.

The state's major task is not to serve the woman but above all to preserve the family."

"Happy Year of the Family," I say to them.

"Happy Year of the Family to you," Yelena says. "Government crisis centres operate like other government organizations. Their policy is preservation of the family and victimization of the woman. Even if the father is beating children—because violence is a chain—preserve the family."

Times have changed not only in the sense of policy but in how criticism is handled as well.

"Now, we're really careful about our public criticism," Yelena says. "A few years ago, we could write and say this or that structure is working ineffectively. Now, we can't really write that. Can't really openly call upon women to go somewhere and complain or something. We can't really say this particular law enforcement agency in a particular district is not doing its job. We can't say publicly a certain region's resources are lacking and incite women to protest, because then the next day there can be a fire inspector at the door and we may be shut down or fined."

I ask Yelena how she got into this kind of work, and she tells me that she was studying psychology and wanted to do something practical rather than theoretical. So she started working on a general hotline in the small city she was living in. She worked there for two years and realized that 80 percent of the calls were from women suffering from domestic violence. Now she is completing a study analyzing models of effectiveness in treatment of victims of rape. I ask her what, in her opinion, are the most effective treatments.

"In our case," she says, "any method is effective as long as it is a method that exists."

The meeting winds down. The two of them have impressed the hell out of me. "Both of you are so young and doing such important work," I say.

They laugh. "Yes," Asya says. "If in the past we had some future prospects, now we can only console ourselves with the fact that we are doing something positive."

Asya and I make plans to meet later in the week. I am intrigued by her, a girl who has grown up in the early days of a new country in an über-macho culture raised by an activist, feminist intellectual. Someone who's spent most of her young life working in a women's crisis centre and studying the oppressed.

I ask Asya to take me to some of the locations where she interviewed the prostitutes. But she says she doesn't want to return to those places. They brings back too dark memories. So we meet at Noodles, a nice light place on Liteiny Prospekt. She tells me she is a vegetarian, but she eats fish and eggs. I tell her about my friend's philosophy that he won't eat anything with a face.

"This is a real vegetarian," she says.

I tell her I was vegetarian for about five years but Russia cured me of it. She nods.

"When I moved in with my boyfriend, all my friends told me, 'You must start cooking meat or he will leave you.' But he eats during the day at the company. All they serve is meat. So he is happy to come home and have a salad."

Her boyfriend is an economist by day for Lipton, and at night he plays in a surf-rock band called the King-Kongs. They play at hip underground clubs around the city.

She wears a striped sweater with sleeves that just cover her shoulders, loose blue jeans, and sport sandals. Her frizzy hair is held back with a yellow elastic. She has big brown eyes. Her fingernails are manicured and hot pink. There are already a few strands of grey in her kinky hair.

We sit on barstools facing the window. When a group of girls done up in prom dresses with sashes over their shoulders walk by, she scoffs.

She has been out of work for six months. She's been having fun. When not on volunteer duty at INGO, she went beer tasting in Vilnius. Took her mother to a Morrissey concert. And camped last weekend with friends on Lake Ladoga.

She is in a kind of existential crisis herself. She's sent her resumé to human resources agents who keep calling and offering her menial jobs that pay barely twelve thousand rubles, around four hundred dollars, per month. She jokes that if she takes one of these jobs, she'll spend her entire salary on the lunches she'll have to buy.

It sounds remarkably like something Igor would say.

"One of my friends told me that I just don't want to work," she says. "Maybe he's right, and I am just lazy."

Her academic record is good but not excellent. She thinks she waited too long for graduate school and now, at twenty-three, she's too old.

She is thinking she might study languages and is brushing up on her French now on her own.

"I don't know what to do," she says. "It was an awful situation when we were in the forest." One of her friends had invited some of his friends from school—two guys and two girls from Primorskoye, one of the working-class suburbs of St. Petersburg.

One of the couples was married; the other couple was engaged to be married in a few weeks. "We were all very drunk. I was swimming in the rain. Then I noticed that the girl, the fiancée, was crying on the shore. I came to talk to her and learned that her future husband had just kicked her in the face. I was furious, but I understood that if I will say something, he will kick me too. I knew the guys also didn't want to discuss it with him. They didn't want to deal with it."

Everyone went to bed after that. It rained like a monsoon that night. When she woke up, water had come through the tent. Her cellphone had drowned. And the couple about to be married?

"In the morning, everything was okay again between them. The other girl said it's the fiancée's fault because she doesn't leave him. It's not the first time. This is a self-estimation problem of the girl. It is awful.

"Of course, I am against violence in general, but when I talked to the guys, I said that if they deal with him, maybe sometime they'll change his mind. When it was the first time, the guys said something to him, but they see her returning to him again and again. The guys said that he was in the army and when he is drinking he is without any head at all. I remember when school friends went to army. Army takes an important period of a boy's life. If you are taught that way, it's like in the jungle . . . the mightiest survive. Kick anyone weaker than you."

Our food comes. A large salmon, olive, and onion pizza with mayonnaise where the tomato sauce should be—her choice—and two garden salads with oil and balsamic vinaigrette. She bites into a slice.

I tell her that one thing that surprises me when I hear these stories is that Russian women seem to me incredibly emotionally strong, especially those old enough to have lived during Soviet times.

She agrees that women are very strong here, her mother one of them. "You have to sacrifice something for that. My mother sacrificed family building. I was with Grandma all the time. There were times I didn't see Mom for months. She was just working. Now our relationship is very good."

"Wait a minute. Did you say your mom went with you to Morrissey?"

"Yes, I bought her a ticket. Last year, she went to see Radiohead in Amsterdam by herself. She is going to Nepal next year."

"Is she Buddhist?"

"No, she is realist. She is feminist. In Nepal she is hoping to ride a moped."

"What do you think your mom thinks about your current situation?"

She thinks for a moment. "Maybe she is upset that I am living with my boyfriend and waiting for him to come home with the salary. I don't know. Mainly she tells me, 'Stop partying all the time!'"

"What did she think of Morrissey?"

"She liked the music but said he is old and fat."

We leave Noodles and she stops off at a store to buy a pack of Parliaments and a lighter.

"I didn't know you smoked," I say.

"I smoke in the alcoholic perspective."

The woman behind the counter tries to talk me into buying a pizza. Indicating Asya, the woman says to me, "She's so skinny, buy her a pizza."

"No, thanks," I say.

"What, are you on a diet? Everyone in St. Petersburg is on a diet. Eat some pizza."

"We just ate pizza," Asya says. But the woman doesn't seem to hear her.

When we come out of the store, I start to say something, but Asya shushes me. She stands behind a woman punching in a code to enter a courtyard. The lock clicks, the woman opens the gate, and we follow her in.

In the courtyard, Asya lights up. "I have to meet my father soon."

"How is your relationship with him?"

"I met him for the first time when I was seventeen. Does that answer your question?"

He has a daughter with his new wife, who kept him from meeting Asya for many years. And when they did meet, he would show up drunk. Now he's seriously ill, an invalid at forty-nine.

"He is depressed. He is disappointed. He is poor. When I was a child, I was a daughter without a father, and I felt very vulnerable."

It's a very nice courtyard, very green, home to some office buildings and some kind of music school. We find a mother cat with two kittens rolling around under the poplar puffs. Asya doesn't like cats.

I ask her about the challenges INGO faces working with women of her generation. She says there are two. The first has to do with the fact that they don't understand the role of a place like INGO in society and in their lives.

"When a person applies for our services, they sometimes think it means that some specialist will solve your problems. This is the view. We are not solving problems. We can only help empower her to solve her problem. There are real problems in trying to understand how to use the crisis centre.

"I know a lot of people don't like what we are saying. Clients sometimes think maybe we are just dangerous women with nothing to do."

The second challenge is that those girls who aren't in trouble, or who aren't in trouble yet, look down on their work.

"They are all superwomen now, when everything is good. And the image of feminism is so awful. Very unpopular. It's so unpopular, people get aggressive about it. *Men should be masculine!* This is taught in school or university or army, everywhere, and we're getting more and more conservative and the image of feminism is getting worse. I can't really tell why. But I can't be pessimistic. I am drinking with friends and hanging around all day at home waiting for an HR recruiter to call and offer me a job for twelve thousand rubles per month."

One morning a couple of days before we leave for Siberia, Igor calls me and invites me for brunch. "What you want? Borscht or potato with chicken hearts? Mom's cooking."

"Borscht," I say.

"What, you don't like potato with chicken hearts?"

"No, man. I can't eat that." I pause. "Especially not in the morning."

"What? It's my favourite meal anytime."

There is something indescribable about homemade borscht, and Igor's mom's borscht is no slouch. The meat is supposedly chicken but seems too dark for chicken. I suspect chicken hearts may have been slipped into my borscht.

"Last night, on City Bandits, I bought the yacht," Igor says.

"Cool," I say. "What can you do with it?"

"Now I can rob another yacht. I can go on the sea and rob another yacht."

"Man, are these chicken hearts?"

"No." He smiles. "You said you didn't want them, but they are very good for you." He pounds his chest.

So maybe I have eaten chicken hearts and maybe I haven't.

Afterward, we aim to finally finish tiling the ceiling, but we measured all wrong. The tiles are not square on a single edge, some of them are falling off, and there are spaces between them. Igor and his mom argue. She is kind of drunk already and it's still morning.

I tell Igor about my meeting with Asya and INGO. I can see that it triggers bad memories of his own youth, this talk of men beating women.

"Well, man," he says, "this is all terrible." But as with many of these uncomfortable subjects, he doesn't care to elaborate much.

The next day, we take care of some shopping for Siberia. We end up in a pharmacy for last-minute supplies. We buy tick repellent, and when we come to the soap aisle, we stand dumb-founded before a wall of different varieties of soap. Igor picks up one bottle of nuclear-green liquid manufactured by AXE. "Look," he says, holding it out to me. The bottle reads *Anti-Hangover Axe Body Wash*.

"I guess we better get that, then," I say.

He suggests that we spend an extra day in Baikal rather than going to Irkutsk.

"I thought you wanted to see your brother and sister?"

"Fuck it."

"What changed your mind?"

"I discussed it with Mom and she half decided, now I half decided. They never congratulated me on the birthdays, all this shit. Why I need them?"

In a short period of time, he has changed his mind about meeting all his relatives there. I'll never fully understand why he made this decision—or why he decided it with such finality—but it clearly has something to do with loyalty and respect. Those he loved and those he wanted to spend time with were those who respected him and were loyal, even if that loyalty expressed itself in the slightest of ways—a phone call on a birthday.

The next night, Igor's mother is still amped up about her trip to Abkhazia. She shows us two glossy magazines she picked up there. She flips through them and points out all the officials in the magazines. The first president of Abkhazia is featured on the cover. "He's a very good man," she says.

Then she pulls out some classifieds. She dreams of retiring there.

Working for the state for twenty years guarantees her a pension at least double the average Russian salary. She has an old aunt and uncle there. She is excited about the warm weather and about having a flower garden. Before she left, she planted a jasmine tree in the yard outside the balcony. It's pathetic-looking now, after being attacked with a weed whacker by the guy who cuts the lawn. I imagine her vain hopes for it: someday, when she visits Igor, it will shade the balcony of his family.

She is forty-nine. Female retirement age is fifty-five. She doesn't want to wait that long.

She is not very forthcoming with me, because, as Igor has told me, she suspects I am a spy. I try to behave as unspylike around her as I possibly can, and ask few questions.

She tells me that St. Petersburg is very unhealthy. "All of this," she says, waving her hand in front of the window. I know what she means about city life, but outside, in the cemetery region, everything seems green and healthy.

"It's pretty, but it needs to be excavated and replaced," she says. "The ecology here is horrible, the water, air, all of it, so unhealthy."

She heaps dinner onto our plates. A couple of Abkhazian recipes—some eggplant and vegetable mixture and a kind of spicy bean paste with parsley—one incredibly tough piece of indeterminate meat, and a plate of special smoked Abkhazian cheese.

With dinner, Igor has a mug of *chainiy grib*. He offers it to me. It tastes sweet and weak. There is another jar of kombucha fermenting on the table now, this one for his mom to drink after we're gone.

Later, his mother changes out of her colourful nightgown and puts on a nice shirt and slacks and lipstick to go downstairs to the store. While she's gone, Igor tells me that he has been saving money to buy her a place in Abkhazia, and, assuming he gets a new job in the near future, in a few years he will have enough. She will leave the apartment to him. And he will visit her in the summers there, the way he used to visit his grandparents there when he was a child.

When she comes back, she's brought beer for us, a bottle of cognac for her, and a handful of the monthly bills. She and Igor open them and pass them around. The year's property taxes for the apartment, in Igor's name, come to 743 rubles, about twenty-two dollars. The gas bill is 53 rubles, less than two dollars for the month. The phone bill is around 400 rubles.

We go to a student barbershop near Igor's place and have our hair cut by two ditzy apprentices. The salon is a room with a stairwell leading up to another family's apartment. The barber chairs are the cheapest generic office chairs one can buy. Igor's hair is pretty simple, a quick clipper job. Mine is slightly more complex but still requires nothing beyond basic scissors work. Neither of us constitutes the hairdressing equivalent of rocket science.

While the hairdresser is cutting my hair, hardly even looking at it, she explains the difficulty she is having transferring photos to her cellphone. She wants to have photos on her cellphone but can't figure out how to get them off the camera to there.

I have a knack for getting shitty haircuts. I have gotten shitty haircuts all over the world. But this one is ridiculous. These two recent graduates who clearly bought their way through the lowest-rent beauty school around have even managed to fuck up Igor's crewcut. It's different lengths all around. Mine presents as bangs running diagonally from the left side to the right in a crooked line.

Igor negotiates them down to 100 rubles for his and 150 for mine because they're so bad. The girls look embarrassed. I remember the barber from Gogol's story "The Nose." The whole story was like a dream from the subconscious of a barber with a reputation for pulling too hard on his clients' noses while shaving them. I can only imagine the horror show this place would be were these trainees given straight razors.

Igor's mom takes one look at us as we come in and says, "What the fuck happened to your heads?" I look around the apartment, which we were supposed to renovate and which is more crooked and disheveled than our haircuts. It was kind of Igor's mother not to ask, "What the fuck happened to the apartment?"

A month after I left Russia in January 2009, Igor and I talked on Skype.

"I quitted the job!" he said. "I quitted the Atrium!"

"Wait a second, dude," I said. "The country—the world—is in crisis. Everyone is looking for a job. And you quit?"

"Fuck it. There is no profit for me to work over there. No customers. It will die in March, and right now I am just having some fun, sitting without any job, some sort of rest or vacation or whatever."

"What did Anya say?" I asked.

"Welcome to duality, man," he said. "When I was writing this special resignation paper, she was on phone saying, 'Don't quit! Don't do it! Everything will change! I will never call you again!' I said, 'I am writing. It means it's my decision. Fuck off.' She said, 'New job, new girl, huh?' Then she said another day, 'Well, Igor, I am happy that you quitted.'"

"That sounds like progress to me."

"From one hand yes, from the other hand it's the same shit. Anyway, I want to work in IT."

"Why?"

"I don't know. It's with computers, always sitting doing nothing. Good job. My leg is paining sometime. Soon I will have pain in the ass and then I need to get job when I am lying another ten years."

He had only one regret about leaving the Atrium: no more freebies left by tourists. Yes, he was the barman whom you returned to talk to after you lost your high-end camera or umbrella, and who looked into your eyes consolingly while saying that he was sorry but no one turned in a high-end camera or umbrella today . . .

I listened as he plotted out a hopeful future while the rest of Russia, for the second time in his life, seemed to be falling apart. "I think I am going to learn some courses," he said. "I don't want to work as manager or bartender in restaurant and all this shit. Ten years is enough to understand that I was an idiot. Programmers, they're always needing them." I couldn't tell if he was being naive or optimistic, or if he was intentionally deluding himself.

Just a few weeks later, we Skyped again: "About IT school, I was talking to this one guy. He wasn't too crazy about it." And, he told me, the IT schools are too expensive.

Weeks passed. He sat in his apartment. Anya worked her two jobs and then went to her family's apartment and the two of them played dice games together online.

Then: "Tomorrow probably I will get information on being general manager at some restaurant or hotel. If it's okay, then okay, if not, then I am still on vacation. You will never see Atrium again. Soon it's going to be closed . . . Three floors of business centre is gone. No more free Wi-Fi. They are gone. Probably I will get some beer for the dinner, eat, then sleep."

Throughout the spring, he downloaded movies and TV shows from the private servers networked around St. Pete.

Shopaholic. Underworld III. He became a fan of *Big Bang Theory*, and I couldn't help but notice that Anya looked a lot like Penny.

After another month, he was bored by TV. He started planning a trip with Anya to Egypt, their favourite vacation destination, where he would scuba dive and play beach volleyball and she would lie out in the sun.

"And you know," he said, "my best thing when I am in Egypt is to sing 'Strangers in the Night' in the hotel bar. There is one man with piano. I am getting applause."

"Say hi to the pyramids for me," I said.

"No. Pyramids are too far. I will say hi to fish for you."

He started studying Arabic on his own. "I already know all the important words," he said. "'Bitch' is going to be *sharmuta*. *Hasis* like an asshole, and if you are going to say you are the only asshole in all of Egypt, it's going to be excellent."

I first realized something was wrong after three months, when there was still no work and even paintball bored him. "I am taking a break from paintball also," he said. "With Straightline barrel, it's too easy, not so interesting for me. The guys with regular barrel and non-electric are showing me all the hits from my paint."

Then the beginning of the end with Anya. The trip to Egypt was shelved. The marriage proposal was shelved, if not forgotten about altogether. While Igor sat at home with the cats, sending out queries for jobs, watching TV, and studying swear words in Arabic, Anna worked every day. She was the only St. Petersburg employee kept on by the Finnish company during the crisis, and she still picked up shifts whenever possible at the struggling but still-open Atrium.

"Basically, it was problem with Anya again today and all these callings," he said. "I was sleeping. She was calling once on cellphone, once on home phone, then cellphone, then home phone. I was like hearing it but wasn't going to answer. I know this is Anya. Fuck off. I am sleeping. What the fuck you want from me? Finally I answered phone. She said, 'I have very important thing to tell you.' I said, 'What is the important thing you have to tell me?' She doesn't like how I say this. She says, 'Doesn't matter.' 'You are waking me up and saying it doesn't matter?' Fucking duality, man."

"What did she want to say?"

"Basically, she wanted to say she is still at Atrium on day offs. Every time I am saying that I don't give a shit on this shit really, and I don't want to discuss it really, and she is still fucking my brain. While we had conversation, four times she said we must break up. And I am stopping her."

"Why?"

"I don't know. Still loving her. But soon, I am going to be tired about it."

III.

FORWARD

||||||||||||||||||||||||||||||||||||||||||||||||||

"So what to do—nothing to do. We go on living like before."
—FROM THE SHORT STORY "CRISIS" BY MIKHAIL ZOSHCHENKO, 1925

CHAPTER 23
SUMMER 2009

gor's mom's eyes are wet. Surely these are the tears of a mother bidding farewell to a son she worries about, but part of me suspects she's crying over our epic failure at renovating the apartment—it looks worse than it did before we started. She walks us to the car. Kostya, one of the local Piskaryovka stoners, waits to drive us to the airport. Igor gives her a reluctant peck on the cheek and pushes her away. We are late.

Two minutes away, we realize that we forgot his camera. We can't visit the epicentre of the Russian Soul without the good-quality camera Igor pilfered from tourists at the Atrium. Kostya spins the car around. Igor calls his mom on the cellphone and tells her to stand on the balcony with the camera. Igor hops out. He stands below their second-floor balcony. He straddles her jasmine tree or what's left of it after the handyman's weed whacker.

"Drop it, Mom," he says.

"Fuck off," she says. "It will break."

"I will catch it."

She mouths a prayer and releases. It falls right into his hands. We peel off again. We barely make our connecting flight from St. Petersburg to Moscow, but barely made is made.

During our transfer at Moscow's Sheremetyevo Airport, we emerge briefly outside to walk between terminals. Igor takes advantage of a few minutes in Moscow to spit on the city he loathes. He rubs it into the cement with his shoe.

"Tell me, man," I say. "Why is it that you hate Moscow so much?"

He says, "Here's a little joke. Meeting of two Moscow citizens. One was just returned from Petersburg for business or whatever. 'So how was St. Petersburg?' one says. 'Oh, fuck shit,' the other. 'What are you talking about?' 'St. Petersburg, this is village.' 'Why?' 'Just imagine, just imagine. They are still fucking the girls.'"

"What does this mean?"

"It means Muscovites are hating us. We are hating them."

I open my jacket and show him my T-shirt underneath: a championship print commemorating the St. Petersburg soccer team Zenit's 2008 victory in the UEFA Cup. He smiles big.

In the terminal, we pass on ridiculously expensive sandwiches and order ridiculously expensive beers instead. He has begun calling me Subcommander Spock because my haircut makes me look like a Vulcan.

We enter the Tupolev and are enveloped by body odour. Tupolevs are Russian jets with a discomforting tendency to fall out of the sky. The interior of the plane has a cottagey feel; there seems to be actual wallpaper on the walls.

When I am on the verge of freaking out in Russia (because the subway car is too full or the taxi driver's Lada ricochets across the highway or the elevator is the size of a coffin, or because the model of plane I'm on has a spotty historical record and the aesthetics of a country house), I have learned to take great comfort from the calmness and stoicism of those around me.

The woman in the window seat next to me wraps a blanket around her waist then wrestles herself out of her skirt, folding it so the pleats align and draping it neatly over the back of the seat in front of her. I admire her. I would be too nervous that, in some kind of emergency, I'd be evacuating in my underwear. This thought either doesn't occur to her or doesn't bother her or is second to her fear of wrinkling her skirt. She blows up a pink neck pillow, lies back, and closes her eyes.

The woman next to Igor—we are in neighbouring aisle seats—applies polish remover, suffocating the plane with the fumes.

Before we take off, the captain says that it is twenty-three degrees Celsius in Moscow. The flight attendant breaks in and corrects him. "It's twenty-seven," she says.

The plane is full of summer campers. Small children are everywhere, screaming and crying in unison. Igor plugs headphones into his cellphone and plays Metallica's *Kill 'Em All*.

Five hours later, we wander through the Irkutsk airport. We are unsure how exactly to get to Listvyanka, the village on Lake Baikal where we've reserved a cabin of some sort.

Igor stops to photograph a sign that he thinks is hilarious. *Attention Trolleybus!* We sit at a nearby café to order some soup for breakfast, and when the bill comes, they've charged us double. Igor barks about it, and the waiter apologizes. He says that he's more hungover than usual.

He makes up for it by pointing us to the bus transfer station, where we find a *marshrutka* that will, for a reasonable price, take us on the forty-five-minute journey to the shore of Baikal.

Before we left, I visited Soldiers' Mothers of St. Petersburg and its chairwoman, Ella Polyakova. Formed in 1991, Soldiers' Mothers was one of the first human rights organizations in Russia, and today it's one of the strongest. An active player and a seasoned veteran in the opposition in Russia, Polyakova had seen it all.

In 2008, she and a group of protesters had amassed in the middle of St. Petersburg in a demonstration for former chess champion Garry Kasparov's Solidarity Party. A red and white bus pulled up in front of them. The doors opened and two men began throwing off sheep in blue Solidarity T-shirts. Some of the sheep were dead, others had syringes sticking out of their necks. Many of them had broken legs, and they convulsed and bleated in the street. The men told Polyakova and her associates that, should they continue demonstrating, a similar fate awaited them. The bus drove off, leaving the protesters staring at the dying sheep. The police arrived on the scene late and were unable to find the men in the giant red and white bus.

I walked into the St. Petersburg headquarters of Soldiers' Mothers while she was lecturing to an audience of about twenty mostly middle-aged and older women, with a few young boys in the audience. I took a seat in the back row.

Polyakova had bright orange hair and a matching orange blouse, dangly jewellery and trinkets hanging from her ears and neck. She was heavily made up, with high arching eyebrows. Nearing seventy, she was energetic and austere. There was something cold and commanding in her face, but her eyes were very kind.

"What are you feeling?" Polyakova asked one woman whose son's appeal to the military commission had just been denied.

"Fear," she said. "Fear and love." The woman began crying.

"All of you have rights," Polyakova said. "So don't cry. You have those rights, and you are protected by law."

Framed photos of dead boys checkered the wall.

"The state is not a number of officials," Polyakova said. "The state is a being with you in the centre." She drew on the board. She surrounded an indeterminate symbol representing federal officials with flowery symbols representing citizens. "You have rights and can change things by doing something. Write letters to officials. Laws are changing all the time. Every official doesn't know what's going on. As long as we pay taxes, the officials work for us. We are not at their mercy. We pay taxes. We have rights. And officials forget about this. You have rights!" she implored.

The audience seemed taken aback. They looked around at one another with blinking eyes. One woman asked, "What do you mean, we have rights?"

Polyakova performed a close reading of the numerous articles from the Russian Constitution that pertained in some way to their rights to representation and their rights to keeping their sons and, for the boys, their right to keep themselves safe: Articles 20 ("Everyone shall have the right to life"), 21 ("No one may be subjected to torture, violence, or any other harsh or humiliating treatment or punishment"), 22 ("Arrest, detention and keeping in custody shall be allowed only by an order of a court of law. No person may be detained for more than forty-eight hours without an order of a court of law"), 24 ("The bodies of state authority and the bodies of local self-government and the officials thereof shall provide to each citizen access to any documents and materials directly affecting his/her rights and liberties unless otherwise stipulated under the law"), 41 ("Everyone shall have the right to health care and medical assistance"), 45 ("State protection for human rights and liberties in the Russian Federation shall be guaranteed. Everyone shall have the right to defend his or her rights and liberties by any means not prohibited by the law"), 46 ("The decisions and actions [or inaction] of state organs, organs of local self-government, public associations, and officials may be appealed against in a court of law"), 59 ("The citizen of the Russian Federation whose convictions and faith are at odds with military service, and also in other cases stipulated by the federal law, shall have the right to the substitution of an alternative civil service for military service").

The crowd continued to murmur. Was the collective reaction surprise, suspicion, disbelief? All three?

"Now, let me ask," Polyakova said. "Do you feel protected?" She addressed a seventeen-year-old boy with hair to the middle of his back and black spacers in his ears.

"Today, yes," he said.

"And tomorrow?" she asked.

"Maybe tomorrow I will have to protect myself," he said.

"Exactly," she said. "You will have to protect yourself. But you are not alone."

When her lecture was finished, Polyakova showed me around the building.

She led me into another office that had shelves and shelves of alphabetized binders full of sworn testimonies and granted and rejected deferments. A very slight boy with a shaved head who had recently escaped from Kamenka—a military unit notorious for cruelty and abuse toward young conscripts there—sat hunched over a piece of paper writing out a statement in longhand. He wore a light blue denim jacket and matching jeans. He was not alone. He was writing under the coaching of a Soldiers' Mothers volunteer legal coordinator. In the hall, his father was writing out his own statement. His father had travelled from their small village in the Urals when he was alerted by letter that his son was being beaten at Kamenka. They managed to rendezvous after his son went AWOL. He travelled to Moscow and met with officials, who laughed in his face. So he came to St. Petersburg and met with Soldiers' Mothers.

When we returned to the foyer, where the lecture space was, Polyakova said, "It's much easier to solve the problem here than in there." She pointed to the room where the boy and his father sat. "In there, too often, it's already too late."

She introduced me to another volunteer, a woman who sat at a desk and greeted guests. Her son had been beaten in the army. He escaped and was captured and sentenced to five years in prison, reduced to two and a half years on appeal. "I work here to be closer to my son," the woman said.

"Prison is better than the army here. It's a nightmare," Polyakova said, echoing Anna Politkovskaya, who, in her book *Putin's Russia*, famously described the Russian military as "mostly a prison camp behind barbed wire where the country's young are locked up without trial. It is a place where beating the hell out of someone is the basic method of training."

We went upstairs to the kitchen, where there was a cross and a small altar. Polyakova told me that it used to be downstairs but the police almost closed the centre down for promoting religious ideals. So they moved it out of the line of sight, upstairs to the kitchen.

Soldiers' Mothers press secretary Elena Popova joined us. She had been at Soldiers' Mothers only about six months. The previous fifteen years, she'd been a teacher of history and English in a St. Petersburg public school. One day the school director came into her classroom after a student's parents complained about a portrait of slain journalist Politkovskaya in Popova's classroom. The director told her it had to be taken down. She said, "I can't take it down." The next week she was fired.

We sat at a long table and drank coffee. Popova put out a plate of cherries, muffins, and pistachios. Then she sliced a tube-shaped ice cream. She lifted out slices and dropped them one by one into each coffee.

I told Polyakova that I was surprised to find her essentially running a citizenship class by way of educating people to avoid conscription.

"What we're doing is switching on their consciences and their minds," Polyakova said. "The conscience of young men today is ill."

She saw the problem as one that began with corruption in the schools and all aspects of life.

"To show what's going on with young men today," she said, "they are put in a situation in which they can't see a way out. But there is: knowing the laws, knowing the declarations, and being proud of themselves. The problem of protecting people's rights is more complicated now in Russia than in the nineties because we see now that it is not a democracy in Russia. The problem is people have nothing to live for: people are taken from the metro station and put in the army and there are killed.

"This generation, they're disillusioned in this situation and can't accept humanity in a normal way. We face the conflict between the old system to which we came back and the changing minds of people. People can be taken from their homes or taken from the metro and put in the army, and from such an experience form a new conscience—the conscience of an angry man who drinks and is free to do what he chooses according to his desire. Another problem is the immorality of society and the system of values which has deteriorated. A new society is not yet born."

The boy from Kamenka and his father joined us at the end of the table. The boy sat red-faced, looking into his cup. The father's face was also red. He had tight, thin lips. He said to me, "I am a very nice person, but I hope you forgive me for not greeting you with kindness since I am in a very severe situation right now."

Popova put plates in front of them, and the boy ate a piece of chicken on dry bread. He didn't say a word or even look up.

Ella told me that the boy, like so many Russians, came from a broken home. He had tried to kill himself twice. Any legitimate psychological screening should have disqualified him for service.

Fewer and fewer people were coming to Soldiers' Mothers every year. Bribing one's way out of the military, as Igor did, was a much quicker and simpler option than fighting for the elusive *alternativnaya sluzhba* (alternative service in civilian spheres), a process that Polyakova believed was intentionally bogged down in confusing bureaucratese and because of that rarely granted.

"When we use our rights, we change our attitudes to things, we change the whole system of society," she said. "We take responsibility and develop citizens' state of mind."

Her view was that in all her endeavours she was teaching people to create a democracy.

Once, a young veteran from Chechnya came to her for advice on becoming a member of Parliament. She asked him what his qualifications were. He said, "Ella, in the wars, I killed a lot."

"This was his credential for office," she said. "These are the ways our conscience is constructed. In this generation it's very easy to find a young man who will kill another one. Men with no morals and no system, and our officials are trying to make terrorists from them.

"Money and glamour have taken the place of propaganda. Even worse, because glamour is more attractive than propaganda." Polyakova seemed to mean that capitalism and Hollywood and MTV culture had taken the place of the Supreme Soviet. But I was reminded of the Chechen vets, Babchenko and Butov, saying that any writing that glamorized war was immoral.

In Polyakova's view, then, a young man of military age is presented with an interesting decision: go into the military or evade it, usually through bribes and falsifying of medical documents. Either way, the process is an indoctrination—into cruelty and violence on the one hand, into corruption on the other. It seemed to me that this explained so much. A system that touched every man in the country and by extension all the women in their lives, and that directly broadcast certain values, or rather compromises in values, explained everything from why Russian cops were often corrupt to why certain segments of society reacted so violently to homosexuality.

But in her dour prognosis for Russia, there was a glimmer of hope. In the next generation, those coming of age now, Polyakova had begun to see something that she hadn't seen in the generation of the 1990s and 2000s. She mentioned Viktor Andreev, the young man who was the lawyer for Soldiers' Mothers, who, at twenty-two, had already argued two cases before the Supreme Court of the Russian Federation. And another, an underground straight-edge musician, the son of a collaborator with Soldiers' Mothers, who had a band that protested against human rights abuses in song.

"You understand," she said, "these people are already a different type. The next generation is much different from the mainstream. They will give something to the future."

I mentally added Asya from INGO to her list.

She paused and reconsidered how to end her thought. "It doesn't mean this generation is thrown away," she said. She was speaking about Igor's generation here. "They are scared."

Igor and I emerge from the *marshrutka* on a white, dusty road that could be any white, dusty road in Russia except that this white, dusty road is on a lake containing two-thirds of the entire world's unfrozen fresh water supply, more water than all of the North American Great Lakes combined.

Lake Baikal.

When you think of symbols of the majesty of Russian nature, you think of this, the world's oldest—twenty-five million years— and deepest lake. We walk to the pebbly shore and just stare at it for a while. The water is crystal clear. It's home to a couple of thousand species of creatures, including the fish *omul* and the freshwater seal known as *nerpa*. The lake features in several iconic Russian folk songs, and it's regarded as a spiritual place, though few Russians I've ever met have journeyed there. Some 330 rivers flow into it, and it drains into one, the Angara, right here where we're standing.

"Big fucking lake," Igor says.

"Big fucking lake," I say.

Then we follow the directions given us by a family that rents rooms. We find a paved road leading toward a cluster of houses between two mountains, an area known as Krestovaya Pad. Each little wooden house has a menacing dog that lunges at us and barks as we pass. We see an English sign up ahead that says *Rooms Surrender*. Google Translate, we will soon learn, is employed unabashedly here.

We check the address on our reservation. This is it.

Galina, the proprietor, shows us to the particular room that has surrendered to us. It's in a series of log cabins built over their garage. Two beds and a bathroom and a nice view of the meadow and the lake. Galina and her family live in a nearby brick house, and there's an old blue house in the middle that they rent out as well. The property has a covered outdoor kitchen with picnic tables, a one-burner hot plate, a sink, a radio, and some condiments.

We leave our stuff in our room and sit on one of the benches in the outdoor kitchen. A crackly radio plays the Spice Girls. We are the only ones in the outdoor kitchen, and as far as we can tell we're the only ones staying at Galina's place. Igor tells me that he feels as if we've stepped back in time and that we're all alone here. I ask him if maybe the radio is on some kind of nineties station. Why would they be playing the Spice Girls? Igor changes the radio to another channel, and unbelievably, it's playing another Spice Girls song.

"Maybe the Spice Girls play on high rotation here?" I say.

"We are in previous millennium," Igor says.

The DJ interrupts the music. "If you want to know the movie schedule," he says, "give us a call."

We walk back down to the shore of Baikal. A few cars rumble by. Two men sit on the shore dipping fishing poles into the lake. We go into a small, empty café and order two beers. The waitress says, "Why drink here, guys? Go downstairs and buy it in the shop. Same beer is half price there."

"She has good point," Igor says.

We walk down the steps into the shop, which sells, among other things, canned horse meat, the beer known as Shore of Baikal, and our favourite, the always guaranteed-fresh Green Mark vodka. I order a couple of Shore of Baikals, and she charges me twenty-six rubles each. I point to the sign on the door that reads *Shore of Baikal 23 rubles*.

"Oh," she says. "This is just an advertisement."

"So it's not correct?" I ask.

"It's not correct," she says.

We walk back to Krestovaya Pad feeling disoriented and misplaced. We again don't see any people. Only the guard dogs greet us. We see an advertisement for a husky farm farther up the road where they rent quadrocycles. We remember fondly our quadrocycle experience in Gelendzhik.

The husky farm is behind a dilapidated shack littered with children's toys. A skinny, bearded man comes out to meet us.

We shake hands. Igor asks how much for the quadrocycles, and the man points to a sign delineating all the rates. We can take four-wheelers for 4,800 rubles each, nearly two hundred dollars and five times the price in Gelendzhik, or we can tour the husky farm for twenty rubles, less than a dollar. So we tour the husky farm.

There are twelve doghouses mounted on wooden platforms in the marshy yard. The dogs tied to each doghouse do not resemble any husky I've ever seen. They look more like Labs. We step from platform to platform. Flea-covered puppies tear at our shoelaces.

We stop at the hut of one purported husky. I point to it. "You mean to say that this is a husky?"

"Yes," he says. "It's a special breed. Not the usual type. More rare."

Many of the strays I saw on the streets of Moscow resemble huskies more than these creatures.

"Are you sure they're huskies?" I ask.

"Oh yes, we're sure," he says. "Pretty sure."

I wonder if we have come across another tall-tale teller.

I start to wonder about my own story, and the turn that my and Igor's buddy movie has taken, landing us in eastern Siberia on the banks of the largest lake in the world, paying twenty rubles to look at false huskies during the global economic crisis. Ella Polyakova is doing important work trying to keep young men from cruelty/corruption indoctrination and teaching the citizenry of a still-new nation how to truly be citizens. Asya is helping women who don't have anyone else to turn to while searching out her own identity. Denis Butov and the Art of War guys are building community among otherwise emotionally stranded vets. And here we are in eastern Siberia, at the metaphorical epicentre of the Russian Soul, a concept that Igor could not care less about, feeling rather lost. Igor doesn't seem scared, as Ella Polyakova put it, but he no longer has the carefree attitude someone like Asya has. For Igor, the moment is a perfect metaphor for the future: wide open and uncertain.

CHAPTER 24
SUMMER 2009

We walk down the street, along the shore of Lake Baikal, toward the centre of town.

The Listvyanka specialty is hot smoked *omul*. Related to salmon, the omul is unique to Baikal. We pass the little post office and the Limnological Museum, an Uzbeki restaurant, the surprisingly upscale Hotel Mayak, and the newly opened Nerpinary, which advertises freshwater lake seals that sing, dance, and do math.

Tourists and villagers are easily distinguishable. A wedding party from Irkutsk vamps in a parking lot near the shore for their photographer. Tourists go by with expensive backpacks and travelling gear. Villagers carry coolers of omul or bushels of strawberries or shallow yellow plastic crates of raw shashlik, or they pull wagons full of beer.

As we enter the market, all the fishmongers shout at us: "Hot fish, hot fish. Hot omul!" Rendered in English, the call doesn't sound particularly catchy. But in Russian, instead of saying literally, *"Omul goryachy!"* ("Hot omul"), they add diminutive endings to both words, as in *"Omulyok goryachenky!"* Diminutive forms are common in the market. They suggest closeness, friendship. I am your pal. Come, buy from me. Also: My fish are cuter.

Dozens of stalls, and stall after stall: omul. Omul after omul after omul, their body cavities held open with toothpicks to show the succulent smoked meat inside.

The fish is an endangered species, but one would not know that judging by the market stock.

Igor insists that we get some. I tell him it's an endangered species and maybe we shouldn't. He blows me off completely. The same reaction as the quadrocycle guide who pitched my plastic water bottle into the forest. Sometimes I wish I were the type who took a stand on principle, but I am weak and easily swayed. I was a vegetarian before I started coming to Russia. And now I will eat omul once Igor decides which monger we will buy from.

He considers for some time, strolls along, looking skeptically at one monger's fish and then another. They all look exactly the same to me. They look good. Clean-eyed. They smell like fresh smoked fish should smell.

Finally, he addresses the fishmonger bearing the closest visible resemblance to Jabba the Hutt. She does not play the diminutive game. She is not your friend. She says firmly and convincingly: "My fish is the freshest here. Luzhkov, you know, the mayor of Moscow—when he is in Irkutsk, he buys omul only from me. I have an order tomorrow from him. I'll smoke his fish tonight myself."

This is all Igor needs to hear. He likes her style. He explains we'll be here for a week. That he is a serious customer. She introduces herself as Yana the Fishmonger. Igor introduces himself as Igor Yurievitch. When she repeats his name and patronymic, she uses the same intonation as the cops on the train and in Novorossiysk.

She wants one hundred rubles per fish, but Igor proposes we pay eighty per and that, if these are good, we'll buy omul only from her every day for the next ten days.

She looks us up and down. I imagine her doing complex math, judging our capacity for ingesting omul, predicting how many omul we'll eat times the twenty rubles per fish the deal will cost her. Her face contorts into a snarl as she considers this. Then she smiles. "All right, boys," she says. "Eighty it is."

She opens an Igloo cooler in which the freshly smoked fish are kept warm. Each whole fish is wrapped in newspaper. Igor selects two. She approves of his choices. She puts them in a plastic bag for us.

As we walk away with our omul, I ask Igor, "How did you choose Yana?"

"I always go to the loud one," he says. "She usually has the best, and if she is loudest, she is getting the most business. High turnover means fresh fish. It also means you can easily get discount from her."

"What if she has crap fish but she's just loud?" I say.

"Actually," Igor says, "I think they all have exactly the same thing. But now, when we return and the others say, 'Buy from me! Buy from me!' I will say, 'Yana has the best.' Then they will try and sell me, saying, 'I have the best.' I will say, 'Give it to me for free.' And they will say, 'No, with discount.'"

As we leave the market, two ladies are battling over placement for the fold-out tables on which they sell strawberries.

There is a small tourist market at the other end. It's the same crap as at the tourist markets in Gelendzhik—Putin matryoshkas and wolf cub fur hats and T-shirts with McDonald's insignias that say *The party is over!*, and folkloric wooden toys and seal figurines. There's a small, locked workshop in the back of the market that has another Google translation on it: *Danger. Homemade Production!*

We sit on the beach at a little round glass table and eat our omul. It's a compact fish; imagine an average-size river trout. The steaming white flesh slips off the bones.

"This would be a great place for a horror movie," I say. "The sea monster that lives here has to be much bigger than the Loch Ness Monster if we imagine that a creature, like fish in an aquarium, grows to the size of its environment."

"And the omul are his angels and the *nerpi* are his army."

"And everyone who eats omul before swimming in the lake will be punished."

"If he's getting revenge on every swimmer who ate omul, this is very busy sea monster," Igor says.

We have been told that for every minute you spend in Baikal, you add a year to your life. I throw off my shirt and swim out, pushing through the shock of the cold until my limbs start to numb, and I swim back. The water is frigid, colder than the coldest cold springs in Florida, colder than ice baths my mom made me take when I had a fever.

"Congratulations," Igor says. "One month added to life. No, let's see. If one minute makes one year, you were there for, sorry, man, no—it's one week maximum extra life! No more."

Then he steps in. He walks in to his knees, holding up the wet ends of his shorts so that they don't touch his legs.

"Take a photograph of me quickly so I can get out of here," he says. I take his photo, documenting his having entered the limnological symbol of the Russian soul, and then we dry off.

Others, especially little children, swim far out into Baikal. "They must have insulated skin like seals," I say to Igor. He agrees. We listen to the chaotic sounds of dozens of languages—Italian and German and Chinese and Japanese—and we wonder where the Russian tourists are.

A cruise ship goes by too close to the shore and sends a series of large waves across the beach. A family sitting near the waterline, their lunch spread across a blanket, is suddenly ankle-deep in water, and the retreating waves reclaim their omul along with their purses and a bottle of vodka. They scramble to retrieve their things in the cold water. No one offers to help. Another man splashes into the lake to catch his canoe that broke anchor.

I notice three armed guards leave an armoured car idling on the street as they get out to buy omul. People on the streets carry steaming omul wrapped in newspaper the way Parisians carry baguettes.

On the way home, we stop at a kiosk and buy a bottle of vodka and a few more Shore of Baikal beers. A babushka from the Republic of Buryatia is selling *lavash* that she bakes in a big stone oven. We buy two circular loaves for fourteen rubles total, and when we give her the money, she flashes a huge golden smile.

We return to the hotel and sit in the outdoor kitchen and drink vodka, which inspires me to offer a little thesis: "Gelendzhik is a soulless place, resorts, capitalism, consumption, et cetera," I say. "Baikal is all soul, even in this, its most touristy zone."

"Every Russian wants to see Baikal," Igor says. "But the place is overrun with Western tourists. You Westerners think that bears are walking in the streets of Russia. But I didn't see any bears. Only Swiss."

I tell Igor about a Russian academic's theory that all Western stories about Russians fall into two categories: Those Scary Russians or Those Crazy Russians. Partially this is a function of Cold War mentality and partially it's the fact that the popular image of Russia is a fixed stereotype from somewhere around 1989. There are new nuances and frameworks, of course, but the typical male Russian character in the popular Western imagination used to be Sean Connery in *Red October*, diabolical yet sometimes contemplative and righteous with a thick accent and a powerful job as a submarine commander, and now he's Viggo Mortensen in *Eastern Promises*, diabolical yet sometimes contemplative and righteous with a thick accent and a powerful job in the mafia. The typical female Russian character has been downgraded from Brigitte Nielsen's character as Ivan Drago's wife in *Rocky IV* to the generic prostitute/mail-order bride.

How did the Russia we'd seen match up with that? Bears don't roam the streets, but men evade army service en masse and far too many beat their wives and slaughter Chechens, who slaughter them back. Cops are easily bought off and they shoot holes in the walls of my favourite banya.

Beyond all that, there was the high-level crazy/scary stuff: the imprisoning of oligarchs who crossed the Kremlin; the bold-faced murder of crusading journalists and human rights activists; the fact that, in informal nationwide polls to determine the sexiest man in Russia, Putin often came out on top. These things were crazy and scary, but they also could happen anywhere. As I write this, a recurring feature has recently been born in the magazine *New Republic* called "Is Russia Weirder Than Florida?" in which the authors present news items that occurred either in Florida, my home state, or in Russia, and you have to guess which is which.

But no, no bears roam the streets (well, maybe if you go farther east), and Igor takes exception to the stereotype.

"You are the crazy-scary ones," he says. "Always bombing somebody and eating McDonald's and having Mickey Mouse. So it's not soul or no soul. It's not crazy or scary. It's big question. Fuck it."

It's big question. Fuck it. I repeat these words in my head. There is some beautiful eloquence there. And of course, from the point of view of the Russian media, more bears roam the streets of Canada than the Motherland, and if the occasional cop fires off a round in the banya in St. Petersburg, that's nothing compared with the constant coverage of ordinary citizens shooting up their schools or offices in the United States.

Galina, the owner of the hotel, comes out to sit with us. She asks how we're finding the village. Igor tells her about his negotiation at the fish market. Galina tells us that she knows Yana the fishmonger. "Everyone knows Yana," she says. "She has the best fish."

Igor boasts that he got a discount.

Galina is impressed. "Yana is very strict with the prices," she says.

We return to Yana the Fishmonger. She tells us that she sold seventy-five kilos of fish today.

"Probably she is boasting," Igor whispers to me.

But she is, essentially, like the attendants on the train, Igor's friend now. He has broken down the hardest fishmonger in the village. Victory.

Three Swiss guys arrive at our place and we invite them to join us for a banya run. They have heard about the banya, but they have never been. On the way, it begins to rain.

Robert, one of the Swiss guys, covers his head with his jacket.

"It's ecologically pure rain," Igor notes.

The Listvyanka banya is run by Yunez, a Lithuanian guy with a punched-in nose who owns the combo hostel/banya nearest to Baikal. Igor negotiates with Yunez to get us into the banya. Yunez begins explaining the mechanics of the banya to Igor, who takes offence. "I am Russian, you realize. I have been in banya since I was a little fucker."

"Okay," Yunez says, "you explain it to all these foreigners, then. If you need any help, there is a manual."

In between steams, I read out loud from the manual, another product of Google Translate:

Treatment and prophylactic action of Russian bath on a human body . . . At first the person comes into a steam room and 10–15 minutes are soared, even before washing then cools down and has a shower bath cold water. And so 2–3 times . . .

It is impossible to reject aside and psychological effect from visiting of Russian bath—pleasure, pleasant sensations. The bath removes stress, creates effects of comfort of an organism and rest, that medical and preventive an effect also has. Not casually both Russian bath and a sauna is widely used by sportsmen. Regular [банные] procedures weaken muscles, reduce weariness, train a hormonal exchange and vegetative nervous system, promote improvement of sports results and creates perfect conditions for working capacity restoration . . . Russian bath is counter-indicative: at oncological diseases; epilepsies; active inflammatory process of internal bodies; ischemic illness with a stenocardia of IV inactional class; insufficiency of blood circulation above a 2-stage; hypertensive illness of 3 stages; amypcardian heart attack if there have not passed 6 months; hypertensions to a bronchial asthea about frequent 3–4 once a day attacks; infectious diseases in the sharp period (at a heat); pulmonary heart . . .

"Somehow," I say, "this explains it perfectly."

"I told you before," Igor says. "Banya is unexplainable."

"We are glad you guys are here," one of the Swiss guys says. "I think we would not have understood this manual on our own."

"Let's go counter-indicate our pulmonary hearts!" I cry.

My dream is to go direct from the banya into Baikal. After wading into the massive lake up to his knees, Igor does not share my dream. I try to persuade him.

"The water in those buckets is from Baikal. I am not going in this water again," he says, indicating the buckets of water Yunez prepared for us in the shower area.

"Yunez probably took the water from the tap."

"His tap is from Baikal. All water here from Baikal."

"We are going, man."

"I will sit here and smoke."

I am much more taken with the idea of the soulfulness of this place than Igor is. Probably this is a good indication that I am much more of a sucker than he is.

The Swiss guys and I tug on our shorts, and I lead the charge out of the banya and across the street into Baikal, where we are quite a spectacle, three Swiss guys and an American, red, splotchy skin steaming as we splash into the lake. I stand it for as long as I can, but my legs start throbbing after thirty seconds and I have to get out.

When we return to the banya, Denis is a little wobbly. He sits down and his eyes roll back in his head.

"Don't worry about it," Igor says. He's seen this many times before. "Give him a minute."

His Swiss compatriots are silent. A few seconds later, Denis comes to. We force him to drink water and he steadies.

"Whoah!" he says. "Good rush."

Sitting in the banya with the Swiss guys, we discuss how cheesy Europop sounds somehow much better in Russia. The country has a liberating effect on tackiness and cheesiness. The eighties lip-synchers Milli Vanilli even sound good to me here in Yunez's banya on the banks of Baikal.

As we leave, Yunez pulls Igor aside. "Go on the website and leave something in the comments section that says you feel at home at my place, that you loved staying here, every day at Yunez's place is like a holiday and comfortable for children. Something like this."

"No problem," Igor agrees.

The Swiss guys want to have a party at our outdoor kitchen. So we buy another bottle of vodka and when it runs out we buy another and when that runs out another, and so forth . . . Somewhere around the second bottle, we forget that we pre-paid Andrey, the hotel owner Galina's son, for an excursion to the island of Olkhon starting at six in the morning. Somewhere around the third bottle, I guess, I go to bed.

CHAPTER 25

Ever since I'd heard it, Ella Polyakova's statement during our conversation about Soldiers' Mothers had been ringing in my head.

She seemed to think that Igor's generation, on the whole, was irreparably affected in every sphere of their lives by the simple fact of trying to live in the corrupt and unpredictable world of post-perestroika Russia.

Of course, there were those of Igor's age and experience who were not as cynical as he about their ability to impact society—poets and writers and intellectuals and journalists and activists among them. (And it would be members of this generation who would emerge as the de facto leadership of the popular opposition in late 2011.) But Polyakova's theory was that it was the younger generation who would reveal the wrongs, find another way, and bring the new Russia into being. And I had come across several folks who made me believe her.

Polyakova herself had introduced me to Viktor Andreev, legal council for Soldiers' Mothers. He was about six foot five, dressed in blue pinstripes. He had very light blond hair, bangs poking into his green eyes. Handsome and with the slim build of a dancer, he reminded me of a young Baryshnikov. His shirt also was striped, and there were only a couple of stubbly patches of hair on his face where he shaved. In his early twenties, he had already brought two cases before the Russian Supreme Court.

Both cases had to do with the provisions relating to mandatory conscription. The first challenged a not uncommon policy in which police locate draft dodgers in the subway or some other public place through ID checks and take them to the military enlistment office, where they're essentially forced into service. The second challenged the system that allows only military-approved doctors to provide physicals for military fitness. Andreev argued Soldiers' Mothers' position that the military commission should accept evaluations from any doctor. He lost both cases, but still it seemed quite the accomplishment for a young man not even twenty-five.

"I think Russian young people have no essential values and aims," he said. "They want to live, to eat, and to entertain each other, but have no spiritual values."

He told me that, unlike almost every person he knew, he had not paid and would never pay a bribe, for anything. He did not wish to be complicit in the system of corruption. He insisted on paying for his own, very bad hundred-ruble (about three dollars) cups of coffee when we met.

He was currently using his own conscription as a test case to challenge the constitutionality of the alternative service provision to mandatory military service. He had lodged an application to claim alternative service as a conscientious objector, and if it was denied, as he expected it would be—the previous year, only one young man in St. Petersburg had successfully applied for alternative service—he would use its rejection as the basis for his case, which would allege that the process of application and procedure for appealing for alternative service denied citizens' civil rights.

"After all of this, in the end, when my application is approved, then I'll present them the documents about my medical condition," he says. "I have problems with my back. Everyone in our country has problems with their back."

He was also working on filing complaints in the European Court of Human Rights for cases that had been rejected in Russian courts, which are known to operate under political influence. One of the cases he was appealing to the European courts involved a St. Petersburg military unit widely accused of allowing its seasoned officers to systematically pimp out younger recruits in a prostitution ring. When the case failed, the recruit on whose behalf Soldiers' Mothers brought the case was thrown in jail and, in a countersuit, Soldiers' Mothers was fined fifteen thousand rubles (about US$500) for defamation.

I asked him if he was worried about his safety, taking on the most powerful players in the fight against corruption in Russia.

"I think it's not dangerous for me until I reach a certain point," he said. "If I launch an application saying that the military draft should be abolished, it would be very arrogant and would be very dangerous for me."

Many in the West are familiar with Anna Politkovskaya, a journalist for the opposition newspaper *Novaya Gazeta*, famous for covering the wars in Chechnya and doing critical investigative pieces on Russian government officials. She was shot in the elevator of her apartment building in 2006. Her death is widely believed to have involved Chechens or Chechen groups.

Far fewer know Olga Bobrova, who essentially stepped into her shoes at *Novaya Gazeta* as a correspondent in the Caucasus region.

I met Olga on the one-year anniversary of the Russia–Georgia conflict. The Caucasus was heating up again. Not long before, there'd been a suicide bomb attack against the president of Ingushetia. She had a flight back to Moscow from Ingushetia and came directly from the airport to meet me. I wasn't sure exactly what to expect. I had in mind a Politkovskaya type, slight, with close-cropped hair and clunky glasses, a determined, no-nonsense face.

But Olga could not have been more different. She had long blond hair and wore a leopard scarf around her neck, a frilly net shawl over a frilly black blouse, sparkling white pants, modest heels decorated with reflective glass. Her nails were painted neon purple. Her lipstick was orange. And her travel bag was Louis Vuitton; I did not have the eye to determine its authenticity. She travelled back and forth between Moscow and one of the most dangerous parts of the world with the total contents of that Louis Vuitton bag weighing in at about three kilos.

The first thing she said to me after our introduction was "We get quite a lot of visits at *Novaya Gazeta* from Western journalists. They're all trying to make a heroic picture of us, that we all wanted to be journalists since kindergarten. It's not true. Don't make a hero out of me."

She insisted that her status as a journalist was more of a fashion choice than a crusade. Olga went to the Russian State

Social University. She chose it because of its beautiful forest campus on Losiny Ostrov, just outside Moscow. When deciding her major, she wanted something that "suited" a woman, she said. She thought journalist or lawyer, and ended up a journalism major.

She started working for another liberal newspaper but soon joined the staff of *Novaya Gazeta*. Her first North Caucasus assignment was covering the notorious and tragic hostage takeover of a school in Beslan that ended with the deaths of nearly four hundred people, most of them children. Politkovskaya was poisoned on her way to cover Beslan, and Bobrova found herself drawn to the seemingly hopeless chain of lawlessness and corruption engulfing the region. It had been her beat ever since.

After the shootings of the human rights lawyer Stanislav Markelov and the *Novaya Gazeta* staffer Anastasia Baburova in central Moscow in January 2009, one of Bobrova's colleagues questioned her decision to continue reporting from dangerous places and on dangerous people. Her colleague took her to the corner of the office where the portraits of murdered *Novaya Gazeta* journalists hung. "Why are you going to Ingushetia?" her colleague asked. "There's no space left on the wall for your picture."

When she had been in the field for a long time and things seemed to be getting dangerous, she would go to Vladikavkaz, the capital of North Ossetia, and have her hair done for psychological piece of mind. She participated in a training program at *Novaya Gazeta* in which an FSB officer coached female journalists on survival techniques, such as saying they were four months pregnant if they found themselves in a bad spot. The hope being that even rebels and terrorists might respect a pregnant woman. She was skeptical at first, but she had used the technique many times.

I asked her, given all this, why she chose to do it. "I don't know what to tell you about why I'm doing it," Bobrova said. "But I'm doing it."

CHAPTER 26

To me, some of the most inspiring members of this younger generation were young activists affiliated with the organizations Shto Delat? (What's to Be Done?) and Vpered (Forward). Shto Delat? was something like an activist think tank, and Vpered aligned itself with workers' causes throughout Russia and, to some extent, led the far left of the Kremlin opposition in the country.

A friend put me in touch with Oleg, who had become something of a celebrity among the student left the year before when he led the sociology students' protests at Moscow State University, which is essentially Russia's Harvard. We agreed to meet one afternoon at Patriarch Ponds in the centre of Moscow.

Oleg was about five foot five, with a student's shaggy blond haircut. His friend and Shto Delat? colleague Oksana joined him. She wore a wide black skirt and a baby-fist-sized crystal around her neck that matched her purple blouse. She had long, straw-like red hair.

They sat on the embankment at Patriarch Ponds sipping red

wine from a box. I joined them, and one of the first questions Oksana asked was how to say *swan* in English. I told her. And then I asked what kind of ducks these were.

"I've never in my life seen golden ducks like that," I said.

"I've also never seen them," Oleg said. "Maybe it is some kind of reaction from the pollution in the water."

Then they suggested we go have something to eat, and since they were poor leftists, we went to Oksana's apartment, where they prepared macaroni and cheese by boiling pasta and melting cheese over it. Her bookshelves were packed with philosophy in French and English, as well as a prized collection of Hegel in German.

Oleg clanked the fork against his teeth with every bite of macaroni and cheese. He wedged the utensil into his mouth and then pried it out, making a scissoring sound. He was twenty-two years old.

The Moscow State students revolted, according to Oleg, because "everything is infected by political and nationalist thought." For example, he explained, the *rektor* of the most prestigious university in the country would say in front of classes: "As a sociologist, I can tell you it is scientific truth that Jews are greedy."

When Oleg was seventeen, he had his first formative run-in with the police. He wasn't doing anything political. He and some friends went to Tver', about two hours from Moscow. They were standing around, drinking some wine, and one of them happened to have a pocket knife. The cops said, "Give us all your money if you don't want to have a problem."

Oksana told me that her next book—she was a philosopher—would concern human relationships with animals. She stretched her black cat in her lap. "Derrida said that a cat needs only one word to accomplish everything. Meow."

Later, we went to the park in front of the circus at Tsvetnoy Bulvar. Oleg didn't want to take a cab. Too bourgeois. He preferred the subway, but Oksana didn't like the subway. "It's underground," she said.

"It's a very proletarian form of transport," Oleg said. The proletarian argument won out.

When we got there, we stood near the clown statues. We drank beer. The young Moscow leftists slowly began to arrive.

Oksana told us about her friend's theory that the problem with the LGBT movement is that it's desexualized. She added that this is a Deleuzian construction. Oksana tried to represent her friend's views: "He believes that sex is bourgeois and you can only truly critique it when you are outside of the grip of sexuality."

Mitya, chubby with a shaggy beard, explained to me that he was not enrolled in any university because he was self-educating. He asked if I would join them at the protest for workers at a car factory in a few days, and I said I would.

Visibly shaken, Oleg's girlfriend arrived. Someone asked her what was wrong and she said she had just come from Lars von Trier's *Antichrist*.

I told them I'd been travelling all over Russia. I had been to more places in Russia than all of them combined, most of whom had never left the Moscow region.

"Can you tell us something about our country?" Mitya asked, laughing.

I chose the anecdote about arriving on the remote end of the island of Olkhon, around six hours north of Irkutsk. We pulled into a small village on the banks of Baikal, and the first thing we saw was a huge yellow banner with large lettering that said *Internet café*.

When my arrangement to stay at a friend's place fell through, Oleg invited me to stay the night. His grandparents, whom he lived with, were out of town at their dacha. It was an old intellectuals' apartment: the books of the poet Marina Tsvetaeva, Dreiser, a book of prints by Rubens, a photo of Oleg as a teen looking dangerous and pissed off, paintings on every inch of wallpaper-covered wall surface—still lifes featuring cognac, port wine, a bowl of cherries, flowers.

We drank Chilean red wine and Oleg and his girlfriend smoked. She ate corn directly from the can and chased it with grapefruit juice. She had calmed down as the immediacy of von Trier's vision wore off.

Oleg loathed the opposition party fronted by chess champion Garry Kasparov. "They are very elitist and aim to take political power. Vpered does not want to capture political power, but Another Russia is involved in the big sphere of politics. They only want to capture power. They don't want to help students, teachers, workers, people. They are very good guys. They believe their ideas are very good and their ideals are very good, but it's also Russian politics." He was suspicious of personal political aims under the cloak of any politician, whether with the Kremlin or the opposition. There was not a single candidate in Russian politics whom Oleg would support.

The next day, Oleg took me to meet Ilya Budraitskis, the spokesman for Vpered, at a Moscow bar for artist types that's always dense with smoke.

Ilya was wearing a Magic the Gathering hoodie, which, I came to understand, was his de facto uniform. When he wasn't reading Marxist political tracts, he liked Roberto Bolaño. His musical hero was Johnny Cash. Of Lithuanian descent, he held a degree in history and worked as a history teacher at several Moscow schools, including the prestigious Intellectual School.

Ilya told me about the moment of his radicalization. His parents, staunch democrats, had taken part in the defence of the White House against an attempted Communist coup in 1991. His mother was an editor in a publishing house and his father an engineer in a chemical institute. Two months later, they were both out of work, and their family spent the nineties eating potatoes for dinner every night.

But new and exotic stores began opening in Moscow. Class started to show on the streets and in the schools. "To be cool, you needed colourful Chinese dress with an image of Mickey Mouse on it," Ilya said. But he had only one tattered Romanian suit that he wore to school every day. Once, on the way home from school, he stopped in a fancy candy shop called Sweet Sweet Way on Tverskaya. He was transfixed by the sweet sweets. But the security guard gruffly kicked him out, swore at him. Told him to fuck off in his Romanian suit. "This was the starting point of my radicalization," he said. "It had no theoretical base at all, just hatred of the rich."

A few years later, in 1997 at the age of fifteen, Ilya joined his first political group, the Socialist Resistance.

Ilya's story in some ways was not all that different from Igor's. The two were almost exactly the same age. Ilya's parents were also approached by school officials for bribes. If a student wanted good marks, the teacher required gifts, which sickened his idealistic parents. "To study normally, you or your family needed to participate in this corrupt system," he said.

Oleg and Ilya had worked together on the campaign against the sociology department faculty at Moscow State University, a campaign that they both agreed had been a failure. They had tried to force the university, in particular a powerful member of the sociology faculty, to renovate the curriculum, which was outdated and rife with right-wing ideology and bigotry. Instead of discussion about sociology as a science, Oleg and his fellow students sat through lectures about how greed was a genetic trait of Jews and the death penalty was righteous and just and should be implemented in Russia.

Their campaign received some media attention, but ultimately the handful of student protesters flunked out or left the university, including Oleg.

"The main weakness," Oleg said of their efforts, "was the passivity of the majority of the students versus the small minority involved."

It's a sound and obvious point: the voice of many is simply louder than the voice of a few. But this was also the main weakness afflicting the larger anti-Kremlin protest movement in Russia.

The Russian protest scene, if you could call it that, was absurdist theatre prior to December 2011. Ilya explained that, long before the start of an action, a typical opposition demonstration in Moscow would be surrounded by steel fencing. A metal detector run by the police would be stationed at the entrance, and the police and special forces officers assigned for security often outnumbered the protesters.

Basically, such actions afforded protesters the opportunity to communicate their messages to themselves, the media, and the police, who were there to ensure they couldn't communicate their messages to anyone else. Political protests in Russia were, as much as anything, performances for the West—video clips and sound bites to air on the foreign media.

Ilya likened the existence of the Russian opposition then to Bill Murray's *Groundhog Day*. "Every three months they organize a March of Disagreement," he said. "Every three months they apply for a permit. Every three months they're refused. Every three months they come out anyway, just to prove that they still exist. The only point of these actions is to show that the opposition still exists."

At the end of that first conversation with Ilya in 2009, I asked him where he saw himself in five years. He wasn't sure about himself personally, but prognosticated about Russia's future. "What I can tell you for sure is that in five years this society will change. In what way, I'm not sure." At the time, I took it as the idealism of a young revolutionary. Now, he sounds like a prophet.

We left the artists' bar, and as we walked past a McDonald's, Ilya said, "McDonald's is popular here because of its bathroom. People all over the city go there to pee."

Oleg took out his lighter. He fumbled with it and it dropped, exploding when it hit the ground. The sound was about what you'd expect from a good firecracker. The three of us stood there in shock, each trying to process what had just happened. I have seen thousands of lighters fall to the ground and never once seen one explode. A freak accident. Oleg seemed reluctant to reach down for it. "Wow," he said. "I am a real extremist!"

CHAPTER 27
SUMMER 2009

Someone bangs on the log cabin door. "The bus is ready!" a voice shouts. I glance at my phone. Ten after six. We're late. The voice is Andrey's. Andrey is Galina's son, ski instructor in the winter, tour guide in the summer. "The bus is ready. You have five minutes or we leave without you. No refunds!"

Initially, we had been so excited about an excursion to Olkhon that we placed a hundred-dollar deposit on the trip. Olkhon is a natural wonder, the largest of twenty-seven islands in Baikal. It has a 1,500-person population, a large part of which is Bury, the largest Aboriginal group in Russia. At the top of the island, the widest point, Cape Khoboy, it's seventy-seven kilometres wide.

In this hungover state, my enthusiasm is dampened, but I don't want to miss it. I jump up. "We'll be right there," I shout.

"Okay," Andrey says through the door, and his footsteps clump down the stairs.

Igor lies sideways on his bed. Only his torso is actually supported. His feet are on the floor and his neck hangs back. His position suggests the limbo. I kick him. I punch him in the arm. The only vital sign is his snoring.

I shower, washing myself aggressively with the radioactive-coloured Axe anti-hangover. It does not work. My head feels like a hollowed-out stone.

"Dude, get up," I say to Igor. He hasn't moved. I dress and Andrey bangs on the door again. I open it. "I can't wake him," I say.

Andrey steps into the room and stands over Igor. Andrey has an impressive demeanour. He is tall and calm. He does not seem to be upset over our tardiness or our general condition. Certainly he is not surprised by it. "You don't want to go to Olkhon, brother?" Andrey gently asks. Igor's eyes open.

"Olkhon?" Igor says. "I want. Is it time already?"

"It's time," Andrey says.

Igor sits up, shakes his head. He stands and reaches for his back, wincing slightly. Then he walks directly out the door in the clothes he slept in, lighting a cigarette as he goes.

We climb in the four-wheel-drive van with automatic doors. In addition to Andrey, two couples and two blond women are already in the bus—seven respectable people and us. Igor greets everyone, apologizes for having kept them waiting. I charge to the back and collapse into a corner seat.

Igor introduces himself all around and asks where everyone is from. In clipped, one-word utterances, they all reply, "Moscow."

"Jesus Christ, Jeff," Igor says to me. "We are on a bus full of Muscovites!"

He begins chatting, partly to himself, partly to Andrey, the driver, who only nods and smiles in response. He speaks in generous helpings of *mat*.

Lena, one of the blond women, turns to him after a while. "Excuse me," she says. "Is it possible for you to not use such language and also, if it suits you, as I'm certain it'd suit us, to stop talking at any point."

"Of course, madam," Igor says. "Your wish is my command."

The drive is five painful hours from Irkutsk. The roads are mostly paved, but part of the excursion involves stopping at all the most magnetic places on the way so that the Muscovites can tie ribbons with wishes onto trees.

At one particularly magnetic place, Igor and I brace ourselves next to a fence post so that we don't puke.

The Siberian sun burns a bright red. But countering the heat, there's a constant and relentless cold blowing off Baikal.

We get out of Andrey's van and board the ferry named *Gates of Olkhon* that takes us to the island. Andrey bids us farewell at the shore. After the short crossing onto the island, one of his partners meets us. He drives a UAZ, a bus that is nicknamed "loaf of bread" for its loaf-like shape. We pile in. As the loaf of bread wobbles up and down the washed-out dirt road, Igor announces, "I am starting to realize that we are on Olkhon."

Perfect circles about six feet in diameter dot the fields on either side of us. Lena asks the driver what they are. "UFOs were coming," he says. "They appeared more than two years ago. Before was burnt and now only brown grass."

"Aliens visit Russia a lot, it seems," I say to Igor.

"Some sort of it," Igor says.

As we drive across the island, the landscape goes through spectacular changes. At one point it's idyllic, like the Caribbean. Aqua water, sparkling sandy beaches. A little farther on, we're traversing barely navigable roads through dense forests. Then, for twenty minutes, there's such thick low-lying fog cover that we can't even see the lake twenty metres away. We stop in the fog at a convenience store where a few Buryati sit around eating sunflowers. They sell us old bottles of water. There used to be a settlement here, but everything except the store burnt down. It's like something out of a horror movie. A few kilometres down the road and we're back to the Caribbean.

At some point, Lena takes out her wallet and I catch a glimpse of a NYC MetroCard. She just came back from there, she says in English when I ask her about it. She softens toward us a bit when she realizes I am a foreigner.

At our final destination on the tip of the island, the tour group wanders around.

By the natural law of groups and couples in groups, Igor and I end up paired off with Lena and her friend, Anya. They are stewardesses for a private airline. They flew a group of businessmen here and are now staying at the Hotel Mayak, the very definition of opulence in Listvyanka.

Lena endears herself to Igor after their initial antagonism by saying that, to her ear, he speaks perfectly clear, if profane, Russian with no St. Petersburg accent. Lena wears a long, flowing black dress. Open in the back, the dress reveals some burn scarring along her back that somehow makes her even more beautiful. She has more than a touch of that Moskvichka arrogance. Anya wears a tight T-shirt and jean shorts cut such that half of her skinny ass hangs out. She hardly makes a sound. Igor and I speculate that she is on prescription drugs or something. She literally says nothing, just sits, smoking and looking uninterestedly about. Lena, once she has taken to us a bit, proves to be as chatty as Igor.

It is surprising to them, Lena tells us as we walk across the northernmost point of Olkhon together, that the two of us are travelling together. They look at us as if we are a true spectacle.

"We have known each other for ten years," Igor says.

Igor blows out his flip-flops. He flings them off a cliff's edge and the wind carries them into Baikal. He spends the rest of the trip barefoot.

We had been promised lunch on this excursion, but the driver doesn't seem to know anything about it.

Igor and I and Lena and Anya seek shelter from the heat in the woods, where Igor befriends a group of Irkutsk locals cooking fish-head soup in a pot over a campfire. They invite us to join them around a small picnic table. They have plenty of plastic bowls and spoons, and bread for all of us.

"Have some *ukha*," Igor says to me, using the generic name for fish soup.

"No," one of the babushkas who offered us the soup says. "It is not *ukha*. Right now it is fish soup." She goes into a Baggie and finds a plastic cup. Then she removes a bottle of cheap vodka and fills the cup. She hands it to Igor and they toast. "Now it is *ukha*!" she says.

||||||||||||||||||||||||

As we wait for the ferry to return, Lena mentions that she in part learned English from reading Danielle Steel novels.

"More interesting than Pushkin?" I say.

"Sometimes, yes," she says. "I can still quote it. Would you like to hear?"

"By all means."

She clears her throat. "'You think that just because I won't have sex with you that I don't like sex. Men think that the entire female race is frigid because at any given time she doesn't want to have sex with one man.'"

"Bravo," I say. Short of reading all of Steel's oeuvre, which I won't be doing, I have no way of verifying its accuracy, but it's impressively recited.

Igor sees something floating in the water. He finds a stick and fishes it out. A German baseball cap promoting car racing. It reads *Deutsche Vermögensberatung Michael Schumacher*. He takes it as a souvenir from Baikal. "The island is giving me this hat for leaving flip-flops. Like cosmic trade."

The next night, Igor invites the stewardesses and everyone staying at our place to visit the husky farm and then have a party at our outdoor kitchen. He mentions that the husky farm is kind of a mess so tells them to dress appropriately.

Lena and Anya take a taxi to our hotel. They arrive wearing short skirts and tank tops and stiletto heels five inches high.

Igor greets them. "What the fuck you are doing in these shoes?"

"You invited us to a party," Lena says.

"You will sink into the mud of the husky farm."

So the husky farm is scratched and we commence the party straight away. The girls are cold and unhappy that we'll be sitting outside. Igor brings down one of his sweaters for Lena and a comforter from his bed for them to put across their legs.

A British guy living in Thailand named Paddy joins us, along with the Swiss guys, a real international soiree. There are some others from the hotel hanging out in the outdoor kitchen, but they keep to themselves.

Paddy asks for an explanation of the following: Every morning, he goes into the café down the street and sits down, and without giving him a chance to order, they bring him rice and eggs. He can't figure out why it is brought to him or for that matter why anyone would prepare rice with eggs. He has tried to gratefully return it or to order something else, but with no success.

Lena suggests that Paddy learn a very useful Russian phrase that he might try in this situation and others: *Da shto ty govorish!?* This is roughly the equivalent of saying, "Right, say what!?" It is particularly useful, she says, in the markets. When someone tells him a price, he should say, *"Da shto ty govorish!?"* Igor counters that this will not do Paddy any good because he cannot follow it up with anything. Lena suggests that he follow it up with absolute silence and he will get a better price. Paddy agrees to try it, and he asks her how to say, "Please, whatever you do, bring me anything you want except just no rice and eggs," in Russian.

"This will not work," Lena says. "In Russia, you must show your strength—and where are huskies you promised us?" She swivels around to Igor.

"I already told you, you can't go see the huskies in these ice-pick heels," Igor says.

Lena and Anya seem surprised and disappointed.

"Something smells here," Lena says. "I think it's your sweater."

"No," Igor says, "it can't be."

"I smell something too," I say.

An awkard silence obtains, punctuated by occasional sniffing.

"Sweater is clean," Igor says. "Comforter is clean." A moment passes. Then he reconsiders. "Take off sweater," he says.

Lena's face turns to horror. "What?" she says. "I can't touch it." She reaches her hands to the sky.

Igor comes around and lifts the sweater off her. He buries his nose in it and throws it over the railing. "Fucking cat," he says, indicting Dorofay, who apparently, after shredding our wallpaper job in the apartment, decided to mark the sweater before Igor packed it for the trip.

The Spice Girls come on the radio again, and Paddy says, "Ah, daughters of the UK!"

At first, Lena is a bit too prim to eat the fish, which you open like a zipper and eat with your hands. But after a while she tries it, and before long she has cleaned two of the endangered omul down to skeleton and head.

"Don't you have any wine for the ladies?" Lena asks. We do not.

"We have vodka for you, Lenochka," Igor says.

"Foo," she says.

"What, do you want the foreigners to think that bears don't roam the streets and women don't drink vodka in Russia?"

"I don't care what the foreigners think."

Paddy goes to his room, where his wife, who is six months pregnant and with whom he's travelling the length of the Trans-

Siberian, is sleeping. He brings back a box of cheap wine and puts it on the table. Lena sits waiting for someone to pour a glass for her.

"Is anyone here a gentleman?" she asks. Paddy pours for them. "Thank you very much for the light consummation," she says. She cocks her head, suggesting how proud she is of this turn of phrase.

Paddy's face goes bright red. "I'm glad my wife is not here right now," he says.

"It is a very nice thing to say. It is light consummation."

"It's very nice. It's super-friendly," Swiss Robert says.

"Does this come from Danielle Steel also?" I ask.

Lena looks embarrassed but unsure exactly why.

"This next is a toast for women!" Igor says. We all clink glasses.

Paddy teaches us toasts in Irish and Welsh.

Lena repeats them with seriousness. She says that these will be very useful should she ever encounter the Irish or Welsh on her flights.

One bottle of vodka disappears and then another. Igor and I run to the store for more, neglecting again to pick up wine for the ladies, and they are further displeased.

All night, across the outdoor porch, a girl with a short blond bob has periodically caught my gaze. She started out sitting with a group at another picnic table, drinking a bottle of whiskey and a can of Coke, and then her friends left her alone. Now the whiskey has begun to flow. She stares me down and eventually stumbles over and asks me to dance. Our companions all giggle, and

I dance with her to some George Michael. She is wasted and steps all over my feet.

After our dance, I invite her to sit with us and everyone greets her warmly, and she tells us her story. Her name is Tanya. She lives in Irkutsk. She comes here sometimes with friends and sometimes alone. This time alone. The others were acquaintances from Irkutsk whom she'd run into here before.

"I am here to forget everything," she says. "About my job, about my husband . . ."

Igor talks to her for a while. He gets the impression that she is downshifting just like us.

"You will come back and all these problems will still be there," Igor says with tenderness and as if talking to himself. "Better to solve them than to run away."

It appears that we are at an outpost that attracts characters of very different sorts: foreigners looking for adventure, regional residents escaping from the stresses of their everyday lives in the city, and Russians from the capitals, on business and not, looking for some meaning near a big lake.

Soon Igor and Tanya are dancing and making out. Some eighties music popular in Russia comes on. Bad Boys Blue. "You're a woman / I'm a man / This is more than just a game." But their dance is stunted. Tanya and Igor flow and wrestle, flow and wrestle. Occasionally she tries to steer, and they almost fall over.

"You will not lead. I will lead," he says. At this, she breaks away, stumbles down the steps, and pukes to the side. She staggers to her room in the little blue house without looking back. Igor stands at the top of the stairs. Paddy and Lena are amused. Igor looks forlorn. It is as though we have just watched the entirety of their relationship—from burning hot young love to the inevitable bickering through to the culminating struggle that makes or breaks—play out in one song.

Lena and Anya call a cab to take them back to their hotel, and then the drinking switches into high gear. Though medical authorities have assured me that you cannot feel your liver, I am beginning to experience a small pain where I believe my liver should be.

Paddy has come to Russia, at least in part, to prove to some Russian that he can drink as much as him, and here Igor is. "Drink, Russian!" Paddy shouts to Igor, and he finally steps over the line.

"Relax," Igor tells him. "We will drink." Igor proposes that they arm-wrestle as well. Paddy stupidly agrees. Igor beats him twice.

It's a stereotype, of course, but I have yet to see a Westerner who can hold his own drinking with a Russian. It is best not to engage in such seemingly false and potentially demeaning cultural generalizations. And to be sure, there are plenty of Russians who drink nothing or only very little. But if you compare the moderate drinking Westerner to the moderate-drinking Russian—or even the heavily drinking Westerner to the moderate-drinking Russian—there can be no comparison. Russians—and particularly, in my experience, certain Russian men—can absorb alcohol in quantities that would kill most American frat boys. Sadly, over time, it kills many of these certain Russian men also.

And for all that we may share, there are, I have come to understand, certain physiological differences between us. Russians need to drink almost no water and can subsist, seemingly, on a daily diet of liquids that includes only diuretics, primarily alcohol and black tea. If I do not consume several litres of water each day, my lips chap and fingers crack. In the winter months, I have entered the subway in my down parka and stepped inside the subway car, which is stuffed full with others in down parkas or fur coats. The temperature in the metro car can be the approximate temperature of a Russian banya while outside it's minus-twenty. But somehow, I am the only one drenched in a cold sweat.

As Paddy gets drunker, he eases up on the tough guy routine. He's from the UK originally but lives in Bangkok, where he teaches biology. The trip thus far has been hard on him and his wife, harder than he'd imagined.

We ask his opinion, as a biologist, on the crop circles on Olkhon. What rational explanation might exist for them? His theory, after three bottles of vodka and two punishing rounds of arm-wrestling Igor? Sheep are peeing in perfectly round circles.

Andrey appears, back from some excursion or other, and counter-proposes that they are the product of a kind of plant or brown grass that deposits its seeds in concentric circles.

The next day, the Swiss guys leave after a bit of infighting. Two of them wanted to go to Irkutsk. Robert wanted to stay in Listvyanka. He almost defected, preferring to hang with Igor and me, and only at the final hour did he decide to stick with them.

With Paddy and the Swiss guys and the stewardesses gone, we are again seemingly alone with the bruising dogs of Krestovaya Pad.

As we're wandering around, Anya calls on Igor's cellphone. She's called several times a day every day. He usually ignores it. This time he answers reluctantly.

"I had a bad dream last night," she tells him. "Is everything okay with you? We need to talk seriously . . ."

"It's spectacular," Igor says after he hangs up. "One night I fall in love, and Anya dreams I'm murdered."

"Fell in love? The last you saw that girl, you were shouting at her and she was puke-walking away from you."

"She put her lips to my neck," he says. "It means a lot, man."

We stumble across a little church, St. Nicholas Orthodox, famous because the Decembrists, soldiers involved in an early revolt against czarist rule, once worshipped here. The church is supposedly built without nails. Russian Orthodox churches, even the most provincial ones, go heavy on the gold. The icons, like all good icons, I suppose, inspire simultaneously comfort and fear. Igor crosses himself as he walks in.

He leaves fifty rubles in the donation box and buys an icon, his name saint, Igor, Prince of Chernigov, the bearer of great sufferings.

The smell in the church is rich with incense. Several pensioners light candles, leaving them in front of the portraits of saints after whispering a prayer.

We sit on the church steps outside. "Well, man, there is something in the churches. Some atmosphere, something," Igor says.

"Why did you buy the icon?"

"I don't know. Actually, Mom is always giving me these things. I have, like, three or four at home."

"So why'd you buy another one?"

"I don't have this one. It's some remembrance. It's going to be a good memory."

A phone call comes through. It's Big Al calling from the south with good news. He's arranged an in-person job interview for Igor at a resort near Sochi, where he's working, on the Black Sea. It's basically a sure thing if he can make the interview. Igor instantaneously agrees. He's been waiting for an opportunity, and here it is.

We stop by the post office, which appears to be, from its window display, selling macaroni, and use the dial-up Internet access to sketch out a plan. He'll take the Trans-Siberian with me to Krasnoyarsk, stay for a day or two, and then fly to Sochi.

"Big Al is already ordering deer meat for my arrival!" Igor says.

Soon Igor will be searching for a new life on the Black Sea, where we started this trip. I recall his having, miraculously, found a chicken heart on the beach as we were leaving. And now, just as he said, he's going back.

When we return to the hotel, Tanya is up. She apologizes to us for her behaviour last night. We tell her it's all okay. She tells us that she is returning to Irkutsk tomorrow, and we ask if she might be willing to give us a lift to the train station.

She agrees, and we spend that evening cooking macaroni bought from the post office with her on the outdoor porch. Another group arrives from Irkutsk, but they don't seem interested in hanging out with us. At a certain point I leave Tanya and Igor alone, because it looks as though I should.

Igor comes to bed smitten. It makes me wonder what exactly he's looking for. She's thirty-two, no kids. Nothing like the sophisticated, materialistic, and gorgeous young city girls he's dated since I knew him. Maybe that's why he's interested in the opposite? Or maybe he has no idea what he wants. As usual, he is less than forthcoming on the subject.

"Do you see some future with her?" I ask.

"You can't see the future," he says, "only live it."

CHAPTER 28
SUMMER 2009

I n the morning, we have a final breakfast in the outdoor kitchen. Tanya cooks. She is already mothering Igor, and me by association. She prepares eggs and toast from black bread with, like all our meals here, smoked omul.

We ride in her Nissan to the shore of Baikal for one last look. "You were right, Jeff," Igor says. "I was not believing you, but there is some something here." He looks at Tanya.

Tanya drives us back to Irkutsk along the Angara drain. We stop in a large field and she puts down a blanket. We eat—what else?—omul. And we drink water and soda. I walk around and leave Tanya and Igor to nuzzle and make out on the blanket.

It's still a little early, but I circle back, interrupting them with the suggestion that probably we should go.

They double-check each other's phone numbers in their phones.

She tells us that her husband sometimes gets drunk and beats her. That she used to love him but now they don't communicate anymore. She tells us that she has nowhere to go. Igor tells her that she should come with him to Sochi. If he gets the job there, the two of them can live there together. She says that she would really like that. She says that she has to go home and figure things out with her husband—even though he is a goat. She owes him that. Igor has it for her bad.

"We still have about an hour," Igor says.

"But we better leave a little bit early," I say, "just in case we have to bribe any cops at the train station not to arrest you."

This time we ride in *platzkart*, which means we have no coupe. *Platzkart* is the hostel of Russian train accommodations—a whole train car full of beds but without the coupes, fully open, like a rolling barracks.

Igor and I are not seated together, but we both sit on my bed, waiting to see if the car fills up. People to my left have a Bible with gold-embossed pages hanging in their net.

"And I don't have flip-flops," Igor says as everyone begins the transformation from day clothes to train/sleep clothes.

The guy next to me twists a girl's ring off her finger. She lets out a small cry and the ring settles on the table. He sits for a while with her then leaves, taking the ring.

People put bags down and sit near their assigned beds. Three women and a guy sit with us; two of the women are in their forties and spry and the other is in her twenties. The guy is also in his twenties. They look like boyfriend and girlfriend. They are from Tyumen. One removes a five-litre water bottle filled with beer. She slaps a cold smoked omul down on the table. "Help yourselves," she says to us. It is no wonder this fish is endangered.

"I'm tired of omul," Igor says. I also pass, but we take them up on cups of beer.

They tell us they are coming back from a relative's funeral in Bratsk, near where Igor's relatives whom we didn't visit live.

Igor and I feel fortunate to have such agreeable train companions. Then, at our first stop, a babushka and a girl, maybe her daughter, arrive to claim their seats and kick everyone out. They slam purses down on my seat as they lay claim. They kick off their heels. Igor retreats to his place in the front of the train. My new neighbours start showing each other sexy shorts they bought in Listvyanka and reading each other their horoscopes. The young one uses a fashion magazine as a fan.

The Tyumen group invite me to join them in their seats. I extend the invite to Igor and suddenly we're back to our good time, cramped in a bit on their beds. The older ones are sisters, and Olya and Tolya are brother and sister, not boyfriend and girlfriend. We get off in Zima and buy two litres of Shore of Baikal beer to supplement their five litres. Olya and Tolya buy some as well and they stand with one of the beggars at the station. I buy some chips and offer them some. They introduce me to the beggar, whose name is Tolya too. They seem to know him, but I'm unclear how. Or maybe, as with us, they just met him and already seem like great old friends. I offer him some chips. He declines.

Back on the train, the aunts compete in showing me photos on their cellphones. Natasha's are mostly of her Siamese cat. One of him in a cast. Then everyone wants to have their photo taken with me, the foreigner.

Olya asks me if I want to hear her best English phrase. I say that I do. She clears her throat. Our group suddenly goes quiet. "Who is absent today?" she says.

"This is a very useful phrase," Igor says, laughing.

"Very useful," I say.

Olya and Tolya have lots of questions about North American schools. They have been told that in America and Canada people work and go to school on Sunday. I tell them the truth: some people go to work and school on Sunday and some people, most people, don't.

Natasha tells me about how she occasionally applies leeches to her body to keep the blood flowing. In some pharmacies in Russia you can buy a small vial of leeches. Even Igor confesses that he tried it once. "That's it," he says. "Just to try. Most important thing is this coagulating agent."

Natasha invites me to come live with them. "You can marry Olya," she says. "Yeah!" Olya says. "I'd be honoured to have you as my brother," Tolya says. I look at Olya. She is very beautiful. I imagine it. My moving to Tyumen. It seems, in my drunken state, the best idea going. I would marry Olya and we would have some Russian kids. Tolya and I would go into business together; I have no idea what Tolya does, but I'm sure in Tyumen, he and I, as brothers-in-law, would go into some business or other together. Igor and Tanya would come and visit from the Black Sea occasionally, and occasionally we would visit them, bringing along five-litre bottles of whatever Tyumen-region beer we could find to share with people we meet on the train. I would take Tolya's place giving Olya foot massages and she would return the favour. This is pure derangement—but such seductive derangement. Something like the fantasy Igor was having about Tanya and maybe she about him.

The train attendant stretches a large sheet over the runner that lines the train car's passageway and snaps it into clips that hold it in place. After a couple of hours she flips the sheet. Then a couple of hours later she changes the sheet.

The fantasy starts to go bad. The intimacy of Olya and Tolya, at times, makes me a bit uncomfortable. She feeds him omul with her hands, then he licks her fingers. He rests his hand on his aunt's bare thigh. I spin out a different story, my coming to live with this incestuous family. Olya having been the bait, they get me drunk and marry me to Natasha . . . who seems actually very kind and fun if considerably older than me and, quite simply, not my type. And, of course, why would I ever want to go to Tyumen? If I am having thoughts like this, I need to leave Russia soon, I think.

When the beer is gone, Tolya opens a bottle of vodka, which we chase with bites of fresh cucumber.

It's dark, but the luminescence of the summer Siberian sky shines like a purple jewel. Most people on the car have gone to sleep by now except for the two women on whose beds we sit, a mother and daughter from Irkutsk. They don't drink with us but are very easygoing.

When I find my bed, I am quite drunk. There is no ladder, just a single step, the size of a bike pedal, to put my foot on, and a metal bar to pull myself up.

The windows in the wagon can be pushed open, but they are all closed, suffocating us. A draft is to be feared in Russia. I have seldom seen a fan in this country. I have never seen a ceiling fan, though it's possible they exist here. An air conditioner may be used, but it will never be used at night.

I have tried to discredit the draft fear, but it is simply another example of American arrogance. One friend countered, "You don't believe that drafts make you sick, and we don't believe that caffeine keeps you awake." The train coughs at night exactly as Igor's uncle's cucumber peel–eating dog Marusya had in Gelendzhik. I sleep with my laptop bag wound tightly around my sweating body.

CHAPTER 29

Around dawn, the train car comes slowly to life. People wake up and start making tea from the big samovar at the end of the car. Igor appears beside my bunk and stands at the window, holding the two books I've given him for the trip, the second novel by Klyucharyova and the novel *Sankya* by Zakhar Prilepin.

"I finished them," he says.

"What'd you think?" I ask.

The new Klyucharyova book doesn't seem to have spoken to him the way *Obshchy Vagon* did. He summarizes it: "The main character, former revolutionary now in Moscow, early love has fallen hard. Now is searching for himself. He is considering getting baptized. Basically, this is the story of the man trying to find the reason for living . . . But he found it in this girl. He made a big mistake in cancelling the relationship with her. After cancelling, she was a junkie . . . then he realizes he loves only one woman and she is married to his best friend. And basically that's all. But it's very interesting.

"There is a part with the fucking good emotional transmission like in *Obshchy Vagon*. He is standing near the church, just scared to come in because he doesn't know the rules of it. At end—he is artist—at end he is painting Madonna with his love's face. The rest of it, not so good emotional transmission, but very realistic. Well, actually very interesting book . . . interesting storyline, man. But the first one was better."

Prilepin was a soldier in Chechnya and subsequently an officer in OMON, Russian special forces, and after that a revolutionary with an extremist group called the National Bolsheviks. *Sankya* is about a young revolutionary modelled on the Nat-Bols, as they're called. I didn't know exactly how Igor would react to such an explicitly anti-Kremlin book.

"Prilepin beat Klyucharyova with this *Sankya*," he says. "The story of him carrying the coffin of the father. It's terrible, man. It was raining. He was wet. Out of power. There is still ten kilometres more and mother is crying and going after them."

It dawns on me that the aspects of the books that he latches onto are those that have some immediate application to his life. Was Igor thinking that he had made a mistake in breaking it off with Anya? When he talked about the scene in *Sankya* where the main character carried the coffin of his father, the patriarch of his family, was he thinking of his grandfather's recent death?

"Do you ever think about these kinds of things yourself?" I ask. "Like in the Klyucharyova book, about trying to find the meaning of life?" The woman below me stirs in her bed. Others still half asleep take note of the two guys speaking English.

"When I was young," he says. "Now, just living. It's too complicated. Sometimes I was thinking, we are not living. We are in hell. Because living here is like in hell. In the world. This is a hell. I was thinking that way."

"Life is sometimes not so hot," I say. "And for some people maybe it's hell. But for me, for most of the people I know, if this is hell, it's not living up to its reputation. Maybe there are moments of hell."

"With a position like what you have," he says, "I can say you don't know what paradise is and what hell means. I think in Russia is hell because we are here just surviving."

We arrive in Kras in a crushing heat wave. Thirty-five degrees Celsius.

Yulia and her father are there to pick us up. She's been here all summer while we've been wandering the country like a couple of strays. And now here I have a kind of home. I'll stay here for several weeks before returning to Toronto via St. Pete. Igor will roam farther—all the way back to the Black Sea for the job interview in Sochi—on his own. Igor and Yulia have met a couple of times before. They are not inclined to really hit it off. Yulia doesn't drink and Igor doesn't shop.

We are staying at Yulia's grandmother's place. Yulia, Igor, and I stroll around.

We sit in the square and watch some drunk auntie dancing there. Yulia says she dances there all night every night, by herself. Occasionally men get up and dance with her. Igor nicknames her: Kras Perpetual Mobile.

Igor and I have a feast with the whole family—Yulia, her

mom, grandma, and sister, and her father. I meet Sasha's son Ivan for the first time. He's a huge smiling boy.

Sasha is plotting her return to Moscow now, where it's more expensive but where there are prospects for an actual career. Grandma or mom or father or maybe all of them will go with her to help watch Ivan.

The first toast is to Sasha's new driver's licence. Her immediate plan, when she gets back to Moscow, is to buy that car.

Sasha is optimistic about finding a job in Moscow despite the crisis. Mom is eager to go. Grandma is not so. She is unhappy about going to Moscow, which she dislikes because of the people. By way of example she mentions that when she was there working for several months, during Soviet times, you would visit someone's house and they wouldn't put anything on the table, no tea or even chocolate. "Can you imagine?" she says.

The next morning, it's thirty-two degrees when we wake up at eight. By nine-thirty, it's thirty-five. By ten, thirty-seven.

We walk around the city. Igor asks me if I've noticed anything different about Kras compared with the other places we've travelled. He is shocked that I am so unperceptive. "I can't believe you didn't notice. There are no cats in the streets here," he says. I hadn't noticed, but this is because I hadn't noticed that there were, according to Igor, cats everywhere in Gelendzhik and Listvyanka and St. Petersburg. Maybe I just don't notice cats and therefore do not notice the absence of them. I think I tend to notice dogs more, especially strays. But then dogs, to me, are more noticeable.

The Lenin statue downtown has been turned into a playground for children driving miniature cars and trucks, and miniature ponies with pompoms and neon saddles. Skateboarders flip and spin their boards at Lenin's feet. So much as touching the Lenin statue used to be prohibited. Now it is essentially a jungle gym.

Yulia, Igor, and I decide to visit the Paraskeva Pyatnitsa Chapel at the top of the hill for the daily cannon blast. We can't find the bridge to the cannon, though, and so, with twenty minutes left, we flag a car. This is a fairly common practice in Russia. A lot of cars double as cabs for extra money. But one of the tried-and-true rules I'd always heard was that you never get into an unofficial cab with more than one person in it.

A white Japanese car with the wheel on the right stops. Two guys are in the front seats. They agree they'll take us to the chapel quickly. And I figure Igor is as big as the two of them put together. But as soon as the car starts moving, the guy in the passenger seat flicks a razor-sharp diving knife open. He closes it and flicks it open again, looking at the driver out of the corner of his eye. The car comes to a stop at a light. If we go through the light, we'll be leaving the main thoroughfare. I look at Yulia, who saw the knife as well, and nod to the door. I tap Igor, who is oblivious, but he follows us out in the middle of traffic.

We immediately find a stairway leading to the chapel and rush up it, looking back to see if the guys in the white car with the knife have decided to follow us. They haven't. We make it to the top just as the cannon fires, setting off all the car alarms in the vicinity.

The chapel is built on a spot that used to be a temple for the Tatars and also a lookout point from which to notify the villagers of incoming hostile raiders. Krasnoyarsk and this chapel feature on the ten-ruble note of the Russian Federation.

We buy a small bottle of *gorilka*, small as an attempt at limitation, but after we finish it we decide to go to the store for another small bottle, second attempt at limitation.

Igor goes into the store. There's a long line. When he gets to the front, he asks for a Nemiroff twenty-five-centilitre *gorilka*.

"Maybe you will take one point seventy-five litres?" she asks. "I think it's the only size we have."

"It's too much," Igor says. "I need only 250 millilitres."

"Go over there and look for your Nemiroff while I serve other customers," she says.

"Okay," Igor says. He looks but sees only the 1.75-litre bottles and some *gorilka* infused with garlic that seems awful.

"Maybe you should take two bottles of one hundred millilitres each," the shopkeep shouts.

"No," Igor says. "This is masturbation."

"Now I understand what it is I am doing, then," the shopkeep says.

"But with me, I always close my eyes and think that I am in a dream. It helps me."

Everyone in the line laughs.

She takes a three-hundred-millilitre bottle of Three Old Men and says, "I am always drinking this."

"I am trusting you, then," Igor says.

Igor is proud of his performance as we leave. "Do you know why I did it?"

"Illuminate me," I say.

"After, she understood that if she will negotiate with me, I have a longer tongue than her."

"I see," I say.

"Oh," he says. "And this line about closing the eyes and dreaming, it is from movie *Caribbean Pirates*, right?"

"I don't know, man."

"No," he says. "No, maybe not."

Courtesy of Yulia's grandma, Igor and I have the crowning breakfast of our journeys: a bottle of Bulgarian wine, a bottle of Bochkarev beer, chicken, potatoes, fried fish, smoked fish, two different mayonnaise-heavy salads, and bread, followed by a Tatar pie that is basically rice and apricots and raisins baked into a very tasty dough.

"Tanya is only texting me once per day," he says. "It's hard for you to understand I'm in love with her."

"Is it possible you're in love with her because she seems like the kind of girl who will take care of things?" I say.

"Maybe I'm wanting to care for her because she is caring about everything."

He irons his shirts and pants before leaving. He's got a kind of *Miami Vice* look going.

"You trying to impress someone?" I ask.

"I don't want to look like shit on the plane, man," he says.

After Igor leaves, things are a little weird. He is such a force that, once you've experienced his presence, his absence is a void. But also, Yulia and I have yet to discuss our separation. Did she get what she wanted out of it? Did I? Where will we go from here?

I had never known this stage in a marriage before, but looking back, I understand where we were. It was that stage when we both know that it was over but no one would admit anything. Instead, we were going with the flow, going through the motions, because after so many years, that was automatic.

I spend a lot of time by myself the next couple of weeks there. But there are a few times we go out and about, again not talking about the obvious, not trying to address the underlying problems or talk through them, not communicating, maybe just hoping, if we ignore them, they may go away or work themselves out . . .

One day, on the way back from the grocery store, she tells me about the jazz band she was in in middle school. I'd never heard anything about it.

"We used to practise in there," she says. She points through a window of an apartment building not far from her mom's apartment. It was still the Soviet Union, and a teacher at the music school selected her to sing because she had the lowest voice. He gave her the lyrics, and they practised a few times. She sings me a few bars and then translates the whole song. It is hilarious to picture her as a Young Pioneer in her red scarf singing a song that went like this:

I'm a little girl.
I party all day long.
Everybody hates me
    who is not lazy to hate.
I like to pick up flowers
    and I like to look into the river.
When I grow up,
    I will leave for America.
In America, life is beautiful

But here in Krasnoyarsk,
  I am penniless.
In America, the sun shines brightly
  and I will not be physically abused.
I will have a lot of children
  and I will love them.
But I am still here in Krasnoyarsk
  without a penny.

When the music school director found out about the song, the teacher was fired and the band broke up.

Within a year from that summer, we will initiate the divorce. She will stay in Toronto and I will move, first to Moscow for a year and then back to Florida for a new job. In Russian, "to divorce" is *razvestis*. Both words have these unpleasant, sharp *s* sounds, the sound of something being scissored apart.

I meet my friend Fyodor for lunch. Fyodor is a 29-year-old marketing exec for the Krasnoyarsk professional basketball team Yenisei. I first met him in St. Petersburg while he was there for the writers' festival, and we have stayed in touch. His wide-ranging interests extend from basketball to IT to poetry.

He picks me up in his beat-up Honda Civic on his break from work. He wears a suit. Skinny and pale, with red skin around his eyes, he looks like a well-dressed heroin addict. We decide to go to California Pizza for a slice.

We find a car pulling out of a spot. And by "spot," I mean a thin sliver of sidewalk blocking the crosswalk. Fyodor obstructs traffic in both lanes for a few minutes while the other car backs out, then he manoeuvres onto the sliver of sidewalk. "It's not exactly legal, but it seems fair," he says. This might be the slogan for the Russian approach, I think. Not exactly legal, but fair.

We take a table at the California Pizza in Siberia. I order margherita, light sauce, light cheese, lots of oregano and tomato. And the pizza is surprisingly good. I ask him to catch me up on his life.

He's broken things off with his old girlfriend, Lily, whom I'd met once. He met Katya, his new girlfriend, when he was driving around one day as a gypsy cab to make some extra money. He picked up Katya, and when they arrived at the destination, he told her to forget about money and pay him with her phone number. "Lily was a nice girl, but sometimes it is just the little things," he says. "You dream of someone with dark eyes, and she had blue eyes. Her blue eyes were beautiful, incredibly beautiful, but you are dreaming of someone with dark eyes. So what do you do?"

Fyodor talks a lot about his career. He seems frustrated. He has a good job as far as jobs in Siberia go, but when he describes it, he uses English phrases such as "the HR model." He tells me that the HR model in Russia is designed to use an employee up and spit him out.

He's pursuing a certificate in marketing that can help him take the next step in his career. He had applied for numerous positions in marketing and management, but he couldn't land one.

"I have tried, but I have failed every time." He says this not with sadness or resignation or even real discouragement, merely as a statement of fact.

Opportunities are much more plentiful in Moscow and Petersburg. He has just returned from one of the Krasnoyarsk basketball team's games in Petersburg. He has considered making the move to one of the two Russian metropolises. If he sold his car and apartment in Kras, he could probably afford another place and car in Petersburg. But it'd be a gamble. Further, often when he arrives home from work in Krasnoyarsk, his grandmother, who has a key to his apartment, has left a plate of varenyky ready and waiting for him on his kitchen table. There would be no plate of varenyky waiting for him in St. Petersburg.

It strikes me that Fyodor and Igor are the same age, and they approach their lives, their careers, totally differently. Fyodor has designed his background and education to fit perfectly that which theoretically is in high demand. He has excellent formal English skills and is proficient in IT. He is hoping that the certificate in management will propel him in some way that he has not yet propelled himself.

While we're at California Pizza, a woman from his marketing certificate program stops by. She recently lost her job, which is a problem because she has to be employed in a marketing position as a condition of enrolment in the certificate program. So Fyodor offers to have his father, who owns a family company, draft some paperwork saying that she's working for Fyodor in their company. Of course, Fyodor does not actually work for that company and neither will she, but the arrangement kills two birds with one stone: she gets a job to continue in the certificate program and Fyodor gets some management experience since he technically now supervises an employee. Not exactly legal, but fair.

Afterward, I walk around the city alone.

I watch Kras Perpetual Mobile dance in the square. Then I stop off at the Krasnoyarsk Festival to catch the high-heels race. A mob of gorgeous women in five-inch-plus stilettos. The winner, a beautiful girl in a red and white polka-dot dress, is out in front of the rest by at least six metres. Afterward, I ask her—being a foreigner in Siberia is kind of like being a celebrity, you can easily talk to anyone, even the winner of the illustrious high-heels race—how she managed to beat the others by so much, and she says, "I am a model, so I'm in high heels all day, and honestly, I didn't see any competitors here."

Igor calls after several days. "I got the job, man. Managing a combination restaurant, strip club, and bowling alley. Fifteen hundred dollars per month, apartment, food, everything."

I'm happy for him. His voice sounds really light and sober. We make plans to rendezvous in St. Petersburg. I will be flying through on my way back to Toronto, and he will be returning briefly to gather his things and take the train, the exact same train that had taken us to Gelendzhik, back to the Black Sea to live.

CHAPTER 30
SUMMER 2009

Back in St. Petersburg, Igor and I eat an entire Papa John's pizza together.

He is gushing with impressions and information. More excited than I've seen him since the crisis began.

Big Al and his wife, Katya, work around the clock there. He is the chief cook and she is the restaurant manager. They are trying to make up the money Big Al lost on an apartment deal with a crooked real estate agency in St. Petersburg.

One night, Igor went to the beach at two a.m. He befriended a vicious German shepherd and ran with the dog on the beach all night. He would later find out it was named Mukhtar after a dog in a famous classic movie. He called the dog Dillinger, Dilly for short.

African guys in tribal dress posed for photos on the beach with kids. The kids hung on spits, and the Africans pretended they were cooking them. Dilly and Igor slept on the beach one night.

Igor hands me the notebook he kept. There are pages and pages in it of questions he asked the director who interviewed him. He asked about soda mix (she didn't know what soda mix was) and he asked about Wi-Fi. He had some sketches in there that showed some of his renovation plans. "I want to make modifications a little bit," he says.

He tells me about the prosecutor he sat with on the train from Sochi back to St. Petersburg. He was divorced and had custody of the kids. He was thirty-three but looked forty-four. "I told him about you," he says. "I told him about our travels and our lives. He got drunk and said, 'You are a spy like your American friend.'"

We head over to Piskaryovka and go to the courtyard to have some beers. His friends are there taking turns around the Ping-Pong table.

The courtyard has soccer goals. A statue of a bee and a statue of a bear. A geometric flower garden of marigolds.

His friends from the neighbourhood call me Chev. The English *j* sound doesn't exist in Russian. The closest one gets is the awkward consonant cluster made by joining the sounds *d* and *zh* for a *duh-zh* sound, or, more simply, just *ch*. Also, the courtyard denizens of Piskaryovka are all fans of the series of *Crank* films whose contract killer protagonist's name, Chev Chelius, rolls off the tongue.

Igor's courtyard is like a living example of Ella Polyakova's diagnosis of Russian society entering the twenty-first century. An entire generation that has given up on hope, on anything except surviving the next crisis, one which they fully expect to come along sooner or later, exists here and in courtyards exactly like it all over Russia.

I am probably the first American ever to set foot in this courtyard, and, as Igor says, I am "a point of interest."

One very drunk Special Forces guy eyes me across the Ping-Pong table. ("He is with, like, Navy Seals," Igor says. "But tougher.") Another asks me, "What kind of mushrooms do you have in the US?" They ask me about the population. They are impressed that I know how many states there are in the States. How many provinces are there in Canada? On this count I am not certain, having forgotten my mnemonic for remembering them all. One guy says for certain there are six. They discuss how many republics are in the CIS and how many republics were in the Soviet Union, and no one knows.

I talk to a guy named Kyrill about cars (he wants a VW Golf), Putin (he hates him), the crisis (it's going to get worse).

Another common courtyard topic: gas prices. They want to know how much gas costs in North America. They're incensed that they live in a major oil-producing nation and pay basically the same price as, or more than, we pay in the West.

The Special Forces guy stares at me the whole time. Finally he asks, "Are black people in America like what you see on TV?"

"I think some of them are, yes," I say.

"Are you a patriot?" Igor's friend Andrei asks.

"It's an interesting question," I say. "I'm not a nationalist and it's strange for me to say something like I'm proud to be an American, because it suggests that I'm better than someone else who, through accident of birth, was born somewhere else. But I do think the country is an incredible model of democracy, with great highs and shameful lows. I don't agree with lots of things the government does."

They nod their heads. "We also don't agree with many

things our government does," Andrei says, the implication being, I catch, *But we still love our country . . .*

"Let's go," Igor says.

I wonder what deductions they're making about me/us from my drunken blather. Do I confirm for them that Americans love their country, or don't love it and move to Canada then hang out in Russia? Or do I confirm for them that "we" are like "them," or not? In *A Russian Journal*, Steinbeck always had just the right thing to say about his delegation. I'm not the person for the job.

The Special Forces guy across from me growls, in stilted English: "I fucking hate all Americans." He looks me dead in the eye.

"Okay, see you, guys," Igor says, pulling me up from the bench by my shoulders.

Igor and I take the same path he took fifteen years ago to meet his friends at school and celebrate his last day.

We pass the playground where he spent his childhood. Like countless other playgrounds in countless other St. Petersburg courtyards, the swing sets, once bright blue and red and yellow, are rusted and faded. "Things are not changing here," he says. "New people aren't coming. It's the same." This is his place. This is home.

We pass the technical college, where there is a brick wall designed so that alternating bricks extrude. One of the favourite activities of Igor and his friends when they were boys was scaling this wall. "All the way to the top," he says, pointing to the roof of the two-storey building.

We dodge some sketchy-looking stray dogs laid out on the tracks.

We cross the railway tracks where the regional passenger trains run and where the freight trains bring coal into the city along the path of the only supply line during the siege.

We hop a fence and a platform. We cross the tracks. We squeeze through some bars with barbed wire wrapped around the top of them.

Then we are at his old school, a four-storey white brick building, Gymnasium 192, Bryusovskaya School, named for the Symbolist poet Bryusov.

The yard used to be just a playground, but now there is a quite modern set-up: a rubber track circling a mini soccer field with goals and high nets to catch stray shots. A group of guys are playing soccer on the turf. Some of them are good. There are pull-up bars under which a group of teenagers are drinking beer, and a basketball court.

We sit in the bleachers and watch the games. He points to the ninth floor of the building opposite the school. "In winter, my friend had the apartment there on the ninth floor, and we would make the biggest snowballs we could and go up there and drop them out the window."

Igor arranges for Anya to drive us over to my apartment at Bolshevikov. It's the only way she could get him to agree to see her before he left.

While we wait, I try to explain why I answered the aggressive guy's question about my being a patriot the way I did. "On one hand, I thought okay, this guy loves Russia, so there are two ways this can go. I can say, 'I love America,' and then he will respect me for loving my country, or I could say, 'I love America,' and then he could lower his eyes at me and say, 'I hate all Americans.' Or I could say, 'No, I'm not a patriot.' And he would say, 'This is what's wrong with America, they don't love their country.'"

"Actually, you can say everything. He was drunk. But in this case, I can explain you one thing. He can say everything, but he will never touch you. And if even with the word, because I am standing nearby you."

"I knew he wouldn't touch me. Well, I hoped that he wouldn't touch me."

"You just needed to say honestly, that is all. It's all he wanted."

"But it's just an accident I'm there. One Portuguese just happened to move there and that Portuguese's offspring happened to meet a German after World War II and they moved there as well, and so on, and then me. And now I live in Canada."

"Man. I want just to say you one thing. Enjoy being there, 'cause here it's another story. It's just opposite as I told you before. Here, we are living on our own rules. And you will never understand it." Then he adds: "My friends in the court-yard, they didn't like USA before they met you. Now they say it's okay."

Anya pulls up in her dad's SUV and we get in. The CD player is suspiciously cued to play Whitney Houston's "I Will Always Love You."

Anya has a few things in the car that she's returning to Igor. One of them is a briefcase that Big Al had given him and that he'd left, at some point, at her place. Anya gives him her own gift, a coffee press that she stole from the Atrium. Their whole exchange is awkward and silent.

Anya drops us off at my place on Bolshevikov. She and Igor formally and politely say goodbye. They hug briefly. I walk away to give them a moment.

When Igor catches up with me, he reports that Tanya from Irkutsk is texting him again. "She's living separately with husband," he says excitedly.

Igor and I go to the Glory Pub. They play Charlie Chaplin videos on their wide screen, then DVDs of live concerts, first Phil Collins and Genesis and finally, at our request, Metallica.

"Man," he says. "I don't want to leave this city, just realized it."

Everything falls apart in the run-up to his departure. A few days before Igor is due to leave, we had planned on mushroom hunting. The boots were parked by the door. Plastic bags crammed into them. Backpack stocked with beer and water and bread and pickles.

But we miss the first train. On a Saturday in Petersburg, if you don't catch the first train, the forests are picked clean of mushrooms.

So I sit at his apartment for a while. For breakfast we have a bowl of hot borscht, some juice from a jar of pickled tomatoes, and garlic *lavash*.

On the counter at his apartment are three jars of freshly pickled sorrel. "Mom is doing for wintertime. From it comes very tasty soup."

The kombucha colony is still sitting on the table with cheesecloth rubber-banded across the top. The mushroom, or whatever it is, has waterlogged, flattened out across the surface of the water.

The day before he leaves, we planned to go to the round banya one last time. But he answers the door dressed in full-body grey thermal underwear. His eyes are yellow and bloodshot. He has chills and a fever.

"Sorry, man," he says. "I can't go to banya in this condition."

"Swine flu," I say.

We sit at his kitchen table, which is now filled with jars of new things pickling and fermenting. We eat fish and chicken, and he eats soup with liver and chicken hearts.

He has a forty-two-hour train ride beginning tomorrow.

We sit around watching TV. A report is on about Medvedev clamping down on corruption. He tells me that V Kontakte was hacked and nothing is working, even his beloved mafia role-playing games.

"I have eleven million euro, and I don't know what to do with it," he says.

The next day, I go to meet Igor at the train station to see him off. I buy him two new books and a Fusion five-blade razor as going-away gifts.

His mom is there, all made up. He is standing with his new seventeen-inch laptop in a new laptop case.

Mom is nervous, on the verge of tears again. She tells him that he dressed all wrong because it's going to be hot and to remember to call her as soon as he gets there and to be careful and did he forget anything and she will miss him.

"I kissed the cats," he says. "Little fuckers . . . Well, there I have Dilly and there are a lot of cats. I will rent one."

He tells me to come visit him there. If he doesn't like it, he'll return when the initial three-month contract is up. If he does like it, I'll have a place to stay for the Olympics in 2014.

The train starts to pull away. He kisses his mom. Then she and I walk along with his coupe. He opens the window and reaches his hand out and we shake through the window of the moving train. The St. Pete to Sochi picks up speed and disappears from sight.

EPILOGUE

||||||||||||||||||||||||||||||||||||||||||||

*I would not swap him for a soberer or more reasonable
friend even if I could.*
—E.B. WHITE WRITING ABOUT HENRY DAVID THOREAU

In retrospect, the crisis made the first cracks appear in the facade of the Putin stability. While there were many factors that led to the so-called Russian Spring of 2011, a spring which took place in the dead of winter, when hundreds of thousands of citizens came out in the streets to protest Putin in the wake of falsified parliamentary elections, the crisis was the first signal that stability was not enough. Prime Minister Putin and President Medvedev publicly acknowledged that they'd be switching roles, and Putin would run for re-election to a term of six years. Everyone already knew what the outcome of the election would be.

Igor held his job in Sochi for about nine months and then was laid off and returned to St. Petersburg. "First three days I was back, just sitting and staring at the ceiling," he told me. "But bit by bit, I am starting to come back alive."

Instead of working, he fished, went to the woods to collect mushrooms (an endeavour that he called "silent hunting"), and played paintball. He tried to find work, applied for hundreds of jobs. The situation in Russia was improving, but Igor couldn't find his footing. Another Russian friend once told me that Russians thrive in crisis. They are always ready for it. But what seemed to have awakened life in so many had killed something in Igor. Maybe on our trip in 2009 he had downshifted completely, stalled out.

He had a nice quantity of savings from his ten years of work in downtown St. Petersburg, but he burned through it all until at a certain point, I understood, he was totally broke. His frequent texts with Tanya in Irkutsk ebbed and then stopped completely when she reunited with her husband.

Sometimes we talked by Skype, and he sounded depressed. The interstice between fall and winter seemed a particularly bleak time. "No fishing right now," he said late one October. "Waiting for the ice. Fish are sleeping right now, like bears."

"Are you playing paintball again?" I asked.

"No, I wasn't playing. Two months ago disassembled, oiled everything, and put it back together. I don't want to sell it. It's a good memory, but all guys from my team, they sold everything. Kyrill with little kid, he needs money, doesn't have time to go fishing with me. Another is divorced and living somewhere very far. Another also living very far. I don't know, dude. They don't want to play paintball. Me also. Just a good memory. I'm thinking to go to parachute courses. I found close to me one stop by train and then five minutes by feet. And it costs not so much."

"You want to jump out of planes now? Maybe you should have gone in the army."

He laughed. "I told you, dude. I didn't want to be killed by some Chechens in reasonless war for the oil."

He sounded lonely and he sounded bored. I remembered his declaration about loneliness being his greatest fear and his belief that boredom was what drove people crazy.

One Sunday morning around nine a.m., Igor texted, *Forgive me*. Apropos of nothing.

I replied, *For what, man?*

Ten minutes went by. I imagined it all, the depression finally getting to be too much. How could I have missed the signs? Were there signs? Maybe there were signs.

My phone dinged. *Today is forgive Sunday. It's old Russian tradition and you should say forgive me.* I was relieved.

Forgive me, bratan, I wrote.

I'm forgiving you, bro, he wrote.

He had taken a keen interest in the progress of this book. "I always thought I just had a usual life, man," he said to me once. "But you know, as I told you all about it, I am realizing that I had interesting life."

He wondered when I'd finish it. I think he thought that I probably wouldn't.

I told him that his country kept changing, and that it was hard to know at any given point what the story was.

"My story," he said, "always same."

But his story, as it turned out, was not always the same. He had started going to casting calls to be an extra on crappy TV shows for six hundred rubles a day. I was really surprised at this move. Do many people go from being avid watchers of TV to standing in the extra cattle calls for next to nothing?

At first, it seemed as though he was only doing it to have a reason to get out of the house and to have a little money for cigarettes and food. They cast him in small, non-speaking parts as thugs, butchers, toughs, mafiosi, cops, and military officers—especially military officers.

"Sounds like fun," I said.

"Not fun," he said. "I'm sitting reading a book then they're saying do this do that say this say that. I'm doing it. I go by myself. I'm meeting the same faces there. They have main jobs and this is like their hobby. Sometimes is coming very rich people. Also like hobby. They are giving coffee all day, food all day, and you are sitting and chatting with someone all day. What to tell you? Fishing, mushrooming, TV shows, that's it. The weather is shit. It's always raining."

As with his move to Sochi, his brief flirtation with IT and with Tanya, his ideas about going to live with Uncle in Gelendzhik, I assumed that the acting thing was a phase.

He started posting photos from the set to Facebook and tagging me in them, confusing my friends who didn't know him. There was Igor as a butcher and as a cop and as a mafioso being thrown by a cop and as a zombie. Once he posted a photo of a peasant straight out of a Gogol story, and I didn't even recognize him. He sent video clips from the shows he appeared in. He was often edited out, but even then he still collected his six hundred rubles, and the pay started to go up.

It still wasn't enough to live on, but it improved his spirits, and shortly thereafter he was offered a job in a St. Petersburg hotel as the night manager. It wasn't an illustrious gig by any stretch of the imagination. It didn't pay as much as he used to make at the Atrium. It was something to build on, and it gave him fairly flexible hours to keep fishing and silent hunting and to focus on his new interest in acting.

Within a year, he was making two thousand to four thousand rubles an episode (around US$65 to $135).

"How is your movie career going?" I asked him.

"Well," he said. "I got in episodes with fights, with gunshots, with talking roles, all where I was killed. It's going good, dude."

I could hear the excitement in his voice. He caught the interest of one casting director, who started slotting him for more parts and higher-paying extra roles in movies. On the recommendation of that casting director, he enrolled in acting classes.

"Right now I am studying for the theatre," he told me. "It's fucking difficult, dude. But it's some sort of interesting yeah. You know, these exercises, to show cats, dogs, your senses. All this shit without saying anything. Well, it's interesting. Very interesting, dude. It's not like studying economics or engineering. It's another. It's really another."

At first, it seemed like the most surprising trajectory I could have imagined for him. But on the other hand, it made a lot of sense. Of course, acting was perfect for Igor. He had always been a chameleon: bodybuilder, truck driver, badminton player, barman, muesli cook, barista, fisherman, mushroom hunter, paintballist, Soviet man, citizen of the Russian Federation . . . I had seen him occasionally play the part of Igor, the massive, drunken, good-hearted Russian—especially around other Americans. Not very often, but I knew that he had it within him.

He had consistently eschewed real life for sets imitating life. He sidestepped real war at great cost and then actively engaged in fake war. He detested the fashionable trappings of downtown St. Petersburg and worked inside a fake St. Petersburg at the Atrium. He eschewed the opportunity to try out life in the West and continued living in a fake capitalist democracy. He had a bunch of fake money in a fake mafia game while he was broke in real life. He had always been playing a role in an ever-shifting production. And now here he was, playing a part—and enjoying the hell out of it—in the latest act in Russia.

And not long ago, Igor posted to my Facebook wall, declaring for all to see: *I fall in love.*

I texted him: *What is this* I fall in love *thing?*

Igor texted back, *with a good girl.*

Me via Facebook: *tell me about your love.*

Igor via Facebook: *Her name is Veronica, 33 years old, I've met her on drama classes, She's divorced with two kids. It's complicated. What else, I don't know.*

He attached a photo of a beautiful blond woman in a short black dress showing a lot of thigh. She looked a lot more like Tanya from Irkutsk than Anya or Penny from *Big Bang Theory*.

In December 2011, when I heard about the protests across the country, I emailed Igor to ask what was going on with the revolution in his country.

He replied, *What revolution do you mean? Send me some links about it, probably I've missed it))))))*

After February 4, reportedly the largest protests of this new popular opposition, I emailed Igor to ask if he'd gone, to ask if he'd protested.

He replied: *Protest, ha. It cant change anything—this is Russia dude. Besides it was fucking cold outside)))*

He wasn't alone. I heard this—the "it can't change anything" argument—from many intellectuals.

And it *was* cold in Russia. Minus-fifteen or minus-twenty.

But that hadn't stopped, by some counts, hundreds of thousands of people.

I arrived in Moscow for a few days. I wanted to see the elections for myself. I went to watch the voting process with some friends. After marking the ballot, the voter drops it into a ballot box that looks remarkably like a trash can.

I met with Ilya Budraitskis, who was an elections observer at one of the precincts. I asked him whom he was going to vote for, and he told me that it didn't matter. That even if there weren't falsifications, Putin would win, only by a slimmer majority.

"What's important," he said, "is how the elections will mobilize the people. I think we're heading toward political instability. I don't know what will happen after tomorrow. I'm very interested to find out." Ilya's prediction from 2009 that Russia would change dramatically within five years was spot-on.

That night, as predicted, Putin won. Wearing jeans, he took the stage alongside Medvedev. Both of their eyes were wet. The old-new president thanked everyone for voting for a great Russia. The day after the elections, the enthusiasm of the new popular opposition was dampened. Far fewer people came out to protest the presidential elections than organizers had hoped, and the police reacted far more aggressively than they had during the past few months, a clear sign that the honeymoon was over.

After that, I got on the train to St. Petersburg.

Igor and I met downtown and walked around the city in the snow. We revisited all our old haunts and had a business lunch at Laima, where we'd met thirteen years ago. I took a picture of Igor standing on the bridge under which he'd swam. In the picture he is pointing to the little dock, which is still there, where he worked then as a barman.

We took the *marshrutka* from downtown past all the now-closed restaurants that Igor used to work at along Nevsky

Prospekt, the main avenue, down Liteiny Prospekt where Anna Akhmatova's house was, past the notorious Kresty prison, where his former policeman stepfather was imprisoned for corruption, and on into Piskaryovka, where the cemetery and the land encases all the old bones from the most debilitating blockade in modern history.

When we got to his apartment, he apologized. "The fridge is broken," he said. "I was saving money for your arrival, but now have to spend on new fridge." He cut some chicken from the bone and threw it on the floor for Dorofay. He didn't force me to eat chicken hearts. Several small and large fish hung from a hook over the counter.

I told Igor that his apartment stank of dried fish.

He said, "This is the smell of victory. Man against nature."

On TV, the continuing protests, peaceful in the run-up to the election, had turned violent again. And it was unclear what direction Russia was now heading in. But, it occurs to me, the story of a place isn't only the story of the warriors on the front lines of the struggle, the players in the opposition, those fighting the good fight and those on the wrong side of the aisle. It's the story of the majority who are just trying to live, who are doing the best they can with the cards they hold in a game that's showed time and time again that it's fixed.

I asked Igor his thoughts on the election and the new Putin presidency.

"The main thing is, nothing is changing," he said. "The main thing, they've gotten everything from us, even our choice."

We listened to the TV in silence for a while.

"There is new joke," Igor said. "Someone asks, 'Why did you vote for Putin?' You say, 'I don't like to lose.'"

Later, the conversation, as it often did, turned to the summer of 2009.

"This was the greatest time of my life," Igor said, "travelling around, talking to people. Excellent."

I agreed.

And if we can make from crisis that, there must yet be hope for us.

THE END

ACKNOWLEDGEMENTS

I probably should start by thanking Igor for letting me turn his life into hard copy and apologizing for all the times I brought a notebook to the banya.

A mighty thanks to everyone in Russia who took the time to candidly and openly discuss their lives and experiences with me.

Thanks to Angelina Davidova and Galka Chernetskaya, who ran back-up translating for me in live interviews and who helped in tracking down many of those who took the time to candidly and openly discuss their lives and experiences.

Thanks to Jeremy Keehn who published in *The Walrus* the banya story, "Getting sweaty with a Russian hulk," which grew into this book.

Thanks to the Summer Literary Seminars program in St. Petersburg, Russia, and all the folks who caroused with me the intersection between Russian and North American literature for ten summers, especially to program founder Mikhail Iossel. Without you, man, I'd never know St. Petersburg, and I can't imagine my life not knowing St. Petersburg.

Thank you to Alina Ryabovolova, whose insights about Russia invariably steered me toward new levels of understanding and without whose support I'd have never finished this thing.

Thanks to Josh Knelman for numerous consultations on The Weirdness.

Thanks to the Fulbright Scholar Program and the Hermitage Artist Retreat.

Thanks to everyone at Harper Collins Canada who worked on and looked out for this book, particularly Maria Golikova, Alex Schultz, and Jane Warren. This book was a dogfight to get right. My editor Jennifer Lambert got in the ring with me. Any faults of this work are surely mine, but all of its strengths are at least in part due to her editorial acumen. Thank you, Jennifer, for your patience and encouragement.

And thanks once again, Ellen Levine.